J T n

MW01258494

fondly,
RAJANI
Jan 26, 17

Farewell to Modernism

Rajani Kanth

Farewell to Modernism

On Human Devolution in the Twenty-First Century

PETER LANG
New York • Bern • Frankfurt • Berlin
Brussels • Vienna • Oxford • Warsaw

Library of Congress Cataloging-in-Publication Data

Names: Rajani Kannepalli Kanth, author.
Title: Farewell to modernism: on human devolution in the twenty-first
century / Rajani Kanth.
Description: New York: Peter Lang, [2017]
Series: American university studies V: Philosophy; vol. 225 | ISSN 0739-6392
Includes bibliographical references and index.
Identifiers: LCCN 2016022396 | ISBN 978-1-4331-3455-5 (hardcover: alk. paper)
ISBN 978-1-4539-1899-9 (ebook pdf) | ISBN 978-1-4331-3676-4 (epub)
ISBN 978-1-4331-3677-1 (mobi) | DOI 10.3726/978-1-4539-1899-9
Subjects: LCSH: Civilization, Modern—21st century. | Eurocentrism. | Civilization,
Modern—European influences. | East and West. | Social change—
Philosophy. | Anthropology—Philosophy.
Classification: LCC CB430 .R275 2017 | DDC 909.83—dc23
LC record available at https://lccn.loc.gov/2016022396

Bibliographic information published by **Die Deutsche Nationalbibliothek**.
Die Deutsche Nationalbibliothek lists this publication in the "Deutsche
Nationalbibliografie"; detailed bibliographic data are available
on the Internet at http://dnb.d-nb.de/.

The paper in this book meets the guidelines for permanence and durability
of the Committee on Production Guidelines for Book Longevity
of the Council of Library Resources.

© 2017 Rajani Kanth

Peter Lang Publishing, Inc., New York
29 Broadway, 18th floor, New York, NY 10006
www.peterlang.com

Printed in Germany

For the Keepers of My Flame:
My Daughters—Antara, Indrina, Malini, and Anjana

Contents

Acknowledgments

This Work is unlike any other that I have scribed across a long innings: it sums up, at times (of necessity) *repetitively*, all the recalcitrant ideas I have come up with, across decades of solitary, but due, contemplation of the verities.

I think I do offer, as such, within a *transcendent* critique, a new vista, a new way of conceiving the 'human dilemma': maybe even a new 'paradigm,' and cosmology. It is up to Others, of course: readers, critics, *et al.*, to confirm/reject this claim.

On the intellectual front, I wish to thank the eminent Dr. Amit Goswami, Quantum Physicist *extraordinaire* and celebrity, whose work helped me understand, early on, as much as a lay person can, some of the nuances of the natural, extra-social world—without which many chapters in this book could not have been conceived, or written.

I also owe thanks to Professor Immanuel Wallerstein, of Yale Sociology—whose *'Modern World System'* I had considered to be the best commentary on the subject, in my student days—who very graciously supplied a blurb for the Book, at very short notice, despite his own preoccupations.

I must also acknowledge, in all gratefulness, Harvard Professors Steve Caton and Gary Urton (the Chair of the Dept.), and the Dept. of Anthropology at Harvard, for their steady support of my scholarly endeavors over the past two years.

I also acknowledge the Dept. of Sociology at the Delhi School of Economics, India—*circa* 1968–1970, under the Chairship of the eminent (late) Professor M.N. Srinivas—which gave me the only formal education I have ever chosen to take seriously, and benefited from, anywhere.

In this vein, thanks are due to Ms. Michelle Salyga, Acquisitions Editor at Peter Lang, who saw merit in the Work, sooner than others, and also the various PL Editorial advisers led by Ms. Jackie Pavlovic who helped bring the book to publication.

Finally, a heavy debt of gratitude is owed to the ever gracious Dr. Fadhel Kaboub, Associate Professor of Economics, Denison University, and President, Binzagr Institute for Sustainable Prosperity (assisted by his student, Logan Smith), without whose kind, patient, logistical support (and personally executed, with excessive toils) I could simply not have gotten the book ready, in timely fashion, for Press, in the format I had wished for it.

❄

We live, unmistakably, in an *Age of Quantity*, solely owing to EuroModernist inspiration: and I am trying to bring back, in all my work(s), a *Calculus of Quality* that can help offset that portentous infelicity.

The Critique I offer is a *moral*, hence, a *transcendental* one: and, as such, evades the usual run of intra-Modernist ideological struggles (*i.e.,* Left-Right, Capitalist-Socialist, *etc.*). It is my sincere belief that these ideational binaries are all a thing of the past, as their parent stem European Modernism—or *Late Modernism* in my *patois*—dissolves right before us: in these times.

The world is ready now, I think, in the twenty-first century, for such an overarching, and liberating, transcendence.

The Wheel has turned: and there is a new dawning of consciousness, globally, that will sweep away all the varied confusions—errors and omissions—of Euromodernism, in both epistemics and ontology.

The hour is fit, in the portentous year of 2016, to recover, and restore, genuine anthropic values—*contra* the received legacy of Modernist snares.

The Time has come: and Change is, finally, here.

For myself, it is not quite soon enough.

Preface

Change

Change is here. And a lot more than mere regime change. It is far from overt, and defies easy scanning. But it may be as close as just a couple of years, maybe less. In an inevitable, and inexorable, way, a four-century old system of European domination is starting to unravel.

The odd thing is that, like some antic Greek tragedy, it appears to be virtually 'fated,' though it is anything but: willful decisions taken at the highest levels have engineered this unfolding devolution. It is said that whom the gods wish to destroy, they first make mad: it pays to examine this genre of 'madness,' in particular to discover its underlying method.

One can rule out hubris, despite its very crude and obvious face on at least the Leader of the Band. Rather, it is the wayward trajectory of the inherent expansionism built into the calculations of present, and prior, leaders.

Empire was to the UK what it is to its eminent successor North Atlantic progeny today. At its root, *empire is simply a means of getting something for nothing*. In short, it is *parasitism*—writ large.

For centuries, Britain, *via* its colonial extractions, was able to live wildly beyond its modest domestic resources. The US practiced this 'internally' at first, checked by the very existence of the 'Mother Country,' to engage in external adventurism.

Native Americans, and African Slaves, gave it a very similar booty, that enabled it to 'leap frog' stages. But such means of 'primal extractions' run dry over a course of time, and need to be supplanted. So, in due course, America 'stepped out' and 'trooped its color,' globally.

After WWII, the Old and the New hegemon, settled on a *New Strategy*. In essence, the primary means of this 'rent-seeking' control was to be *financial*.

A ridiculously over-valued pound, together with a global gold-price-cum-interest rate-fixing capability, assured the UK of staying in the game—with the City of London set as a permanent financial hub.

The same status was achieved for the US, *via* the dollar being denominated as a global 'reserve' currency: so it could buy real world assets for scraps of rather unwholesome looking greenbacks. Thus did the old, and the new, hegemon dictate to the largely prostrate world, after WWII.

However, the prostration was not to be permanent: and *Others* rose, albeit slowly, to economic and political leverage. Germany, Japan, South Korea, first: China, Russia, and India much later, started to gain a small measure of counter-vailing eco-political resolve.

Now, none of this could have seriously disturbed the Anglo-American '*ancien regime*,' except for one catastrophic Himalayan default: the Reagan-Thatcher Neo-Lib 'revolution' removed the very possibility of rational regulation (even on behalf of the rulers) from Empire.

Henceforth, it would essay blindly, in finance and other fields, pursuing essentially scorched-earth economic policies in all domains. Elementary caution was thrown to the winds, and the system turned into a wild orgy of Casino Capitalism: from the Eighties on, it was—as it is today—catch-as-catch-can.

From then on, workers, the middling classes (!), the poor, the underprivileged, were *All* consigned to the dustbin: the world belonged, exclusively, to the 'elect.' 'Look Ma,' they screamed, as these elites roller-coasted, 'No Rules.' Such were the likes of both policy makers, and the freshly empowered fly-by-night Pirate-Captains of ruthless Entrepreneurship.

Of course, academic economists, as the designated sycophants/soothsayers of the new regime (their heyday was the Eighties and Nineties: today, they are not 'needed' at all and serve absolutely no function, even that of being lackeys) concocted *ad hoc* 'theory' to suit their paymasters. Government lost even a semblance of public responsibility, and ideas like 'nation,' 'society,' and 'public welfare,' ceased to exist, let alone matter.

The US collapsed as a moral force, as a template of even mundane success: it scrapes the very bottom of the barrel now, in every significant societal index one can think of—reviewed globally. If there existed a 'third world,' it might lay strong claim to be its leader, by right. So, it was more a case of 'Look ma, No brains.'

Me first, and the devil take the hindmost—neither a novel, nor a complicated formula—became the *Mantra du Jour*. And then, predictable events happened: to call them 'crises' is a bit gratuitous since they were exactly the sorts of situations that the New Overseers expected, and oft engineered.

The Era of Taxpayer Capitalism, and Free Marketeers had begun. They could derail the locomotive (accent on the 'loco'), again and again, in a frenzy of reckless profiteering, only to have it all covered, paid for, by their stooges in Govt. It promised to be a permanent joy ride.

However, the Neo-libs had not fully anticipated another, darker, brooding force that now showed its menacingly poisonous fangs. After the (enforced) capitulation of the Soviet Union—*arguably amongst the most egregiously irresponsible acts of state policy in modern history*—the *Neo-Cons* took over much of the conduct of politics. The entire world had to be made safe, now, for the new Anglo-Am Empire.

So, added to the toxic whirlwind of financial derivatives that swept the globe, were the rippling shock waves of the on-going depredations of *militarism*: regime changes, coups, civil wars, false flag events, and such.

It is this strong, but immature, force that becomes the last straw; and delivers, unwittingly, the *coup de grace*. Neo-Lib economics and Neo-Con politics, left to one or the other, might have naturally expired when out of stream—without earth-shaking consequences. But, *in combination*, they are become the engulfing tsunami that bring *All* Issues to an ineluctable head.

Under the latter's auspices, West Asia and Afghanistan, now Ukraine, Russia, and even China, are all sought to be brought under Western 'containment.' Yet, paradoxically, all this is being sought by a largely bankrupt, fragmenting, crumbling, system running mainly on gambles, printing presses, credit creation, borrowed funds—and explosives. It is an incendiary combination. Would-be empires, one would think, need to be made of sterner stuff. So: is this to be seen as tragedy, or farce? Either way, the Game is on, in deadly earnest.

The EU, for now, is performing its allotted task of being a dutiful wagtail: but for how long? There, too, the chasm between Govt. and the people is widening (Greece is only the thin end of the wedge). Apparently, you can't fool everyone, all the time.

On the *autre* hand, the BRICS, and Others—by no means a weightless grouping—are being forced, defensively, to form their own, protective enclaves. So, the global Stage is well set.

xvi | *Farewell to Modernism*

Of course *Darth Vader, Inc.,* can press the big button: and end it for All—including their own ilk. But, somehow, that doesn't seem to quite stack up. There is a natural shrewdness to the human species that may intervene, in the last instance!, to pre-empt that final act of reckless hubris. If so, the Path is clear.

We will wake, after some necessary jitters, to a New World of *Ex*-Hegemons—and ordinary nations, engaged yet again in the ordinary business of life, as they had been, for centuries: until the onset of the Great European Interruption that, in hindsight, gives even the (so-called) 'Dark Ages' a bad name.

A multi-polar world: fancy that! little wonder that Europe/America, with centuries of skimming off the surplus of the globe, cannot accommodate itself to the idea. But they will need to.

Will Capitalism survive? Of course, but of a very different species: a capitalism, itself only one layer of a 'mixed' platter of *concurrent modes of production*, held to responsibility by its various stakeholders.

There may also be no need for a 'reserve' currency (which is merely a requisite of empire), just an accounting one. Indeed, 'world orders,' with all their top-heavy paraphernalia of multilateral agency, will be a thing of the past. And thus the most pernicious 'caste system' of human history will dissolve.

The prospect is far from uninviting. Of course, it is far, very far, from Lennon's millenarian hopes expressed in the lyrics of 'Imagine.' It will be a humdrum world of lowered expectations, but with better distribution of resources, a far higher priority than the heedless, enforced 'growth' of the last century (that has threatened to shut down processes of nature vital to our survival, aside from exacting blood from the new serf/slaves of the 'globalized' world). But humdrum, in an anthropic world, is about as close as we can ever hope to get to an earthly 'paradise,' given the proclivities of the *'paradigm of masculinity'* I often refer to in my writings.

So, alas, the First, individual, 'self-made,' *Trillionaire* (other than the *Ye Olde* banking oligarchies, such as the Rothschilds, that have been within that charmed circle for a while) may never come to pass. The *Few* will still, unfortunately, do better than the many: one of those implacable historical facts of life—but not at all on the preposterous scale that is extant now.

True, other than the BRICS, right now, not too many are involved, at least overtly, in such a hopeful narrative. But that will change. For once, the old, hackneyed saw of *'plus ça change, plus c'est la même chose'* will be patently wrong.

It's almost enough to make one an optimist, despite the stupefying mayhem of our times.

Foreword

The book you are holding in your hand *Farewell to Modernism* is a very important book. I will emphasize in this foreword only one of the reasons that I think is the most compelling. I am sure as you read it you will discover many other reasons to consider it important. You know there is a new physics (new? Ha! It has been around for almost a hundred years!) called quantum physics that is supposed to have replaced Newtonian physics. You may also know that the message of this new physics is integrative—among other things it integrates science and spirituality which is the basis of religions. But have you wondered why this message is having difficulties in getting traction? I have; I am one of a substantial number of maverick scientists who keep trying to effect a paradigm shift in our entire worldview due to the paradigm shift in physics.

In view of the polarization we see today between science and religion, an integrated worldview would make sense, wouldn't it? Perhaps the idea of integration is all theory, no back up by experimental data? No, that is not the case. Quantum physics says unambiguously that there are two domains of reality: the first is a domain of potentiality where all objects are instantly interconnected waves of possibility; this instant interconnection is called nonlocality—signal-less communication; the second domain is our familiar space and time; it is the domain of actuality where there indeed are independent separate objects only able to communicate through signals going locally through space taking time unless they are "entangled when the nonlocal communication channel opens up. And this nonlocal instant interconnection has been verified by myriad experimental data both for the micro and for the macrocosm.

Why is this so important? What does oneness remind you of? It is *the* ancient mystical/religious message, no? Underneath our separateness, we are interconnected One. Some of you are enthralled by the message; it seems to agree what you intuit anyway. Sociological data says that maybe even as much as 20% of Westerners are like you. But the rest of Western society, the 80%, and importantly, among this 80% are most of the professionals especially scientists, either neglect the message or actively resist it. Oneness is an Eastern thing, it is Eastern mysticism, they say for one thing. Perhaps the data at the macrolevel is not as convincing as it should be for another! I have addressed this last concern in all my books and it is not based on facts. But let's take up this East-West thing.

A young philosopher (sociologist) named Rajani Kanth was appointed assistant professor at the prestigious Jawaharlal Nehru University in Delhi at age 21. He was of course thrilled; but the challenge was to find a research program to keep himself busy and make his mark. The problem that fascinated him was the supposed rift between Eastern and Western modus of thinking and living immortalized (?) by those famous lines of British poet Kipling: East is East and West is West/And the twain shall never meet. Is there such rift and what exactly is the basis of the rift? young Rajani asked himself.

The answers he found are revealing. Socioculturally, Easterners are community oriented; they live in a joint family, they are expressive of how they feel, family is more important to them than external achievements, etc., etc. Kanth calls this mentality huddle mentality, heat-seeking, mammal-like. Westerners on the other hand (especially more recently) take pride in their individuality, in being independent separate objects "free" to accomplish anything. This is reflected in the economics of capitalism which the West discovered and now is almost exclusively followed by everyone. In capitalism, if both producers and consumers alike follow their individual selfish interest then the invisible hands of the free market is assumed to keep the economy going.

How do Westerners today do that, keep themselves to individuality whereas human beings throughout history—East or West—seem to live in social communities? Kanth wondered. The answer is, today they suppress emotions and follow the cold dictate of reason. They are cold-blooded, like reptiles. (If you are a woman reader, you will object. Women are 'cuddly' everywhere. Kanth is aware of that but he reminds you of the fact that the Western society has been very male dominated until very recently.)

And then the important question. How did it get this way? The answer of this book is of course the worldview of modernism, but what do you think modernism is? Common sense simply dictates this: be modern, follow science's two prong approach of theory and experimental verification whenever applicable in preference to the old tradition—religion which is based on revelation, theory and faith. But this is the catch. This simple dictate does not define how modernism was actually practiced by Europeans who brought this worldview to the world.

Euromodernism has four defining dicta, Kanth points out: (1) A dogmatic faith in science; (2) a philosophy of rampant materialism; (3) a "self-serving and triumphalist" belief in progress; and (4) a "readiness to deploy illimitable *Statist Violence* to achieve policy ends. Items (1) and (2) together is sometimes called scientific materialism and I have pointed out many times in my own writing that this is like a religion. What took even me by surprise is that there is enough case for items (3) and (4) if we examine carefully the history of *how* Euromodernism came to its present dominant position.

But how do you impose these dicta on an entire people, initially very divided for that matter? You know Europe was not one nation. And conspiracy theories don't work. True. But there were tools that were discovered, reasonable and successful tools for manipulating a society to progress in the intended direction: capitalism, democracy, and liberal education. The power mongers from generation to generation used these tools to inject individualism deep into the entire Western male-dominated culture. This is Kanth's main point. And I am impressed that he makes his case well, sometimes with wit, often with cutting sarcasm, but always with persuasive reasoning.

But all is not lost, says Kanth. Now that quantum physics has demonstrated that there is oneness behind our individuality, the winds of change will take hold. First, he notes that the recent unleashing of greed that caused the great recession is symptomatic. It suggests that the system is self-destroying. You will enjoy Kanth's poem—an eulogy to that effect titled *farewell to modernism*.

Who will pick up the pieces after Euromodernism's self-destruction? Kanth is hopeful that women will. Women all over the world are warm, mammal-like; they will bring back community, will replace *homo economicus,* the selfish individual of Adam Smith capitalism with *homo communus,* the community way of being that Eastern cultures still covet and preserve to some extent. So the Eastern countries—China, India, Russia, maybe the entire BRICS group—they too will play a role in the revival of civilization.

xx | *Farewell to Modernism*

Well, I cannot, nor do I want to, give you the taste of all the beautiful prose that Rajani Kanth has written to make his case, but I tell you this: you will be impressed and you will be moved, and you will think. How could (relatively) so few influenced so many for so long with untrue at best incomplete ideas? Well, that is the power of culture!

What is culture? As we interact with other people in a society and look at how they are responding to stimuli, there are neurons in our brain called "mirror neurons" that simulate in our internal experience the behavior we are witnessing; so if we are on automatic pilot we start behaving the same way. So our internal experience growing up with the same people tend to be homogenized. Of course there is also that nonlocal way of communication since we are people not machines, but that works only if you are open to feelings. Thinking tends to exclude nonlocality. So do you see how the male dominated society in the West became so homogenized in their individualistic culture? You can also see how women in the West escaped the cold reptile male culture to a considerable extent. Because they were allowed to remain open to feelings, the necessity of motherhood and all that could not be ignored.

This homogeneity of the internal experiences of people living in the same geography is the culture: it is our internal "we." The word society we reserve for talking about the "us" thus generated in an objective way.

When we grow up in a culture, we become culture-bound. Let's face it! Majority of Western scientists go on supporting the archaic Newtonian worldview and materialist philosophy because, culture-bound as they are, they cannot help it.

Kanth goes as far as to posit that Euromodernism produced a culture that is autistic, incapable of feeling even sympathy, let alone empathy, with people's suffering. Some of the history he quotes and some of the history he reconstructs of how Europeans came to dominate the whole world with their myopic autistic thinking is downright painful, especially if you are a Westerner, especially if you are a woman. But still, remember, what Jesus said, Truth shall set us all free.

And so it will. I will end this foreword with an afterword. There is a movement now, *quantum activism*, activism to replace the modernism based on Newtonian physics with true modern spirit: make your worldview as much as possible based on scientific truth which evolves becoming closer and closer to Truth and that scientific truth right now is quantum physics and the degree to which it agrees with our experience of who we are suggests it is very close to Truth. And quantum truth is inclusive: Not individual and locality alone, but also community and nonlocality. And quantum activism is getting traction everywhere. Yes, East and West (and North and South) have met under the same quantum umbrella;

and they all like its warmth. And they will build a new *modern* culture based on integration and transformation.

I agree with Kanth: women with their natural huddling instinct will lead the post-Euromodernism movement. I find evidence of it everywhere; 70% of the participants of quantum activism are women. But men are joining in ever-increasing numbers. And young people. Everybody knows, old paradigmers (the power mongers) never change, but they do die. In the future, I see Rajani and I working together to develop the steps to a *quantum* modernism.

The bottom line is this: read this book, take your time, think out of the box (straitjacket?) of Euromodernism, and this will change your life.

Dr. Amit Goswami
Theoretical Quantum Physicist
Emeritus Professor, University of Oregon

Introduction

Challenging Eurocentrism: 45 Theses

It is high time, in this Late Era, the *High Noon of Modernism*, to articulate a true Cosmology for the Sciences and the Humanities, replacing that tendentious legacy of Misogyny and Misanthropy bequeathed us by the European Enlightenment, namely, *Modernism*. In that vein, I offer the following *Theses*, for due consideration, not for '*debate*' or '*argument*,' which is the rather fruitless Modernist Way, but for serious, sobrietous *reflection*.

There is no God's-Eye View of the World: so, all is couched here in the implicit belief in the *Suchness* of Things, in the inherent *Maybe-ness* of Phenomena, and in their Ineffable *Many-Sidedness*, Methodological Tenets of Ancient Jain Philosophy, *circa* fifth century BC which, like so much that is unknown to Modernist audiences, is amongst the World's foremost Scientific Traditions.

1. We are, contrary to the ruling precepts of Judeo-Christian Ideology, *Self-realized, and Self-realizing, Animals at all times*: notions of *Progress* and Regress, thereby, carry no valency [except as purely *arbitrary* constructions].

2. Nature has programmed us in many ways: so life on Earth, in its Cosmic sense, is beyond Anthropic notions of Good and Evil, no matter how inescapable such judgments might appear to be.
   Theorem# A: *Men are endowed with the Instinct to Kill, Women with the Instinct to Nurture, quite regardless of Culturally specified Roles and Responsibilities that mediate such Drives.*

Men and women constitute therefore *Two Distinct Sub-Species,* occupying differing ontic and epistemic spaces. Their respective '*Cluster of Traits,*' I title the *Paradigm of Masculinity* and the *Paradigm of Femininity.*

3. As *Hominids,* we are endowed with no special tilt toward either Equity or Justice; recall that Nature, proverbially, is '*red in tooth and claw*': and so are we.

4. Our *Species-Being* is *Trans-Human,* it's what we share with the broader *genus* of Hominids.

5. The '*meaning of life,*' if one exists at all, might simply be *To Be,* not *To Become*: and life is only '*solitary, nasty, brutish and short*'—under uniquely *Modernist* ontology, epistemology, and practices.

6. Modernism, was first erected in Europe, *whence its synonymity with Eurocentrism,* on the *Metaphysical Triad* of: (a) a near blind 'Faith' in *Science,* (b) a self-serving, and Triumphalist, Belief in *Progress,* and (c) a Philosophy of rampant *Materialism* [a *Fourth Adjunct* would be the readiness to deploy illimitable *Statist Violence* to achieve Policy Ends: to cite even the great Libertarian, J. S. Mill, it's quite right to '*force people to be free*'].

7. *Modernist Civil Society* is a fateful innovation, set apart from the Two *prior Universal Archetypes*: the hoary *Natural Society of Tribe,* imbued with the Cooperative *Paradigm of Femininity,* and the Masculinist *Social Frame of Empire,* run through with the eternal *Dialectic of War.* It appears, epistemically, when *Masculinist Greed* overcomes the more mundane Masculinist drives for *power and domination,* subverting, in process, the complex of *Feminine Hospitalities* implicit in Familial/Tribal society.

8. Modernism constructs a rabid, Masculinist, '*Political Economy of Interests*'—the fount of All putative '*Social Contract*' notions of Society—extinguishing wherever possible our Primal, Feminine, '*Moral Society of Affections.*'
   Theorem# B: *It is this Gratuitous Ravagement of the Gratuity of Kinship and Affinity that lies at the base, and is the Root Cause, of All our Modernist Alienations.* At its very Zenith, this Path leads us only to our emergent, contemporary reality of a *Casino Economy,* a *Video Culture,* and a *Techno-Fascist Polity.*
   Theorem# C: *Anthropic Society is based on Reciprocal, Affective Ties, not* '*Social Contracts.*'

9. *Patriarchy,* an *Anthropic Universal,* repeatedly unseats all our naïve Plans for Amelioration. The best one can do here has already been achieved

historically by *Tribal Society, to imprison Men's murderous impulses within the healing Matrix of Natural Affinity/Kinship* [in effect, the *Anthropic Utopia* has always been both *Immanent* and *Pre-achieved*: it is in no need of the gratuitous *Caricature of Modernist Invention*].

10. Modernist *Utopianism*, More to Marx, which has martyred millions is, at best, a plaintive protest at our uninspiring Anthropic Fate; at worst, the devious plan of dangerous madmen seeking, as ever, *Absolute Power.*

11. Indeed, all Modernist Agendas, of the Left or Right, need to be categorically rejected as specious.

    Theorem# D: *Men, in their Collective aspect, are not to be trusted with Power, and Modernist Patriarchs, devoid of many 'natural stabilisers,' least of all.*

    Theorem# E: *All Modernist Paths, Left or Right, lead only to swift and sure Perdition.*

12. Modernist Ideologies are both banal and destructive: they hold aloft the barren/dissembling/tendentious slogans of *Equality* and *Freedom,* the better only to ensnare us into serving the greater Glory/Greed of the Ruling Orders.

13. *Modernist Nation-States* [constructed on the notion of *bellum omnia contra omnes*], much as *Civil Society,* are *imposed, Inauthentic Entities,* uniquely European in provenance, and devoid of *Anthropic Meaning,* that serve only to deceive and/or Alienate the *Subject Orders*: they neither correspond to, nor serve, *our Real Anthropic Needs/Natures.*

14. *Civil Society*—the Preeminent Domain of all our Anti-Social drives and the High Icon of Liberals—is itself held together only by sheer Force, Economic Dependency, and Propaganda.

    Theorem# F: *Economics is but the Crown Jewel of the Hegemonic Ideology of Civil Society, i.e., Modernism. It is a Program that uniquely promotes the Modernist Agenda, not the 'Science' it pretends to be.*

15. Democracy, reducing to a mere *Voting Rule,* is oft the preferred internal tool for *Ruling Strata,* when in a *State of Equipoise,* to Resolve Differences, wherever possible, without bloodshed. As such, it is far from being a *Modernist* invention. But it is a *patent fraud* as far as *Subject Peoples* in Civil Society are concerned, and functions merely as an Ideological Instrument of *Mass-Deception.*

    Theorem# G: *Tribal Formations aim at, and achieve, Consensual, and hence Convivial, Modes of Existence, far beyond the imagination of Modernism.*

16. Modernist Institutions that rule the globe today are uniquely *Germanic* in origin: *i.e., German Protestantism wedded to Anglo-Saxon Mercantilism*. As Max Weber well understood, *Protestant Theology* and *Capitalist Ideology* are near-identical and homologous.

17. Indeed, as an aside, *Northern Europe* first annexed the Legal/Commercial accomplishments of *Southern Europe* [the so-called *Renaissance*], which was part of a larger *Pan-Mediterranean Civilization*, itself fertilized by Egyptian/Indian/Chinese ideas, and next garnered the Ideational/Material resources of the colonized *Non-Europeans* [*viz.*, the so-called, *Enlightenment/Industrial Revolution*]. *The North produced little, but knew How to Appropriate*: to this day, that basic pattern, of a globe under the Domination of Anglo-Saxon institutional *Hegemony*, has not yet altered.

18. The *only* instruments that Northern Europe truly perfected, above all other Anthropic Species, are the mechanisms material to *Waging War*, and the means ideological of Defrauding Peoples, *that is, Cannon and Chicanery*. To this day, it is these that remain the Twin Bases of their near total *Hegemony*.

19. As Hominids, *i.e.,* as Mammals, it is not Liberty and Equality we seek, but Care, Reciprocity, Consideration, Nurturance, and Warmth.
    Contra Marx, our *Species-being* is *not* expressed in *Labor* [that, regrettably, is a uniquely *Protestant* notion] but in *Play and Conviviality*, albeit within the frame of societal and cultural norms. It is this, immanent, "*Sympathy of Life*" that Modernism destroys.

20. The Life-or-Death struggles that bestride the world today are now inevitably between the *Mammals and the Reptiles* [*i.e., between Civilization and Modernism*].

21. Darwin published far too late for Marx to renounce his inescapable *Judeo-Christian Ideology*, carrying idealistic, delusional, and fantastic notions of '*Human Perfectibility*.' Unless God, perchance, is an Ape, we are probably not molded in His/Her/Its image.

22. *Modernism is the ultimate Iron Cage within a Bell Jar*: there has been no societal order on this Planet that demands more *Incessant Labors* from the many, and yields us less Leisure and *Conviviality* than Modernist Civil Society.
    Theorem# H: *Universal Egoism [Hegel] breeds only Universal Discontent [and Existential Despair].*

23. Within Modernism, there is no such thing as a meaningful '*Social Science*' divorced from the eternal *Agendas of Domination* and *Resistance, i.e.,* the perpetual Masculinist struggles between, what Karl Mannheim termed, *Ideology* and *Utopia.*

    Theorem# I: *Indeed, Modernist Social Science is simply the secular version of Judeo-Christian Ideology, and is equally Protestant and Monotheistic.*

24. Further, this *Modus* of Science is neither a necessary nor a sufficient condition for Emancipation from Modernist Grids.

    Theorem# J: *Anthropic Oppressions are first Felt, and then possibly Acted upon: they do not require to be Theorized, except as an effete Exercise in Abstraction.*

25. The Newtonian, Reductionist, Materialist philosophy undergirding Modernist Science, is both false and obsolete. Matter is not dead and inert: but conscious, self-aware, and, occasionally, articulate. *We, ourselves, are living Testimony to that.* Indeed, we have moved, within European Thinking, from *Deterministic Physics* [1600–1925], *via Indeterminist Physics* [1925–1995], to *Self-Deterministic Physics* [1995–?] today. Regrettably, however, most Modernist Science/Ideology, Left or Right, is still trapped, somewhat immaturely, in *Phase One* of this dramatic Evolution.

26. Modernist Science has long monopolized a species of *Instrumental Knowledge*; but there are, and have always been, great *Competing* Traditions, ruthlessly suppressed by Modernism, that are now, albeit slowly, reviving globally. Aside from *Reason*, the Human Ape is pre-given both *Instinct* and *Intuition,* even upon rare occasion, *Revelation,* the latter tapping into a reservoir of what Jung called, after Vedic Philosophy, the '*Collective Consciousness,*' a species of *Quantum Interconnectedness*: and Modernists barely know the power of the latter for having neglected/ disparaged these Bountiful Avenues, for centuries.

27. The Fundamental Hominid Condition is *Autonomy* and *Self-Regulation, not* 'Liberty' or 'Freedom' which are mere Modernist dissemblings:

    Theorem# K: *Both Capitalism and Socialism, the Tweedledum and Tweedledee of Modernist Discourse, deny this Natural Condition, and so are, sooner or later, Prefigured to Perish.*

28. The only meaningful 'freedoms' are not freedoms at all, but vital *Anthropic Necessities*: Freedom from *Want, Fear, and Indignity*—and no Modernist Formation has ever been able, even if/when willing, to guarantee those, in practice.

29. *Civilization*, in the sense of the *Pacification of Anthropic Existence*, is effected by near *invisible Gender Struggles*, not *Class struggles*, which are *Masculinist* struggles primarily, if not exclusively, about *Power*.

    Theorem# L: *Women, via their Paradigm of Femininity, are the Trustees Eternal of Anthropic Civilization.*

    Theorem# M: *Stated simply, Women Build inescapably, and incessantly, in this area: and Men, equally invariably, and uninterruptedly, Destroy.*

30. Aside from *Gender*, and *Inter-Tribalist*, tensions, *Change* arises within Anthropic Society also through the continuous *Dialectic of Random Individual Deviance* pitted against the *Norms of Group Conformity* [similar, homologously, to unexpected '*mutations*' in Darwinian Evolutionary Theory].

31. Theorem# N: *It appears almost a Natural Fact that Micro/Individual behavior is 'Free' [i.e., relatively Unpredictable] whilst Macro/Group behavior is more 'Constrained' [Predictable].*

32. As *Herd Animals*, we follow *Totemic Charisma*, quite naturally; and can be led/misled, willy-nilly, as such leadership chooses. [Anthropic *Politics*, thereby, is *not*, necessarily 'rational.']

    Theorem# O: *Charismatic Leaders, thereby, are often the Characteristic Tools of Radical, overarching Anthropic Change, for better or for worse.*

33. Yet, despite these Ills/Oppressions of Anthropic Existence, there appears to be a *natural shrewdness* [likely a 'survival' instinct] to the species that asserts itself, *if only in the last instance*, usually forestalling the ever cumulating Doomsday Plans of our *Totemic Leadership(s)*.

34. Anthropic Culture is *Particularistic*, and emphasizes *Uniqueness* and *Difference*; Modernism Standardizes, Universalizes, and Homogenizes, only as prelude to Conquest and Control.

35. The Provenance of what passes for *Morality and Ethics* lies in the Natural, Anthropic *Species-Need* to rear the vulnerable newborn, safely and securely, in the torrid war zones that Masculinity creates spontaneously.

36. Given the *Natural* Role of Women as the very *First* Natural Caregivers of Children, they become, in effect, the *Original* Bearers of all Human Civility.

    Theorem# P: *Indeed, Women and Children, together, form the Fundamental, Constituent, Anthropic Units.*

37. *Women, Workers, Traditional/Tribal Societies* all live in an Implicit or Explicit *Moral Economy* and, in varying degree, form the *Natural*

Opposition to Modernism. They define, now as ever, its enduring *Natural Limits.* One might also add that Modernism has functioned, since about the sixteenth century as the Colored Man's, Women's, Tribals', and Workers', overwhelming Blight, Cross, and Anathema.

38. We flourish most naturally in *Packs and Herds, i.e.,* in *Families and Tribes* [our *Natural State*], and inevitably, and transparently, rot and decay in '*Civil Society*,' succumbing to *Anomie* and/or *Angst*, or worse.

39. Theorem# Q: As *Being Natural Creatures, the more we dwell apart from Nature the more Pathologies we adopt and assimilate on a continuing basis.*

40. Contrary to many views, it is *not* the Planet that is endangered by Modernism: *We are.* Indeed, if Modernism lasts much longer, it is *We* who will be gone, *not* the Planet. In fact, in terms of Species' 'rise and fall,' we may well be in the Critical Margins today.

41. Freud, prototypically trapped within *the Dialectic of Civil Society*, and in uniquely Modernist fashion, was *wholly wrong*: our manifest Discontent is not *with Civilization*—but, *au contraire*, with *the pathetic dearth of it in Modernist Society*

42. *Religiosity*, far from being a Sop or an Opiate, is simply the *Collective Intuition* of a larger Cosmology than afforded by the *Bleakness of the Anthropic Prospect, i.e.,* it is the ultimate *Search for Transcendence* intrinsic to our Anthropic Natures. *Its Truth-value, case by case, is an Open issue: not a Closed one.*

    Theorem# R: *Religion is the Spontaneous Metaphysics of the Species, and also the Evolving Repertory of its Natural Ethics.*

43. *Modernism fears Religion*, not for its *Reactionary, Delusionary* leanings, but for the *exact opposite*: its *Revolutionary/Revelatory* potential. In fact, the Protestant Revolution was uniquely *Modernist, i.e., reactionary,* seeking to dull the Moral/Ethical force of hoary, Fundamentalist Christianity, an impediment to its own Materialist, Misanthropic Ambitions and Agendas.

44. The Meaning of *Anthropic Alienation—a uniquely Modernist Condition*—and, more importantly, its *Antidote*, must now be abundantly clear: We need (a) to Relink with our *Internal* Mammalian/Hominid Natures [*i.e.,* immerse ourselves within the *Affective Values of Kinship*, real or ersatz], and (b) Realign ourselves with/within the *Rhythms of External Nature.*

45. If/When we do, rejecting the Bane of *Eurocentric Cosmologies*, then it still is/will be, despite its inherently enigmatic nature, both a Bounteous, and Self-Fulfilling Universe, as the Bushmen and the Aboriginals, and legions of Native Cultures, have *always* known.

Note

1. This Paper was presented in a Special Event at the American Economic Association Meetings, Chicago, January 4, 2007: *'The Challenge of Eurocentrism: A Global Review of Parameters: Festschrift Celebration of the Life and Work of Rajani Kannepalli Kanth.'*

Part I

In Crisis

1

Today

Hollywood and TV show the Unspeakable. Pentagon discusses the Unthinkable. Wall Street engages in the Irreparable. The Media dole out the Unbelievable. Deep State ploys, and False Flag events, proliferate. Yes, it is—it must be, '*exceptionalism.*' We, the People, cannot expect Equity. We cannot ask for Justice. We cannot require Security. We cannot demand that elected representatives fulfill their mandates.

We cannot insist on rights without our gracious high Judiciary agreeing, usually, with the Executive Branch. Millions of us cannot expect gainful jobs, let alone meaningful ones. Nor can we ask that explicit corporate plunder of the eco-system, such as fracking, be abated, if not stopped. We cannot stop GMO pollution. We cannot ask for a ban on BGH. We can't even ask for full-disclosure labeling. We stopped asking for truth from the Government (at a single-digit approval rating, for Congress, that much would seem obvious). We can't get it from the Corporatists, given their inalienable privacy rights (rights that, apparently, don't exist for us). The largest trade agreement in history, the TPP (Trans-Pacific Partnership), that is expected to seriously erode state sovereignty in favor of Corporate rights, is going ahead with the populace, and the Congress, kept out of the loop: about 600 Corporate lobbyists will write that law, as similar groups have done, in similar legislations.

They can make war, even nuclear war, without our consent. Democracy is quite a prize, is it not? If only the run-of-the-mill dictators understood that, they would all switch (I won't refer to the fact that a recent, Princeton/Northwestern study, 'officially,' styles the US as an *Oligarchy*). They can, frankly, do what they wish—as they do, *willy-nilly*—as they have for eons. As I have mentioned, only the fig leaf has been shed: all else is business as usual. Now that we have 'led' the 'free world' for decades, perhaps it is finally time to try and join them (leaders and the led, need not necessarily share any kindred: after all, consider the Pied Piper and his 'following')? Meanwhile, society, in its essential form, atrophies.

A glance, now (2014/15) at its economic visage (2016 has not achieved any marked melioration, in this regard).

Using only official data, Debt is up: the National Debt is over 17 trillion, with about a trillion added every year all the way from 2005 to 2012. Corporate debt, outstanding, stands at over 9 trillion. The Deficit was over a trillion in 2013. The Debt/GDP ratio in 2013 was 101.53% (the Bank of International Settlements [BIS] considers a ratio above 90% to be unsafe). And, mostly, it's debt of a kind that does not generate income, nor pay back the principal. Total, public, and private credit market debt outstanding is about $60 trillion. The total Debt/GDP ratio is over 400%, if all public and private debts are added. The Financial sector has been at *Zero Net Worth* for decades, and the Federal govt. at minus Double-digits Net Worth since 2008.

You and I, in such a position, might think we were *insolvent*. They don't: since they can always shift the bill on to us either by bail-outs, and bail-ins, and/or via an inflation tax (the Keynesians who, ideologically, take public debts to be harmless, fail to notice that: (a) not only is much of this debt, public or private, not being expended in anything even remotely approaching a productive, beneficial manner, but that (b) its repayment burden is mostly shifted on to the weaker strata of taxpayers). So, Debt-financing is become a Great Redistributive Device, *if you wish to play Robin Hood in reverse.* Now, using alternate calculations, on what is called 'generally accepted accounting principles' (GAAP-based accounting, as deployed, by John Williams), as apart from the cash-based accounting models of the govt., *actual* federal deficit hit a record $6.6 trillion in 2012, with actual Federal Debt over $86 trillion.

Savings are down to 4%, fallen by 13% since 2013. 1 in 3 Americans now has zero savings for retirement. Official Unemployment is at 6.3%, alternate calculations (including the millions of discouraged) would put it higher than 10%. Unoccupied homes exceed the numbers of the homeless. Yet, paradoxically, we can 'house' a full quarter of the world's prison population. Poverty is at 13%, 1 in 7 stay hungry, and 3.5 million sleep where they can.

The GDP, in my own rough and rude calculation(s), adjusted for real inflation, has not budged since 2008. My rule of thumb now, based on casual observation of recent numbers, is: discount official GDP growth figures by 50%. Multiply Inflation figures by a factor of 2.5. Multiply general Unemployment percentages by a factor of 1.5 (to obtain *Minority* Unemployment rates, use a factor of 3).

We are now more vulnerable in both Finance and Economy, since 2008. The Fed Balance Sheet is worse by almost 4 trillion (and is, itself, now more leveraged than Lehman Brothers at the time of their collapse). The notional value of the Derivatives market is at about 1.4 Quadrillion (*i.e.,* 23 times World GDP) from the modest 600 Trillion in 2009. In 2012, just one bank, J.P. Morgan had $72 trillion, about the size of World GDP, in notional amounts of derivatives on its books. The notional amount of derivatives held by US commercial banks in 2012, was about $223 trillion, with the four largest US banks accounting for 93% of these contracts (the US GDP is 17.5 trillion, by way of comparison).

The US Big Banks are liquid, but not far from *insolvency*, in particular given the potential derivative loadings referred to: they are, on average, leveraged as per the Basel III approved rate, at 33:1—which is higher than Lehman ratios at the time of its collapse (the new rules, for 2014, require the eight biggest bank holding companies to maintain top-tier capital equal to 5% of total assets, so the Debt/Capital ratio is now being raised to 20:1).

QE has gone, since 2008, ever straight into asset-price inflation: finance, and real estate. The so-called 'tapering' is idle talk only—to reassure creditors: in fact, recently, tiny Belgium bought $242 billion of Treasury Bonds. *Belgium, with its GDP of $500 billion!* So, we might all guess who actually made the purchase, regardless of the proxy used. The weakness of the dollar is unmistakably evidenced in the strong price of gold (despite unceasing efforts on the part of North Atlantic Central Banks to short it). Stocks (like real estate and the dollar) are overvalued, with corporations buying their own stock, owing to the cheap, or rather 'free' money, policies. Besides, the stock market now has no appreciable (positive) effect on the real economy. That disconnect, including the baseline asymmetry between risk and reward, took place years ago.

The European Central Bank (ECB), led by the Fed, has taken the next step in this downward spiral by going into the no-man's land of *negative interest rates,* just one step short of, and ahead of, the coming bail-in (where bank deposits can be legally confiscated) that kicks in, in January 2015, as EU Policy. The ECB is also, similarly, expanding its own balance sheet, encouraged by the US example, so the EU is now heading in the same direction—of insolvency (and break-up). They all know the Big Banks are likely to implode.

Real Estate is doing better, but only at the speculative peak of the realty pyramid where big investment banks are involved. At lower levels, homeowners in serious delinquency are but daily fare, back at 2009 levels, with 1.9 million mortgages at risk, or slightly under 5%. New mortgage applications are down 21%, with prices up by 11%. Consumer spending has only kept up, if at all, with Price Inflation. So it's vaunted 'increase' is delusive. There is no monetary policy aimed at price stability, any more, or full employment, as required by statute. It is engaged only in staving off the inevitable plunge of the dollar—and protecting the balance sheets of the Big Banks.

In effect, *Finance Capital* dominates the Anglo-American world (just 5 of the biggest US banks have holdings valued at 56% of the US GDP (Jamie Dimon, of J.P. Morgan, recently, treated a $6 billion trading loss as a 'tempest in a teacup'), and is gaining that same position within the EU. But, a few of the known activities of the really Big Banks make Al Capone seem like a small town pick-pocket: from LIBOR price-fixing, gold-price fixing, money-laundering, tax evasion, inside trading, misleading clients, and foreclosure abuse. Yet, who can hold them really accountable?: after all, many of their top executives interchange as sobrietous Government regulators (and *vice versa*)!

M2 (cash + checking deposits + time deposits) velocity has been eroding steadily by about 2% since 2000 (Banks are not lending across the board, consumers are not expanding expenditures, and only student loan debt is 'taking off,' standing at $1.trillion plus: it is estimated that each graduating student will be saddled with over $25K of debt), and is at a historic low of 1.56 today.

M2 supply growth is averaging at around 5.2%, since 2008. Given these numbers, nominal growth rates cannot exceed 3% by much: and, after splitting for inflation, real growth is close to nil. The Money multiplier has fallen off from over 8 in 2000 to about 3 now, whence the Fed's balance sheet expansion is not readily translating into broad monetary expansion (owing to the standstill in velocity). The Fed, recently, asked the Top Tier banks, in 2013, to prepare 'stress tests' against a 'severely adverse scenario' that visualizes the following data: the jobless rate peaks at 11.25%, stocks fall almost 50%, and US housing prices slide 25%, while the Euro area sinks into recession.

Developing economies in Asia are also experiencing a 'sharp slowdown.' I would think that the 'severely adverse scenario' is about as close to realism that the

Fed has ever gotten, and more imminent than many imagine. There is no serious fiscal policy, since investible capitals are diverted into feeding bubbles: in the bond market, the dollar, and real estate. More importantly, the domestic economy does not figure, as an issue, in any serious way. Why?

Because the Corporates are quite ok with it all: since they are doing well. They employ, manufacture, and in many cases, base themselves, notionally, *Offshore* (to escape taxes, regulation, and decent wages), *the very essence of so-called Globalization*, to great advantage. Why should they, or their Government (let there be no doubt), worry about domestic Growth, or Unemployment? In non-economic areas, the slide is steady and steep, and a snapshot of other indicative data is anything but reassuring.

Number One in the World's Crime Index at 4.7 per 100K population, the developed world's highest homicide rate, and the world's highest rate of gun violence, the United States spends more on the military than any other nation, and more than the next four rivals taken together. Not one American city figures in the top 10 cities in the world for livability. We spend more on Health than any nation, yet figure 37th in the WHO Health Index. We are still number One in Air pollution. We have 50% more First-day deaths of the newborn than all the industrialized nations taken together. All of the above is, possibly, gross data: on a subtler scale is the issue of the eclipse of basic civic niceties.

Concealed weapons are legal on many college campuses, and AK47's may be openly carried into fast food establishments as part of that very same legality. *This is reminiscent of a satrapy of backwoods Afghan warlords, not a society of refinement or grace.* Civilisation? Yes: in its *Anglo-Norman Avatar.*

Let's take up another area, Education: in an OECD survey on Education (reported under the banner of 'The Decline of America') young Americans finished dead last in a twenty-six nation sample: in reading, numeracy, literacy, and problem-solving. We spend 5 cents per dollar on education, 68% on foreign wars. *The 'Aim': a perfect Idiocracy, on steroids.* Worse, many schools are militarized, criminalized, razor-wired, and kept under surveillance: with gun-toting security guards, as part of the 'zero tolerance' policy: girls arrested—yes arrested—for using perfume; others expelled for burping, and doodling; with a seven-year old actually arrested in the cafeteria for nibbling his pop-tart into the shape of a hill.

In even more sinister fashion, 'disorders' like ADD and ADHT are being used in brute diagnoses to make paying customers out of normal kids, and placing them on Anti-Depressants, in Prozac-organized 'National Depression' screening days. Half of all school kids watch Channel One TV in class every day, with 80%

of its programming crammed with commercial adverts for popular consumer items. And so it goes. Orwell was writing, it would seem, but a puerile, G-rated, kindergarten version of extant reality. So, what can one expect?

Well there is Always War (even, perhaps, a nuclear one: after all no other Power has ever claimed a 'first-strike' right), in the plural: that may be the only 'fiscal policy' the regime is willing to consider. *Perhaps, if peace were a four-letter word, it might get used more often:* thereby alerting the populace as to what might appear, to many young folk, *who have never known the nation not at war,* to be a novel alternative to the *status quo.*

In fact, the governors have already achieved a certain kind of success in the behavioral domain: recent psychological studies find the young down more than 40% in *empathy*, a necessary step toward 'mainstreaming' the sociopath and psychopath as the norm rather than the exception. It will stimulate War production with stable employ (unless it is nuclear)—if subject to sudden attrition during action—and, importantly, may divert people from their (many) domestic woes. However, it is my guess that many have, by now, seen through the spin. And there are, possibly, term limits, even to bizarro worlds.

But, until the next collapse—triggered by a plunging dollar, and bringing with it a bond and stock market slump, one can, likely, expect more of the same. The *Why* of it all can now be answered, since most analyses that reach similar conclusions elide the issue. Capitalism—in simple terms, the profit-motive, embodied in Corporate entities, and channeled *via* markets—unless restrained, either by custom/convention, or by regulation, sees a profit opportunity in each and every domain of life: and will seize it, if allowed to (and their 'private interest' is often in direct conflict with the public interest: besides, why leave matters as vital as employment and income to the chance vagaries of a blind market driven only by alternating bouts of greed and fear? It is as irrational, as it is iniquitous.)

And no society has allowed it as much Open License as we have. But, it can be so restrained, and held accountable, wherever communities are serious about it, albeit at cost. The 'profiteering disposition'—*Me First, All Others Afterwards*—is by no means confined to the investing class, but is become a sort of an *American Creed*, and accounts for much of the unconscionable behavior witnessed daily, across the board, as the business norm. In that regard, Wall Street Banks, in 2008, only acted out what is inherent in this rampant philosophy of Societal Darwinism that is not significantly apart from prevailing corporate norms. *As Marx had it, eons ago, capitalism not only has no values but, worse, derides all values.*

The *Amoral Society* is what it produces, at the end of the trail. So, we are little other than the apotheosis of Scottish-English Free Trade ideology, though the latter came wrapped, as in Adam Smith, with redoubtable 'moral sentiments.' That wrap was doffed a long time ago, perhaps falling overboard into the Atlantic on a particularly rough crossing, by those New World pioneers. Too bad they didn't lose their conquistadorean temper of empire, *en route*, as well. It is highly instructive that China is Number One today, on the same material scale that Europe invented as the universal yardstick—but has no interest in the 'full spectrum dominance' so beloved by Anglo-American ruling elites.

So it is not enough to rein in Corporate greed by *fiat*: a much larger, and perhaps more necessary, task is to *reseed culture* itself with more socially empathetic norms than are available: and that would imply a moral revolution on a scale akin to the Reformation. That is the 'civilization' that Gandhi spoke of, decades ago. Until then, reform will only be followed, after a hiatus, to a return to the same *status quo* (Vidal, wisely, called us the *United States of Amnesia*).

I call the Post-WWII version of this Unchained Midas Machine the '*Post-Human Society,*' with a book by that title, authored in 1992, published in 2015 (Kanth, 2015).

2

The Root Cause

Few, in these times, are into seeking *Ultimate Causes*. Most wouldn't know how, even if they really wished to know. A few slogans, a few headlines, a few 'talking points' are enough to set off the ritual tirades. This applies to both the 'left' and 'right' amongst the ruling tribe of *EuroModernists*. Whilst they may have some topical value in describing viewpoints, those two aging postures are also strictly *passé: for they are both internal to Modernism, and serve only to prop up the Edifice*.

Democracy, by now, should be understood to be what it really is, stripped of its banal rhetoric—the pre-eminent tool to: (a) protect a regime from outright revolt, and (b) to allow Corporates full control, behind the scenes, over all key variables that matter. So, whilst the populace gets into a merry frenzy trying to figure which of the two Mutt and Jeff, or Dastardly and Dastardly, candidates is the real McCoy, the real governors attend to real business—unnoticed.

Yes, we are always passionately involved with giving our rapt attention to the monkeys, whilst the organ-grinders remain well out of sight: the above is not just true of candidates, but also of Political parties. In office, they all conform to the Centre. No, the Corporates didn't set up 'democracy' to let us vote them out of business (despite the nostrums of 'political science').

❋

Where Corporations are people. Where Money is free speech. Where Legislators, like petty voyeurs, are given but only limited sneak previews of new Laws, if at all, by the Corporates. Where Corporate Courts openly undermine, and disdain, popular sovereignty. Where journalists critical of the State credo are viewed as possible 'terrorists.' Where false flag events are staged to suppress rights, and increase surveillance. Where not wrong-doers, but whistle-blowers get prosecuted. *This, no less, is the Grand Apotheosis of the Great European Way, of all those grandiloquent 'declarations' with which Europe announced its godlike 'Enlightenment,' and perennial superiority, over all Others.*

Yes: we are all convinced, by now that Hitler and Stalin were but early novices, mere upstarts, and anticipators, of the high norms of the US-UK world of 'full spectrum dominance,' and hegemony. For 'Europe,' after WWII, is not even a shade of Europe as it was, but merely a mix of vassal states of the Anglo-Saxon Empire.

❋

So, why is it all the way it is?

And how did we (well most of 'us,' the *sans-culotte*, within and without Europe, didn't have a smidgeon of choice) get here? No, it's not a failure of Capitalism or Communism. For, they are but *artefact-avatars* of a much larger 'gila monster' by name of *(Euro) Modernism*, which was uniquely European in provenance. Indeed, no other society on earth had ever produced such a novel, daring, and revolutionary, societal philosophy. Stated succinctly, it is in the willful privileging of individual self-interest over and above communal and societal welfare.

In subscribing to that one fateful principle, Europe had stood anthropic history on its head, and set itself light years apart from its own history—and the history of all peoples. The profit-motive, capitalism, *et al.*, were merely the derivatives of that, more primary, notion. After that, naturally, came the Deluge. They made human society not the instinctual, natural, entity it is, but rather a 'rational,' 'contractual' entity, *i.e.*, into a 'civil society' monstrosity of *'universal egoism'* (Hegel), where each uses the other, and society itself, as but means to a private end.

That was the original death knell: and it is still ringing. And that is why the Doomsday Clock keeps getting moved closer to midnight. And that is why humans, sloughing off their mammalian mold turned reptilian: wherever under the sway of that terrible ideology.

❄

We are a *tribal* species, leaning on affective ties, forged *via* kinship, real or fictitious. That is our real, natural, *species-being*. It is in that matrix that we, as a species, thrive. Stripped of that, we are lost, like most Modernists (be they European or not, since most of us now are under its thrall), succumbed to *angst*, normlessness, and worse. Constitutions and Rules of Law are the formalized, desiccated, synthetic substitutes for the life giving ties of conviviality that fail miserably. Go ahead, I dare you: hug your Constitution, kiss your Rule Book, and then tell me, if you will, of the nature of gratifications earned, or solace gained. And so we run about seeking it, instinctively: if ever in all the wrong places.

Instead of love, warmth, and all the natural cravings of a societal animal, they gave you the chimera of personal 'freedom' to live on. I say chimera because the freedom they offered the populace was but the tendentious, dissembling ploy; the ruse, the doggy-biscuit handout with which to hide the far greater freedom they reserved strictly for themselves: *to dominate, exploit, plunder, rule, and govern—for, and by, themselves*. Now that's a Faustian deal, an *Ex Parte* deal they handed out, in the Modernist Revolutions, to those, who in the main, did not ask for it: and at grievous cost of surrendering their antic birthrights, customs, compacts, cultures, and autonomies.

Liberty, Freedom? Yes, Alexander Selkirk had it all. And we are all the worse for it.

❄

What is to be done? No, it is what is to be *Undone*, if the Doomsday Clock is—ever—to be turned back. We can learn our social alphabet all over again from the 'savages,' the Aboriginals, the Bushmen, the Andaman islanders, all the 'peoples without history.' They still hold the keys: of conviviality, commensality, and co-operation. We could (still) rediscover the '*Moral Economy*', that unique anthropic sanctuary usually tended by women, for millennia. Sound utopian? Hardly: because the nucleus of the Moral Economy, the human family, is with us still, despite all the Policies (not necessarily willful) to dismantle, debase, and debauch it that have been around for centuries in the Modern era. Yes: and it is, still, *en generale*, neither free, equal, nor 'democratic.' Yet it suffices, as nothing else does.

For, as I have said before, *the greatest human need of all is: to huddle*.

3

Crisis, Disaster, Catastrophe

Up the Down Escalator

When I consider there is a just god in heaven, wrote Jefferson, I shudder to think of the fate of my country.

And that was when sins, of omission and commission, were still a cottage industry—not a Transnational Enterprise. But, regardless of a 'god' that is/is not just, it would yet be meet to shudder, in these latter days. Now back in the Nineties, with the Soviet debacle in mind, the joke was that the highest stage of Communism was Capitalism. Since then, we know, without undue hyperbole, that the highest stage of Capitalism is a freshly renewed (*neo*)*Feudalism*.

Such, the ironies of a *devolutionary* history. Except, it's no irony: it's tragedy—of Himalayan proportions. *For these are the bad old days of False Flag, Black Swan, Parapolitical, and Deep State, events that have tripped over each other, day after day, to return us all to antediluvian socio-political spaces.*

The unabashed rollback of 'rights' and liberties—which were a dubious matter for the many, even at the time when they were *not* so viciously trampled—led, as ever, by the Anglo-Am hegemonic powers, *today*, is unspeakably staggering. Of course, it's also a potent warning to the naïve who see only 'progress' written into societal evolution since the Enlightenment, as part of their blind—or is it bland?—*Eurocentric* hubris.

One clean, swift, putsch: and we were all transported to the terra infirma of a profiteer's dystopia with complete union between the state, the corporate sector, and the media. What various erstwhile dictatorships could not achieve, despite trying, may now been effectively secured, ironically, within the lead countries of the 'free' world. We lurch on now, mostly in shock and stupefaction: how many political traditions are now eating humble pie, if they are eating at all?

For some two decades now, I have been writing/speaking, of the very foundations of the larger mindset that has garnered such bitter fruits. For, at the base of all human edifices, material or ideational, rest *metaphysical suppositions:* and when philosophical error is at their heart, dire consequences follow. *To repeat: no (accurate) economic or political idea about human society is tenable unless it rests on a prior elaboration of a realist anthropology of humans.* Such a realist *Anthropology* has been absent, in the European tradition, for centuries. The Enlightenment concocted imaginary ontologies of 'human nature' (applied to economy, polity, and society) be it of Hobbes, Locke, Smith, or Rousseau, to serve topical, policy ends. Classical *'progressivism,'*—'Socialism' in particular—was merely a secular version of Christian redemption, so was equally specious in what it 'assumed' about our *species-being* (Darwin's great, if incomplete, work arrived too late even for Marxian speculations).

In 2007, I provided an outline sketch, in two *Festschrift* Lectures, of a *non-Eurocentric* Anthropology that is true because it is verifiable, and verifiable because it is true (these constitute, in this work, the *Introduction* and the *Postface:* they are also available on YouTube—*Kanth https://www.youtube.com/watch?v=ZDwQrp fom9M*). If properly understood, it can help correct the more facile errors of past theorizing—in the direction of caution. It shows us we live not in an ideal world, but in a real, Darwinian world whose unflattering traits are part of our daily, lived experience. I will refrain from drawing out its implications, save to say that *we can't simply invent utopias, willy-nilly, and expect human society to conform to our specifications.* And we are now at a dark pass, perhaps the darkest!, in human history: and clinging to defective paradigms will not at all help us even imagine, let alone find, a way out. The forces that have brought us here will take us even further, and faster, toward perdition: and we do not have the luxury of decades of rumination.

The Anglo-Am empire is a new *Neo-Feudal* Colonialism continuing on the great European tradition of Empire that was unsettled in the early decades of the twentieth century. It is now back in the saddle, breathing fire. Europe is yet on training wheels, in this regard (save France, which at heart, *never really gave up the idea of* empire—a necessary adjunct to their own deep-rooted chauvinism as the self-styled flag-bearer of European Civilization—parsed as *'liberté,' 'egalité,'* and, inevitably, *'banalité'*). The only remaining obstacles to its world domination remain China, Russia: and its own quite formidable folly. Right now it is this latter that checks its pretensions, rather than any serious resistance on the part of Russia and China. At any rate, at this point, anything is possible, only because even a minimal 'rationality' is far from being its present governing trait.

The dollar, and its related banking system, can collapse, any day, though not unexpectedly. A national emergency could then be declared. Indeed, this could happen even prior to any such collapse. *Two,* quite separate, strategies might then be followed. *One way* is *War,* which would, in outline, be World War III. In such a war, born of chaos, and frustration, quite anything is possible. The current Imperials cannot hope to win such a war, in any arena. But they can level *Others* to their own dismal levels of disarray, thus achieving a certain 'parity'—which is not improbable.

The *Other Way* would be to utilize the national emergency to remedy the deep malaise. Policy would have to systematically re-engineer the entire world economy—and start afresh. Either strategy would, in some degree, spell breakdown, in the short run, with deep social strife. So, come what may, the chariot is out of control: and cannot be pulled back from the precipice. As it currently stands, the Fed, for all its jawboning, will continue its titanic 'easing'—to serve its mission of keeping the dollar, and the banking system, afloat. If it didn't, interest rates would spike, the securities market would collapse—and so would the banks. This won't do: *since the Fed is, naturellement!, their bank, not the nation's.* And no one is, or has ever been, powerful enough, to tell them what to do. Of course, a miniscule, nominal increase is conceivable mainly as face-saving eyewash.

So, the current stalemate will eke on until it can crawl no further. Of course the pundits of the hour will still, bravely, see 'light' at the end of the tunnel—even if that be only the effulgent façade of *Nemesis.* And what is that point?: when the world starts to sell off its dollars. *Then, the deluge.* To conceive of that as just another 'Great Depression' would be foolhardy, as it would spell not merely a collapse in the supply-chain, but a currency slump—together with rocketing prices. The original Depression did not carry the latter two derangements. Of course, 'eventually', Special Drawing Rights (SDRs)—issued by the IMF as an alternate currency, or, even the 'Amero'—and such, will be brought in, though not without due discord. But even this takes time: and the interim will not be an equable one even were *Option#2* to be chosen.

So, oddly enough, given the disasters to come, these may well be the only 'good times' we will know, for a long while. But, then again, human history has never been a bed of roses. Beyond the mundane certainties of the proverbial 'death and taxes,' lie the three near-eternal scourges: *racism, sexism, and empire* (the last is, admittedly *itinerant*, depending on fortuitous circs. that cannot be dealt with here). *For some four hundred years, regrettably, the outstanding fact of world history has been the conquest, annexation, pillage, and mass-murder of non-Europeans by Europeans (to be joined, in this pastime, later, by their North American Offshoots).* Since the beginning of the twentieth century, they have shown, even beyond the scale of dynastic, religious, and ethnic conflicts of prior times, an equal readiness to quite *destroy themselves* in the process.

World War I and World War II were, *primarily,* European-inspired, *inter-Imperial* Wars (the resources, human and non-human, of the *Non-European,* mostly colonized, world were imperatively commandeered to serve this effort: *India, e.g., in all irony, fought on behalf of its oppressors).* World War III may well be a *Europe (inclusive of North America) turned against its entire Periphery,* globally, *in an All-out War that will end War itself*—for rendering human civilization near-extinct. A steep price to pay, one would think, for everlasting, universal, 'peace'! And yet how very Darwinian, in a way: after all, more than 98% of species that have ever existed have gone extinct.

What is so special about us?

4

Anatomy of a Crisis

I have laid out, in some detail, the structure of the collapse at hand. It is a crisis, specifically, of Anglo-Am Capitalism, an over-determined form of 'greed-run-riot.' *Culture* (or the lack of it?) is, thereby, at the very root of the problem. Not surprisingly, culture is excised from (social) scientific discourse in the Eurocentric idiom, true to its self-avowed 'materialism'—to its great detriment.

Easy to see why: *culture is, above all things, difference.* Modernism seeks, instead, a flat, homogeneous, monotonic, uniform, world, ideal for conquest, manipulation, and control: and smooth capital accumulation. Whence the spurious, epistemic cant of 'we are all equal,' *etc.* (a rhetoric quickly abandoned on the *terra firma* of the glaring divides in income, wealth, power, privilege in relation to race, class, gender, religion, *etc.*).

And yet where is culture (or its absence) not visible? Iceland and Switzerland (and a few other such in Europe), for example, could not have given us, nor even imagined, such a crisis. They have rather humble 'tribal' value limits that set bounds to how far they can let society be debauched for profit (even when led by their Trans-Atlantic hegemon).

I have said that we, as a species, for all our vaunted 'modernist identities' are but tribals under the skin: Europe has proved that for centuries—as it is doing now, yet again. Similarly, no Eastern, or Non-European society, even in full capitalist encoilment, like China, could have traveled this far. They would have been halted by a certain prudential restraint that is almost instinctive. But not so, apparently, for (*i.e.*, the rulers of) John Bull or Uncle Sam. *They are a breed apart.* But, matters run even deeper. It is not even a crisis of Capitalism, *per se: rather, is it a crisis of European Modernism (EM) which is the mother matrix of both Eurocapitalism and Eurosocialism* (which are the Tweedledum and Tweedledee of Modernist discourse).

For years now, I have been posting a critique of this paradigm (defined in my *Eurocentrism Lectures* cited earlier), in my writings: to fairly stark incomprehension. A fateful step was taken when Europe, starting in the seventeenth century, switched over, in epistemics first, to a '*contract*' model of society, from its previous '*organic*' *modus* which it shared with human society at large. Suddenly, what was a natural, unconscious, immanent, *End* (for better, or for worse) became a willful *means*—to individual fulfillment (or lack of it). This step removed the dominant European tribes, radically apart, from the rest of the social universe—and their own previous history. There was no 'looking back' for them after that: and, to this day, they remain, in a fundamental sense, incomprehensible to both traditional societies (such as the Masai, or the Bushmen), and to the uneasy or reluctant modernizers (such as the Myanmar, or Bhutan) that try to 'walk that walk,' either under temptation or duress.

Rudyard Kipling's romanticized 'East is East and West is West, and never the twain shall meet' apothegm is only true when understood in the above terms. Indeed, it makes no realist sense in any other frame: unless it be one of outright racist chauvinism (in which *genre*, he was but one of the many, shining, exemplars of his time). Today's China and Russia (the historic *Other*) know the *game* of the artful manufacture of a crisis in the Ukraine: but they cannot really grasp the mind-set undergirding it's breathtaking insanity. Nor did Khrushchev (not to mention a petrified world that watched it all play out in shock) understand the how/why of a Kennedy ready and willing to press a Doomsday button, in the so-called 'Cuban Missile Crisis,' though he knew it was all too real.

Speaking figuratively, I have previously identified the struggles today, albeit within a Modernist world, as between 'Reptiles' and 'Mammals,' *i.e.,* between the cold-blooded and the warm-blooded. Such is the affective divide between the Anglo-Ams, and the 'rest of the world's—philosophy.

There is, also, a slightly different way in which this issue might be posed. I have suggested that the world has always known morality and immorality: *but amorality was a unique European invention*, itself related to, and a consequence of, the societal model that replaced the 'balance of affections' reality of real, anthropic society with the 'balance of interests' notion. Hegel expressed this latter trait beautifully, and succinctly, when he termed this so-called 'Civil Society' as the world of *'universal egoism.'* Invented in Europe, it nonetheless overfilled the hollows of America—itself an 'artificial' construction—as nowhere else: it is this outstanding feature that makes it the most radically inventive, and most lethally toxic, entity amongst the entire Comity of Nations.

Stated simply, there are no inherent normative limits to both its imaginations and its practices: all others are limited, in greater or lesser degree, by the dusky overhang of moral nuance and idiom. After all, it was itself erected upon the greatest holocaust in modern history, as well as upon its largest slave society. It also, in that very same vein of perfunctory insouciance, dropped nuclear devices on a large, hapless civilian population. *Culture, i.e.,* conventional morality, no matter how wispy and fleeting, sets limits in all other nations as to whether, and how far, they can go in any direction: in America (a fast waning) 'legality' is the only remaining, real, structural bound—since an amoral stance is utterly libertine, indeed wholly profligate, in its egregious spread.

Of course, once the 'law' itself is widely understood (as is becoming more and more true today) as being but an ordinary commodity bought, sold, debauched, like any other, then alas: even that mild barrier is of no further consequence. In sum, everything is a *'game'* (recall the Benthamite trope of 'Pushpin being as good as poetry') in its feral discourse—and the evolution of 'game theory' is itself of significance in this regard—and a (virtual) video game is as good as a (real) war game. In fact, the 'drone' as a remote controlled instrument of casual techno mass-murder, maladroitly, joins those two worlds in macabre synthesis.

I have mentioned Nietzsche and Kierkegaard as important philosophers who, presciently, glimpsed the approach of this fatal impasse in human affairs; and quite understood its terrors: the one (latter) taking refuge in religion, the other (former) in self-induced dementia. Of course, the putative 'progressivists' of European thought dismissed that entire genre as being 'romantic' and retrograde. One would think that the developing realities of the twentieth century would bury the linear mythology of 'progress' forever.

Anthropic society is a matrix of affective reciprocations: *i.e.,* it is, before anything else, a *moral* entity. Its replacement, in Modernist zealotry, by rational, material, 'exchanges' of tangibles, cools the social temper, injects iron in the soul, and 'alienates' each from each, and one from all. Marx understood much of this emergent domain of 'alienation' but, given his perhaps unconscious Judeo-Christian layering, failed to see that the new chasm was also a rift between society and nature (since society is, inexorably, a natural entity): *i.e.,* his lack of a full

Darwinian understanding prevented an understanding of humans as *animals* in the first instance (as I have written, the idealist extremes of socialist fantasy are but the secular version of Christian redemption). It is our animal nature that is, inexorably, 'social': *the 'family,' e.g.,—and despite cultural variation—is both a natural and a societal entity simultaneously.*

Instead, the dominant strand of classical European anthropology, down to Levi-Strauss, in the second half of the twentieth century, in the inescapable Judeo-Christian (henceforth, J/C) vein, continued to postulate a spurious 'opposition' between nature and culture, such that the latter is require to 'transcend' the other: doubtless because, to put it in Marx's words, 'Man is the sovereign of all Creation' (*i.e.*, descended from 'god,' so to speak, not apes). The consequences of philosophical error, I have suggested, can be calamitous (and a realist anthropology needs to be the basis for any and all speculations about utopias): so women, and 'primitives,' ended up classified at the bottom of that totem pole as *naturvolk* (as opposed to the more genteel *culturvolk* at its elite upper end) to their everlasting detriment.

Of course, Women and the *Other* have never fared very well in any of the taxonomies of materially stratified societies, east or west. The issue is particularly egregious in the European instance only because, unlike traditional societies, Europe retains all the biases of such societies whilst hypocritically parading, and wrapping itself in, the lavish lexicon of liberation. At any rate, the European became, as per this conceit, a ravening 'civilization-monger,' on the side, even as he sought to impose his own material brand of philistinism (pillage/plunder) on the *Other* (in the specious name of the various catechisms of 'Progress'). This Game is still on, in dead earnest: but with potentially calamitous effects for *All,* since the old option of a unilateral, *one-way*, genocide is no longer an option.

So, I have defined the real stakes in the struggle, globally, today: primarily it is one of saving the moral existence of our species from the sweep of those profoundly out of touch with their own anthropic natures, with the simple *desiderata* of the basic reciprocities of human society, and with the larger, universal, nature of which we are but an aliquot, infinitesimal part. In short, *the moral will be pitted against the amoral:* a unique struggle quite unprecedented in human history. We shall—*All*—either prevail in this, in this dangerous decade: or disappear from the planet, like 98% of all other species that have ever existed.

All this might have saddened, if not really surprised, Darwin—or so one would imagine.

Part II

The Economy

5

Where We Are

To repeat, in parts, some comments from a previous chapter: Hollywood and TV show the Unspeakable. Perhaps, if peace were a four-letter word, they would use it more often, to the millions who are under their spell. Pentagon discusses the Unthinkable Wall Street engages in the Irreparable. The Media dole out the Unbelievable. We, the People cannot expect Equity. We cannot ask for Justice We cannot require Security. We cannot demand that elected reps fulfill their mandates. We cannot insist on rights without our gracious high judiciary agreeing with the executive branch. Millions of us cannot expect gainful, let alone meaningful, jobs.

Nor can we ask that explicit corporate plunder of the eco-system, such as fracking, be abated, if not stopped. We cannot stop GMO pollution. We cannot ask for a ban on BGH. We can't even ask for full disclosure labeling. We stopped asking for truth from the government (at its royal 3% approval rating). We are not obliged to get it from the Corporates, given their privacy rights (rights that, apparently, don't exist for us). They can make war, even nuclear war, without our consent. They can, frankly, do what they wish—and they do that, willy-nilly—as they have for aeons. As I have said before, only the fig leaf has been shed: all else is business as usual.

Meanwhile, society decays. Debt is way up, Savings are down. And debt of a kind that does not generate income, or pay back the principal. The GDP, in my calculation, adjusted for real inflation, has not budged since 2008.My rule of thumb is: discount official GDP growth figures by 50%, multiply real inflation figures by a factor of 2.5, multiply general Unemployment by a factor of 1.5. We are now more vulnerable in Finance, and Economy, since 2008. The Fed Balance Sheet is worse by almost 4 Trillion (and is itself now more leveraged than Lehman Brothers at the time of their collapse).

The notional value of the Derivatives Market is at about 1.4 Quadrillion (*i.e.,* 23 times World GDP) from the modest 600 Trillion since 2009. The US Big Banks are liquid, but insolvent, given the above, and hopelessly over-leveraged (their required debt/capital ratio is about 20:1: Basel III allows a 33:1 ratio). QE has gone straight into asset-price inflation: finance, and real estate. The tapering is idle talk only: recently, tiny Belgium bought $242 Billion of Treasury Bonds. Belgium, with its GDP of $500 billion!: so we might all guess who actually did.

Stocks are overvalued, with corporates buying their own stock, owing to the cheap, nay 'free,' money policies. Besides, the stock market now has no appreciable (positive) effect on the real economy. The European Central Bank (ECB) has taken the next step in this downward spiral by going into the no-man's land of *negative interest rates*, just one step short of, and ahead of, the coming *bail-in* (where bank deposits can be legally confiscated) that kicks in in January (2015) as policy.

The ECB is also expanding its own balance sheet, encouraged by the US example, so EU is now heading in the same direction—of insolvency. Real Estate is doing well, but only at the top of the realty pyramid where private equity is involved. Consumer spending has only kept up with Price Inflation. There is no monetary policy aimed at price stability any more, or full employment, as required by Law. It is only into staving off the inevitable plunge of the dollar. The velocity of circulation of money has been falling by 3% since 2008 (Banks are not lending across the board, and only student loan debt is 'taking off,' standing at $1.2 trillion). M2 supply growth is stationary at 6%. So nominal growth rates cannot exceed 3%: but discounted by real inflation it is close to nil. The Money multiplier was about 8 before 2007, it is less than 3 now, so growth in Money supply is also at a far lower rate today.

There is no fiscal policy, since investible capitals are being diverted into feeding bubbles: the bond market, the dollar, and real estate. More importantly, the domestic economy does not figure in any serious way. Why? Because the Corporates are quite ok with it: they are doing well. Why should they, or their government, worry about domestic Growth or Unemployment? So, what can one expect?

Well there is always *War*: that may be the only 'fiscal policy' the regime is willing to consider. It will stimulate war production: and, more importantly, maybe divert people from their domestic woes. But even this traditional ploy may not be tenable: too many have seen through the spin.

6

More Endgames

There's news of the marvel Trading outfit which, unlike us ordinary mortals who have good days and bad days, racked up over 1230 consecutive, successful, trading days in the 'too fast to fail,' High-Frequency Trade Market. Imagine that, as well as the odds! No matter: give those calculators a rest. These are Endgame Scenarios, each more of a 'black swan' event than the other: so we may well have to gear up for a next-generation genre of 'lilac swan' events. Yes, Virginia, fantasies happen.

Also, twelve bankers have, putatively, committed 'suicide' since January—one deploying a staple gun: know how many staples it takes…? That's a current switch from the old cast of 'lone, crazed, gunmen' who, conveniently, removed Undesirables from this world. No matter: it's another one of those contemporary tales that make these times so memorable.

Used to be, Economic commentators (these are the folk who know even less about the economy than economists) once talked of 'business cycles' to explain hard times (for the many, not the few). Now they don't. In fact, the term 'economy' is itself *passé—finance* is the favored proxy for now. Too bad the breaking crises cannot be alphabetically engineered by the global dealmakers for the sake of sequential elegance: Ireland, Iceland, Cyprus, Greece, Detroit—and (now) Puerto Rico—make for a somewhat messy alphabet soup. Who's next? Ukraine?

No, that's strictly a Dr. Strangelove affair. It's just side-entertainment, whilst the barbecue spit is being stoked.

And the redefinitions are legion: McDonald's is getting hamburger flipping recognized as 'manufacture'—and larger moves are afoot to include the *Non-Factory* stages of production to also be included in the same net. So Apple—which, until recently, 'produced,' as per the older usage, next to nothing in the US—can now become one of its largest manufacturers. Not to mention Silicon Valley. The idea is to anoint '*Factory-Less Job Producers*' with a more favorable designation. Suddenly, the US could be declared, once again, a leading global manufacturer! O, wouldn't it be lovely! Poor Germany, Japan, Korea, and China: if only they could come up with some plain old fashioned home-baked Yankee ingenuity!

Now, there's a challenge for our more venturesome economists: there might even be a Nobel Prize in this game of accounting fabrication? And why not? They have been awarded it for less. Only we know that the real economy is no more than a New-Wave reality show: they, being behind the times, still take it all too seriously—as if life were really about those sordid factories, production technologies, and jobs! At any rate, since business cycles are out of style, we could speak instead, perhaps, of crime waves of a rhythmic nature: say, hypothetically, a QE being followed by a credit and housing bubble; then a crash of one, or both—then a bail-out/bail-in (as per choice), then back again to square one. Quite a show: even if it lacks now, in these latter-days, that vital element of surprise. After all, over 45% of graduating Seniors from Princeton apparently opted for finance, with Harvard and Yale not too far behind. Genius goes where it spots opportunity. And one does not need to be a genius to spot it nowadays.

There's no Professor William Black, this time around, and don't we/they all know it. So we can all try and be entities too big to jail. Remember Collateralized Debt Obligations, and Credit Default Swaps? They will soon be obsolete: so, why not introduce a new, omnibus cover-all, neologism-series called PFS's. It's my own patent: it stands for *Pre-Immunized Fiduciary Stratagems*. Now, that allows for *all* that they can invent—now, and in the future: a nice, standardized item that can be carefully sold to the lay world, as the newest miracle prop to 'liquidity.' Of course, these have no need for collateralization: the entire tax and deposit base of the country is now a captive stand-in for that!

Exciting. But, sadly, not all the populace 'gets it.' I've seen bumper-stickers in Utah that say things like: 'Ban Mormon Weddings: Stop the Spread of Bigotry,' and, 'Legalize Adulthood for Women.' You see what I mean: here's a brash new world awash with all these mushrooming ways to get rich, and there's these old, reactionary, folk continuing to crib about those bygone bugaboos of women's and minority rights. It's enough to make one want to ask Congress to criminalize living in the past (in addition to criminalizing protest), with atavistic, hackneyed, 'employment and equity' sloganeering. Ugh!

Whatever happened to that old spur to civilization: faith in *progress?* Oh, wait: the phone's ringing. Guess the NSA just tipped off Wall Street—or, perhaps, the other way around. It can all be pretty confusing. But, as they say, (the New World) Order comes out of *Chaos* (as does, regrettably, a richly deserved, wholesale, *collapse*). Though there is no real cause for despair (especially since CNBC, and CNN, have said so). Reminds me of the one about the guy who tells his buddies he talks to God every day; when asked if he really believed that, he turns on them, in all incredulity, to say: what! Would God lie to me?

You see, we can simply declare victory, in all domains, every day of the year: we can claim to be the strongest economy, the greatest military power, the brightest lamp of liberty, the world has ever seen. I'll bet at least the little nation of Grenada (remember Grenada? Now that was a War we truly won, thank goodness, unambiguously, and hands down; more medals were, thence, naturally, awarded than actual soldiers who landed there) will acknowledge some part of that not-immodest set of claims. In fact, that might well serve as the very first 'PFS' wager on record.

Postscript: all right—so irony and satire are not a good fix for our times—but, we may have reached a stage of *desensitization* to the horrors of daily economic and political fraud, where it only hurts, like that old, apocryphal, quip about the WWII soldier's wound—when one laughs.

7

Free Markets

Remember that hackneyed Economics, Friedmanite, maxim that goes: *there's no such thing as a free lunch?* How could you not? It's cited *ad nauseam* in virtually all media—not least by those who have had nothing but free lunches/gratis dinner all their lives. You know of whom I speak: the kind who bail out banks—and then cut food stamps, in the name of austerity. Well, time has turned the tables on that little junket of political casuistry. For now, there is a new, far more indisputable, *mantra* afoot, inspired by the more newsworthy exploits of Wall Street. Here it is: and note it well, for the Media may not post it on prime time.

There is No Such Thing as a Free Market.

Thus do we live—and learn (leastways, some of us). Now, I must say one feels a little sorry for Milton. Could be he never had a free lunch in his life—or so one might surmise. I was mighty lucky: my mom always gave me free lunches. In fact, she made it a point to say, each time:

Rajani: this is yet another free lunch. Tell that to the Monetarists, the Supply-Siders, the Neo-Libs, and all those Voodoo Econ types. That's what moms do, day in and day out: dole out free lunches, don't you know. They've done it for eons. Then there's Mother Nature: she gives it away, too. Ok, so slaves did it too, for their owners, every day of their unpaid lives: like the serfs before them.

Seems to me the ruling elite, everywhere, is up to its gills in free lunches, gratis dinners, and a rash of cocktails in between. But Milton may have a minor point: workers and poor folk don't get any freebies—yep, those gala free luncheons, with which the 'free world' abounds, sure don't 'trickle down.' You know the kind. Like those 3-Martini tax-free corporate lunches, complete with insider-trade tips, in off-shore, exempt, tax-havens. Or, how about the Ponzi-scheme free lunch? I hear that's a biggie. 'Course, there's also the Bail-out free lunch, and the Bail-in free lunch, very popular on Wall Street, and elsewhere, that starts Monday morning, and can go on till the year 2016—or till the Regulators run out of cash.

Or the Gold Price-fixing free lunches that those upright bankers get up to in London twice a day: or all the Interest-rate fixing lunches in between. Then there's the Reserve-currency free lunch, where you can print a lot of money and buy out the world's real resources because everyone's stuck with having to hold your money. Now that can last decades.

So, don't go getting disheartened by these Friedmanite naysayers. In fact, tell you what, if Milt ever came by, I would say to him, come on in, I got a free lunch for you—and all your Chicago Boys, too. Maybe that'll help cheer, and loosen him up a bit.

That was what my mom might have said, had she cared for the con art of econ: but she didn't. Instead, I was brought up believing that the best things (and, even more, *non-things*) in life are free—or should be. Like education, health care, mass transit. A decent society: where basic needs were met, for all, regardless of the canon of the 'ability to pay.' Where the rich(er) would wish to be generous 'trustees' for the welfare of the poor(er). Gandhi called it *Sarvodaya,* or the welfare of all. No, Milton would not have understood, his mantras were of the mundane kind: but it's what innumerable tribal societies, not yet devolved into hierarchical structures, also practiced, for millennia (like Australian Aboriginals).

Bet it was all free in Eden, too (all those loaves and fishes—I admit, I personally don't care much for the latter, being vegan, but maybe it was all metaphor?—*just given away,* if I recall that sermon right). Until that First, Corporatist, Reagan-Thatcher-Friedmanite misfit came around, put a fence around it—and started this whole *meum* and *teum* thing.

You know the rest of it: double-entry bookkeeping, compound interest, and bottom lines. Possibly, a really embittered misanthrope founded Capitalism. Maybe, his mom didn't pack him a free lunch? So, next time you have to deal with a Friedmanite, buy him lunch first: you may find him a kinder, gentler, soul afterward. Alas, not really. These folks have proved themselves to be quite incurably hardcore.

8

Les Folies Tragiques

The Droll Schoolgirl's Guide to the World as It Is Today

Economic 'theory' has not merely trailed far behind reality, but has lived in another dimension of space-time altogether. Ordinarily, this would not be an issue at all—since the 'economy' (*i.e.*, the production, consumption, and distribution of goods/services) has always been 'managed,' by societal overseers, quite independently of such niceties.

However, the danger of economic theory is that it serves not so much to explain, but rather to *rationalize/legitimate* reality (*economics is the crown jewel of capitalist hegemony*, its most committed apologist), usually *via assuming what requires to be proved* (I have written elsewhere that *all of classical economics is just a parable—nursery pap—to suggest that laissez-faire optimizes all/most outcomes*). That latter ploy is sheer, if perverted, genius: *let me assume what I will, and I can then, of course, prove anything!*

The '*argument by assumption*' plan is equally astute: if one raises any empirical objection, one gets the sneer that in a *model* 'realism' is not an issue, despite the fact that *the putative 'model' can be—and is—used to commend this or that policy that bears entirely on the real world.* Indeed, a Dr. Pangloss could learn much from such a versatile *modus*.

The doughty Joan Robinson was once asked by a student, on a visit to India, why anyone should study economics: she said, pithily—*'to protect oneself from being deceived by economists.'* That is as true now as it was in the Fifties, when she said it.

Basically, the tedious arguments between Neoclassicals and Keynesians (the tiresome Tweedledums and Tweedledees of mainstream economics discourse: two schools *divided by a common fealty)* are so much gratuitous 'noise.' *They are much ado about nothing: of course, their theoretical dissonance(s) stem(s) from their choice of tendentious 'assumptions' about the nature of the capitalist economy, despite their common standpoint of accepting it as legitimate.*

If *any* of their maxims got in the way of the *powers-that-be* (that own/operate/control the 'commanding heights' of society) and *their pet choice of policy—they* wouldn't last a day. So, their content (slight as it is) can be 'stretched,' as needed, to serve Policy. No: *one does not need to know 'economics' to operate the real economy*—I know someone with but a 'lite' degree in English Literature who presides, successfully, over a Bank. Better still, there is a trading caste in India—the Patels—who are world-masters at successfully managing economic units, in the most trying locales: yet are, mercifully, ignorant of any economic 'theory.'

Keynesian *'accounts'* were devised originally to *raise money for the War* (that was, more or less, the prosaic *subtitle* of the paper, authored by Keynes and Stone, *circa* 1940, that introduced standard GNP calculations): and it is really no more than a self-contained *accounting* system (now imposed on All by *diktat* by the UN/World Bank).

Keynes was *Policy-driven,* much like Ricardo; and his ideas—even the '*General Theory*'—are little more than *short-run policy guides* ('In the long run,' quoth he, 'we are all dead': as Joan put it aptly again—yes, *but not all at the same time).* One of the key architects of Bretton Woods, *expansion via government debt* was his great contribution to economic policy. *So, we owe the scandal of cataclysmic debt financing, (or, more correctly: its legitimacy), today, at least partly to his ingenuity, with modern governments emulating the hoary practices of feudal monarchies. No doubt, the City of London, and its tight coterie of investment bankers, could not have been happier: en passant, recall he was a City man, a Director of the Bank of England, and his early Treatise was on money.*

'Progressives' are enamored of the 'jobs-creation' side of Keynesianism, *whilst wholly innocent about its financing,* and other societal, implications (again Joan put her finger on it: jobs, *without reference to their content* is, surely, an error—no doubt we could all be employed by the Navy, mining the world's waters...). *Is there anything 'progressive' about running trillion dollar debts, with Unemployment barely touched, as it is today, and the homeless expanding their numbers, and Arms expenditures rocketing sky high?* Possibly not.

To repeat: Keynes fabricates, *ex hypothesi,* an *accounting* system for the macro-economy: and it is only as good/bad as his definitions. There are other, indeed far better, means of scaling the same phenomena—that also take into account (*fuller*) social costs and benefits. *Indeed, the Capitalist economic story can be told from many points of view: workers, consumers, employers, government, public welfare, etc., that are by no means consistent with each other. Inevitably, however, it is told from the vantage of the Investing Class, i.e., the 'animal spirits' loaded Entrepreneur-Hero. Therein, its fatal Elision(s).*

To make the point: here we are, at the worst turn in economic fortunes that the world has experienced in modern history—and what has *economics* to say about it all, either in diagnostics or in cures? The pundits will, if pressed, mumble their old *mantras,* Austrian, Keynesian, or whatever, and that's that: as John Kenneth Galbraith has said, *economists give advice not because they know anything—but because people, all ingenuously, ask/expect them to.* Can one imagine a *real science* like Physics failing similarly, were there to be a similar crisis in the *natural* world around us? Why does economics fail the real world test? *Because the real economy, unlike the pristine analytical one, is driven/rent by political and societal forces, which quite disable its pious nostrums.*

The truth wants telling: even the hypothetical, stand-alone, 'economy' of economists' fantasies can only retain a measure of logical coherence at the *Micro* level. But, in the *Macro* instance, there is no such 'logical' *economics,* culled from its ontological matrix in society, even analytically speaking: only the *real-life force of societal determinism. In effect, the 'economy' is a heuristic abstraction only* (which is why economics fails, dramatically, every time*). So, Microeconomics (Neo Classicism) is but a tendentious parable operating in never-never land: and Macro-economics (Keynesianism) a pathetical, and expurgated, parody of political analysis.*

It is both sad and ironic that the 'progress' that Europeans value so highly about themselves has simply meant moving from the canonical dogmas of Religion to the canonical dogmas of Economics, both equally 'other-worldly,' and delusive—though performing the same vital societal function, of serving as a sop, numbing the wakeful intelligence, and justifying any and all means of societal exactions. As I have argued elsewhere, even the *utopian* strain in European thinking, *e.g.,* 'socialism'—now all but vanished—is but *the secular version of the Christian Vision of Salvation:* the road to hell, in both cases, being paved by a similar, benign intent.

The truth is much starker: we speak of the 'economy' and 'economics,' as if such terms represented something *universal*—they don't. We are speaking of a *capitalist* economy, and an economics of *capitalism*, as first developed within *European* society, sixteenth century onwards. There are a plethora of possible 'economies,' far more benign to the human condition, many of whom were over-run by Euro-Capitalism in process of creating this '*Post-Human*' economy, based on insatiable greed and illimitable expansion, and which, since, has been rudely thrust upon the world. *So, 'getting the economics right' is very far from being the issue: we need to find ourselves a better, more hospitable, economy and society.*

Not only is the *Profiteering* impulse to be radically reined, but the *Patriarchal* one (which drives it) as well: the oppressions visited upon farm-workers and factory-workers, historically, pale in comparison with the non-unionized, far less noticed, servitude of *house-workers* (mostly women, to this day), in particular when they encounter, as is often the case, the *double-jeopardy of being (not necessarily willingly) both factory/farm and house-workers contemporaneously.*

And still the extant ills do not expire: for the *empire* has not merely been exploitative, misogynist, misanthropic (in the largest sense), anti-social, and ecologically disastrous; but also, for good measure, racist/chauvinist, and—at times—*genocidal* as well. So much for the boons of progressive *Euro-Modernism*, and if it is objected that *all* historical empires may be similarly tainted—*for, where is Man not evil?* —then this rather obvious riposte becomes inevitable: *why then pretend to be god's gift to the world, and the choice haven of 'liberté, egalité, and fraternité'?*

Seems to me, it's much more of a pathetic case of *venalité, banalité, and duplicité.*

❄

At any rate, stated simply, a conjoint Anglo-American '*alliance*' has (*tried to,* that is—more often than not successfully) run the world since the late nineteenth century, these irascible cousins (together with their *country* cousins, Canada and Australia), unified by the challenge of gathering socialist movements and the 'inter-imperial' struggles of the Two Wars, globally. Today, the 'alliance' has been solidified, yet again, by the far humbler rumblings of so-called 'fundamentalism' (Islam beyond the border, Christianity within), and the need to curb the pretensions of their restless *ex-Colonial* charges.

Now one must not pursue the '*national*' nature of the 'alliance' too far: in mature capitalisms, 'nation' quite loses it import—and powerful *Corporatisms* take over (Marx pointed out the mordant irony in the fact that virtually all British institutions bore the adjectival '*Royal*' prefix, except for the, yes: '*national*' debt!). Yet, even Corporate empires require a captive '*field of play,*' wherefore the 'national' affiliation retains some import; besides, the need to deploy instruments of *state power* leaves the Oligarchy very little choice (Corporates could still field their own armies and navies, but the important issue of a general *legitimation* restrains them) but to exercise such suzerainty within the nation.

At any rate, the dominant interests, in this period, have been, all but unnoticed, the Great Financial Houses: Rothchilds, Morgans, et al., who have controlled Policy from 'behind' the scenes—via Two rather facile mechanisms: (a) *complete control over finance/money/banking,* and (b) *complete control over media (public opinion).* Contrary to common understanding, (a) is quite unworkable (in a formal democracy), without (b).

The preference for '*democracy*' (in its top-down, 'managed' form) is also quite obvious: Napoleon once said that *one can do anything with bayonets except sit on them i.e.,* to rule by force is costly, and at times counterproductive—far better to let the media smoothly channel public opinion in favor of a 'consensual,' 'one-dimensional,' society (the 'agreement' being essentially on One Axiomatic Fundamental Freedom for the dominant 'ruling' strata, *i.e.,* the Great Conglomerates of Antic Wealth: *to get What It wants When It wants, and on Its terms*), in which *genre,* the US was, until recently, way ahead of the pack

That way the public has the comforting illusion of *choice and participation* (it is, to use a phrase of Mosca, but a '*political formula*' appropriate to *statecraft:* an idea that would have been be perfectly comprehensible to the wiles of a Kautilya in ancient India, or a Machiavelli, in Italy). And, generally, that is all that the vast majority of them have time for in the 'rat race' that is so very thoughtfully imposed on them.

Now it took time for the Financial Interest to achieve this level of outright dominance (the complete closure of world media within their grip is, now a *fait accompli:* the Rothchilds, *e.g.,* more or less, leastways by common report, may be assumed to control Reuters and Associated Press, the dominant Wire Services, and the Three Major US Networks). One has only to gauge their involvements in global governance entities, past and present, such as the Bilderburg Club, the Trilateral Commission, the World Economic Forum, *et al.*, to fathom their determined seriousness.

Originally, in European history, *Trading* (Commercial, Mercantile) Capital (such as the East India Company) and Finance Capital (say, the Fuggers of Germany) arose as near-contemporaries. But the nineteenth century saw *Industrial* Capital race on ahead, fuelled by the emergent technologies of the industrial revolution. However, the irreversible rise, and *predominance*, of Finance was quite triumphantly 'signatured' with the creation of the 'Federal' Reserve (the Fed being about as 'Federal' as Federal Express) in the US, in the early years of the twentieth century, capping the 'capture' of the Bank of England several decades earlier.

It's over-riding pre-eminence over other forms of capital dates from the late Eighties (whence the slew of financial crises cascade in grand array: the Savings and Loan Fiasco, the Asian Financial Crisis, the Mexican Peso crisis, the Sub-prime Mortgage Collapse, the 2008 Financial Meltdown, *et al.*, all vivid markers of its ignoble reign), when the spate of official green signals to electronic debt-creation helped amass astronomical funds that gave it overwhelming leverage over all other interests. Thus, Bank/Finance Capital now bestrides the world like an indefeasible Colossus.

There are important differences in the outlooks of these different 'capitals' (or vested interests). Industrial capital, like agriculture, is vested in tools, machines, and the organization of large numbers of people (workers, consumers, the public at large): it is, therefore, altogether serious in its 'societal' approach to business. Returns take years to cumulate: so there is also a fixity and stability to its calculations, which makes for a certain stolidity of preoccupations.

But Finance knows few such constraints: at but an 'entry level,' a person with a laptop with the fundamentals of forward calculations can go 'into business,' it doesn't matter where; and S/he can also bet on any market in the world. There is no necessity for either local fixity, of station or function; nor any concern other than private gain. *It is after all, but a gamble,* using publicly borrowed, or electronically concocted 'funds,' for lavish private gain (the Barings collapse, or the Bernie Madoff episode, amongst others, may be viewed as cases in point). This gives Finance a remarkable 'fluidity,' and a prototypical 'fly-by-night' attitude to the market/world it operates in.

The Classical Economists argued more: *that capital in areas like Finance ('services'), unlike agriculture/industry was 'unproductive' (since a service is consumed at the point of production and expires, and cannot be accumulated)*: another critically useful term that modern economics has quietly elided. Be that as it may, the clear point is that, apparently unbeknownst to its calculations, Finance remains more heavily dependent upon the *prior* existence of agriculture and industry, much as medieval *trade* was parasitic upon *pre-existing* peasant and artisan outputs, than *vice versa.*

Given *human needs which are never allowed to enter economic theorizing!*—a Pizza economy, arguably, *e.g.,* will live/last longer than a Derivative economy, or a Haircut economy for reasons obvious—finance is also *parasitic* in that it 'produces' little of direct societal value, whilst collecting/consuming a vast chunk of it. *Therein, lie its ontological limits.* Even if finance were no more disreputable than any other capital, and all of the above were to be false imputations, it has itself, in the past two decades, more than amply revealed its lusty appetite for outright recklessness and irresponsibility, overtipping the scale of the debauched ruling elites of Late Feudal Europe.

At any rate, at the conclusion of the Two Great European Wars of Supremacy (*and we must recall, importantly, that Wars are to credit and finance, as green fields to locusts*), Bretton Woods installed the joint US-UK Plan for Global Governance (so the UN, the World Bank, and the IMF—and now the WTO—were/are all part of the self-same Agenda). Serious Challengers to their hegemony were really only *Two*: Russia and China (in their 'socialist' guise: It is true that France, within West Europe, with its own Colonial preserves, remained a pesky irritant: but it was, always, really, no more than that). So, the Cold War was invented to counteract the former: and it did. They are still around, of course, but their 'socialism' has quite vanished. And so, by the Eighties, the Cold War, putatively, had been 'won.' Russia capitulated: and well before that, the US had made those initial overtures to China that would ultimately lead to the fairly spectacular *Great Reversal* of China. And only then could Finance Capital, rid of virtually all its major obstacles (with Reagan and Thatcher having turned the state into its own private satrapy), 'take off': and *how it did!* Today, we know this as a vital part of so-called '*globalization.' As pointed out, virtually every mini-economic crisis, since the Eighties, has been provoked by this interest.*

Ironically, though, to lose to the 'Alliance' may only be the necessary step prior to turning into its hapless creditor: as Germany, Japan, Russia, and China can confirm. These last three named shore up the Dollar today, howsoever inadvertently, and allow Alliance partners to live far beyond their real means. *As every banker knows, when it comes to unsecured loans, it's the creditor that is, usually, held hostage.*

Be that as it may, a third 'Challenge' to the ruling Plutocracy was the *Ex-Colonial* world, which was largely pacified by force, fraud, and bribery, as circumstances demanded. Here, a certain, if admittedly *unstable*, measure of 'success' has also been achieved. However, in winning the Two 'Wars' (against Socialism and *ex-Colonial* Nationalism) so called '*religious fundamentalism*'—originally activated by the Alliance itself, reminiscent of the British supported Wahabis, deployed against the Ottomans, to be used against socialism and its allied secular forces— has emerged now as yet another irritant (as an aside, the 'religious' part of the militancy may well be a misnomer: as Lewis Namier once said, but about another century, '*religion can be just another name for nationalism*'). But, it provided a new opportunity: to keep the hyped up 'security threat' argument going as necessary pretext to forge the new 'managed' republic of today—whence the everlasting 'war against terror,' out of all proportion to the alleged 'threat' (one might distinguish two aspects of this 'fundamentalism' which are oft, erroneously, lumped together: the Alliance-inspired *free-lancers*, who catch the headlines, and the *moral nationalists* who tread humbler ground).

In the UK, this '*new hegemony*' aimed at creating a servile populace and Parliament, on the lines of the US, has taken longer to install, and is still far from being *accomplished* (though Tony Blair deftly crafted the mechanisms of *executive bypass* of the popular will, guided possibly by the example of his inept *alter-ego* from across the Atlantic). In both the US and the UK, the *structural change* in formal politics sought was a *concentrate of power in the Executive Branch* so as to wean out Congressional and Parliamentary (*i.e., popular*) oversight completely. A few fat-cats in back rooms, attended by their leaner serfs, deciding the fate of the world could not, perhaps, be realized in any another fashion.

But, to return to the Beginning: Finance Capital requires continuous currency creation and manipulation: and the new, emergent computer technologies made possible a veritable explosion in this regard. As is well known, the slew of 'derivatives' so concocted can now buy out real world GDP several times over. With Bretton Woods guaranteeing Dollar supremacy, a piece of paper could become Almighty—scavenging the globe to purloin and seize real resources (such as oil, *e.g.*) wherever they existed. However, this could only work if the dollar, itself, could be 'secured.' Gold would not do, because 'foreigners' could accumulate dollars, demand gold, and run down reserves. So, the dollar was 'cut loose' from gold, in the early Seventies.

But it still had to be 'backed,' by something, after that severance. The solution arrived at was near perfect, albeit in an imperfect world. *One plank* was to insist that a vital global commodity (such as oil) had to be *traded in dollars, s*o the oil-consuming world would always need dollars. This was, largely, achieved. Then, the *Second plank*, partially in place to help enforce the first, and then some: to build, initially covertly, then openly—the *largest military machine ever created in history.*

Whence, it becomes clear that the dollar would not fall below acceptable thresholds, even as they ran up titanic debts, deficits, and printing presses, nonstop—*because there would always be a demand for dollars*. And that 'demand' could be insisted upon/guaranteed by '*regime changes,*' via the military behemoth, as desired. *So, the dollar is 'backed' today by Oil, the Military, and the Hegemony over world Media (aside, of course, from gold-price and interest-rate fixing).*

Thus was the Bretton Woods Agenda completed, in our times, by these mechanisms. They explain the various interventions (overt/covert) in West Asia, and elsewhere, both planned and achieved. They explain, also, the *generalized Crisis*, the widespread eco-political 'malaise,' that envelops the world today. They explain why a system that, by all accounts, should collapse, has still managed to shuffle on.

Never has so much harm been done to so many by so few.

Where does the EU fit in all of this? Well, it is a junior partner in this Great Game (we must note the Euro-Financiers, the Lazards of Paris, the Warburgs of Hamburg, and the Moses Seifs of Rome, *en passant*, and their behind-the-scenes support for the EU's financial consolidation), and the solid mainstay of NATO, despite erstwhile French coquetting, another important Post-War initiative of the Ruling Alliance (French ambivalence is related to its aspiration for a leadership position, in the game, other than its designated role as second-fiddle to the US: hence its episodic 'sulking in the tent' routines). And NATO participation in the latter's misadventures is steadily rising. In a *One-Size-Fits-All* world, there were few other options presented to European governments, despite the ire of their own peoples. Of course, they too (*i.e.*, the EU), now, are near-stymied by the debt virus carefully intruded upon them in the last twenty-five years, and hence are now 'part of the chain,' part of a 'praxis of evil.' So where is it at, now?

A militarized economy and polity now have put the credit devil (the *mass distribution* of the common credit card, unlike its more restricted prior forebears, was a diabolic move in the Seventies, *intended to serve as the vicious 'salve'—as Capital prepared to move abroad—to the slicing of employment and wages domestically*), in *everyone's* hands. So, when the Unemployed buy food at Walmart today (having lost jobs that are never to return) that is charged to a card—they are, literally, paying *double digit usury on bread*, so to speak (which puts Marie Antoinette and her gang of gallants to complete shame), to the very same forces that created their distress via this *engineered* 'recession' (if what we have, globally, today is a *recession*, the Great Depression was but a minor 'downturn').

The Crisis is a Final one: one can expect no reprieve. Corporations will merrily continue to produce wherever costs are low, and the regressive *domestic* employment and welfare that such a policy induces, is by now a mere political football to kick around as needed, on the media, for public consumption, with little or no serious effort to seek/find remedies.

In effect, the low-wage-high-unemployment catch-as-catch-can economy is no crisis for the ruling elite, but in fact precisely what the doctor ordered. No surprise, really: Finance has never 'needed' the *real* economy, nor owes any fealty to society—*even Adam Smith understood its abject parasitism.* When we consider the fact that a bare *50 Financials now control more than 65% of industrial capacity, globally,* we get an idea of the relative power of unproductive capital over productive assets prevalent today. It is little short of stupefying.

Capitals flow to the pools of highest reward: and, truly, which industrial/agricultural form of investment can today hope to earn/emulate the profiteering of a Wall Street Financial (even be it short-lived like the run of a Bernie Madoff)? *This form of Money only chases money, via near-money, to make more money.* And they are still raking it in: in fact, they are, by now, *'too powerful to fail.'* So, it's a great success: it matters not that economies, societies, and cultures, fall by the wayside, globally. And, what if the bubbles they build collapse?

Well, they control a 'managed' polity that will bail *them* out, at everyone else's expense. Who there, left, to protest? And, if some do protest: so what? For, if protest spreads, unexpectedly, there are ample laws, and machinery, *now*, to contain them all. Worse, we protest only the visible *monkeys* of the realm (politicians, governments, and such), but the invisible *organ grinders* remain comfortably aloof and invisible. *The Republic died a long time ago (some might claim, like most revolutions, at the very moment of its birth). Consume, Obey—Be Silent*: such the unwrit Laws of our Time. *This, above, is the real world we live in.* And what is there, yet to come? And how far, and for how long, can such a *zero-sum game* be played, in the real world?

Well, there is an incumbent *'karma,'* even in such processes (whence the mention of 'limits' earlier on), but a full evaluation of reckonings to come—and *the time frame is not distal*—are fit subject-matter for another disquisition. However, one or two comments can yet be made. The limits may have already been (b) reached: Pandora's box is irreversibly open, and nakedly empty. Whether or not one can fool everyone all the time, *one certainly cannot control everyone all the time. Whence, the writing on the wall: empires fall apart, obeying the antic law of all (forcibly) imposed protocols* (recall, *e.g.*, the Napoleonic *dictum* cited previously).

Both Humpty and Dumpty (!) are off the wall(!) today: though the huffing and puffing goes on—and 'all the king's men' are not exactly rushing in to help. But the distress applies only to nations and peoples: what of the great Financial Houses? As grey eminences, they remain unfazed, their fortunes intact, perhaps even more concentrated. Forbes estimated recently that 174 Corporates effectively control major world economic processes; now, it is my own hunch that, according to the old rule-of-social-thumb, *about 200 families still run everything, everywhere—as they always have* (the *'Iron Law of Oligarchy,'* apparently, may not be breached): so, taken together, these two numbers may well form a conjoint set—and the financials would stand at the apex of such a set.

So, here's a clue: *stated simply, a wholesale collapse is the only 'corrective' that such a system will 'accept'*—though it could carry, regrettably, a related malignancy of fate If conventional means to enforce their agenda—of bringing the entire world within their clutch—fail, one might recall the thousands of nuclear warheads that lie dormant and shining in silos on the ground, on ships at sea, or in the air: will they, if frustrated, yield to these fiery temptations?

Having brought the world to the point of extinction once before, during the Cuban missile crisis, it may not be safe to bet on sanity prevailing, a second time around. For, if they are seen to operate, at some level, within the *cultural* matrix of Anglo-Saxon institutions—*unmistakably the dominant culture of our times*—then it may be portentous to recall the disposition, when facing adversity, of their aboriginal, mythopetic, patriarchal, super-hero: *Beowulf.*

Absit omen.

❉

On matters more trivial: the prognoses of the official economists—whose tribes are legion—alas, have not helped us elucidate even an iota of this simple, verifiable, snapshot of reality. Nor have they *ever* been of any help (*they are like a Fire Brigade who arrive, safely, only after the fire has been put out by others: and then, too, only to try and figure out, forever after, in well-funded, leisurely, parlor room pedantry, why it ever got started*).

Au contraire, given the sullen doldrums of today's world economy, consider the genius of a 'science' whose Illuminati blithely celebrated, in *text-books* no less, in the high euphoria of the last decade(s) of the twentieth century: *the alleged latter-day suspension (!) of so-called 'diminishing returns.'* They felt, perhaps, that wild Wall Street adventurism had, serendipitously, hit upon a new Shangri-La: *a fantasy economy that functioned as a perpetual-motion machine!* That brand of *Nirvana*, of course, proved to be short-lived, and not merely in textbooks.

Now, such 'scientists' can get it wrong, and still greedily embezzle a gratuitous, and *ever politically canny, Nobel Prize*—if they hang on long enough (given the obligatory once-a-year allotment). But, what of the more enduring query: of *what value, this 'science' of economics?* Well, we might just as well borrow a leaf from their own book, and echo that eternal economics drone/dissemble: *On the one hand, on the other hand...*perhaps, on this issue of a show of hands, we might yet have to be grateful that they are, providentially, still primates—not *centipedes?*

It almost has one believing in intelligent design.

9

The Bail-In

So you've barely finished congratulating yourself, for surviving the Crash of 2008. Alas, that's no cause for euphoria. Yes, it's our big, bold, Banks, *again*. Here's the story. They have your *deposits,* on their books, of about 1+ Tril. Their outstanding *derivative* bets likely exceed 500+Tril (leveraged at about 60 to 1). *Globally, 1.2+ Quadrillion of such bets abound, whereas the combined value of All global financial assets: stocks, bonds, and deposits stand at 167+ Tril (and recall World GDP is only about 70+ Tril).*

Now, of course, all these numbers are *guestimates* only, since the era of *reliability* of official figures is past. But the FDIC, you say? It has about 29+Billion in its till: that's less than 3% of Deposits. *And you don't own your deposits; they do. Yes, Virginia, Banks own deposits, depositors don't.* So, when they go belly-up, what happens? Dodd-Frank (the *'Rescue'* Plan, after 2008) does not permit *Tax-funded* Bailouts. So, they just moved on to the next best thing: it's called the *Bail-in (Yes, before it all goes away, no doubt, there'll be Bail-ups, and Bail-downs, as well).* That means when they go under—how *can they not? Just look at the numbers*—they can seize your *deposits* to pay off their owings. *No private Corporation, other than a Bank, can do that (legally, that is)!*

And *you?* What happens to you? Oh, your deposits will get you *shares* in the bank. Now Gandhi, who was something of a bright guy, once called British *promises*, of this and that, to India in 1942, during the last years of Empire, 'a *Post-Dated Check on a Crashing Bank.*' Similarly, these '*shares*' are current checks—but *on an already failed bank.* Ah, promises, promises.

And, long before you ever see a dime, the long line of well-heeled *Derivative Claimants* trump you, *en route* to the cash (if any). Yes, *their* claims run ahead of depositors. So, where does that leave you, the *taxpayer-cum-bank-depositor,* with your antique FDIC illusions behind you: *think?*

Think it's not possible? *It's happened already*: in far Cyprus, Ireland. Well, if it's any consolation: the *next Crash will be the Last Crash. After that, the Deluge.* So, maybe, you can go back to your euphoria: as the poet has it, *where ignorance is bliss, 'tis folly to be wise.'* But wait: there is a *Stone-Age* alternative to this *Bank-deposit fiasco* (interesting how, at times, the evolving Crises of Capitalism have us wishing for the '*bad old days*' for answers: *which doesn't say a whole lot for the notion of 'progress' we're all reared to believe in): i.e., Gold and Silver.* Or, a late-breaking internet-generated hi-tech *salve: Bitcoin, Litecoin, et al.*

But Government, you say, how about Government? Can't they help? Sure they can, and will, you can bet on it: *but, alas, it's not you they will help.* They just might seize your gold (*FDR did just that, in 1933, 'criminalizing' the possession of gold: and similar actions are afoot, right now, in Asia*), and the Bitcoin, too. Curiously, as an aside, Germany, jittery of late, just asked the Fed for the gold it has on deposit at the Fed—and also in Paris—all *674 tons* of it. To put it baldly, it hasn't happened yet. In 2007, and 2011, the Fed actually refused them a full audit of their own cache. It did, however, repatriate some 5 tons: guess you could call that a start?.

You can't complain, now (can you?): as Mark Twain put it, a long time ago, *we have the best government money can buy.* So, you can't expect much help from *that* quarter—*unless you are a Bank, too big to fail.* Well then, maybe *Commodities?* Possibly: though that will be less of a great strategy if the *currency* itself fails. As it could, owing to all these bank–induced shenanigans.

Or, Land? The real-estate bubble will burst alongside the financial one, but land is always worth something: maybe, you can grow food on it, if all fails (worth some, if the currency fails). So, what can you do? Well, here's a thought: maybe it's time for us, *en masse*, to let go of the kind of Capitalism *that seems to put Bankers' Cabals in charge of the National Budget.* And the kind of political system that's, apparently, *up for sale to the highest bidder.*

The Russians got rid of Autocracy, with not a great deal of pain: *can we not do the same with Plutocracy?* Or, of course, one can simply return to the *status quo* euphoria: it is, after all, the gift that goes on giving—*hope to the hopeless.*

Yes, one is 'free to choose.' But it may well turn out to be a *Hobson's Choice.*

10

On Economics

This is not an Age of Integrity.

Latter-day Finance has irrefragably overturned any shard of belief in public probity in the economy, and governments have done more of the same with husbandry of the public household. Whilst such goings-on were glibly attributed to 'oriental satrapies,' in the past, it is clear now that very little is in order—if it ever was—in the torrid 'State of Denmark' we inhabit, far closer home. Who left now to preach to the world about rights, responsibilities, and such anachronistic leftovers of the *ancien regime*? It is enough to give vulgar propaganda a bad name.

But, here, I wish to set the record straight about Economics, rather than contemporary state and society. I have written elsewhere that Economics the '*crown jewel of the hegemonic ideology of Modernism*' (Kanth, 2005). Whilst that sums it up, a more prosaic rendering is yet necessary. I came to economics not *tabula rasa*, like most new students—but with years of Anthropology in my veins. As such, it simply failed to impress. Unlike many who, despite much instinctive dubiety, remain in awe of (its canny resort to) mathematics—it cut no ice with me in that intemperate zone.

Being educated in India, I could differentiate a function twice, whilst still in High School, so its inappropriately deployed math (part of that old bugaboo of physics-envy) held few terrors. But there was that initial sense of shock; surely all its fabricated complexity had to mean something more, substantively, than met the eye! Of course, there isn't: but I did lose a few weeks assuring myself on that score.

I studied Classical Economics first, and wrote a Book on it soon thereafter (Kanth, 1986): it was readily apparent that *economics* was but a higher-order cover for *policy*.

It was a bit like a cannon that could fire in any direction, once one equipped it with the right rations of explosives. Smith and Ricardo (the latter, with more clarity) essentially used it to imply that, barring the odd reservation, laissez-faire (and /or 'free trade') produced optimal outcomes—thereby making of economics the unwitting, and at times witting, flag-bearer of the emergent manufacturing interest.

Malthus, of course, given his 'protectionism' of the landed orders, challenged this tradition: but was over-ruled less by cogent argument than by the more well known stratagems of scientific exclusion. Marx usefully piggybacked on Ricardo, finding in the latter's imperfect 'labor theory' a facile staging ground for his own political economy of rejection. Closer to our times, Keynesian ideas (much like Friedmanite notions) are also quite over determined by clear, and unmistakable, policy objectives. To think that the 'science' was born first in a lab, and then 'discovered' to be of utility in societal struggles is to maladroitly put the cart before the horse: the cloister of invention was all but contaminated, *ab initio,* by the 'task at hand.' As I have said, you get out of economics only what you put in, explicitly or surreptitiously, by way of selective 'assumptions' (much of the 'difference' between Keynesianism and Neo-Classicism emanates, *e.g.,* from the prior 'assumption,' or lack thereof, of 'full employment'). Argument by (tendentious) assumption is quite a wondrous game! Much of this is clarified in my *Against Economics* work (Kanth, 1997a). In that work, I wrote that *'Economics is a self-referential language-game with zero representational efficacy,'* with regard to Neo-Classicism.

To state it all succinctly, economics is a *policy science*—and so, perhaps, not science at all—with no independent content to speak of. Or, put another way, *it is politics—by other means.* Which is why, when I encountered it after Anthropology, it appeared rather tawdry, shallow, fare—all the more astonishing for its high, and smug, pretension to an esoteric knowledge.

In fact, the Anthropology reference is vital: economics fails, as a 'behavioral science,' for *not* being based on anything but a fictitious, deductivist, 'anthropology,' itself erected on inappropriate assumptions. *A false epistemology cannot create a true ontology!* In fact, without a true Anthropology of the human species most of conventional philosophy, psychology, and such fail, similarly (I elaborate a realist anthropology in my *Against Eurocentrism, op.cit.*). My *Breaking with the Enlightenment* (Kanth, 1997b) sketches some of the inadequacies of the heroic postulates of enlightenment thought.

As an aside: even the more Utopian Agendas of European thinking, from More to Marx (which I treat as the secular version of a Christian Redemption) flounder (at incalculable human cost) on the shoals of this radical error/omission. *The human animal is a real, natural species with inherent propensities: and one cannot simply concoct great fanciful ideals—and expect them to be duly 'realised.'*

At any rate, returning to the question: a quick comparison with Physics can help seal this argument, even as to minimal 'relevance': is economics even relevant to fathoming the crises of our time in these 'bad old days'? Could Physics, *e.g.,* ever be so utterly irrelevant in its own domain? What/where are the 'laws' of Economics that might compare to physics? I warrant the only 'law' economics *inherited rather than discovered,* since it was universally known, for eons, is that pertaining to 'supply and demand.' No trader of antiquity—be it Gujarati, Lebanese, or Jewish—could have managed affairs without it. As Carlyle said it, more or less: I have a parrot that I have trained to say 'supply' and 'demand', at due intervals, which suffices to make of that (bird-brained?) creature a tolerably well-educated economist.

It will be found that all of its other putative 'laws' are simply logical truisms, often based on that primary law. And yet the 'science' gets a Nobel (Memorial) Prize—though that is more a savvy benefice of the astute Bank of Sweden, if one examines the history of the process—routinely. And I have provided the clue already: Economics is the very select *Patois of Modernist Discourse* and so is elevated far above the Social Sciences (it of course pretends to be a *Natural* Science: in America, in academe, a dour pragmatics usually allots it, appropriately, to schools of 'business'). Indeed, few such Prizes could be more politically motivated.

Economics imports the metaphysic of materialism into societal life, disingenuously, as a series of axiomatics: a practicing Buddhist, for example, could not pass a Micro-exam for demurring the idea that 'more is better.' So, whilst its science content is virtually nil, its propaganda content is immense. And the propaganda is not *culture-free*: an Australian Aboriginal would also not pass a Micro test. Neither would a scholastic European, prior to the so-called 'Reformation,' which, perforce, made Original Christianity—opposed to the inherent thrust of economics—compatible with Modernist drives.

In effect, we are all, required to subscribe to the *Great European Way* (this is no hyperbole: a Keynesian accounting of the economy is a UN *imperative:* a nation that does not so order its accounts can hardly participate in Globalisation, nor have access to the network of Multilaterals). It is well, therefore, to insert the silent prefix to 'economics': it is *Euro-Capitalist Economics*—about as 'universal' as Samoan cuisine.

So why should we study Economics? It's hardly even *useful:* after all, despite the boastful Friedmanite claim of 'prediction' being the true function of science, what crisis has the 'science' predicted that was not otherwise obvious to the lay person? *Au contraire,* it has miserably trailed behind lay wisdom, as with the Governors of the Fed, the IMF, and the World Bank—in relation to the crisis-ridden decades of our time.

In fact, one could press this point of the *real world bankruptcy* of economics; if economics is a science, and science has to do with prediction: why then can we not predict outcomes in the stock market (which, *en generale,* used to be proffered as an ideal example of a 'free market,' the other being small-scale farming)? And, if it fails in this market, where else can it succeed?

Well, one could borrow a feather from the subject's own materialism: for most professional economists, it is a terrific avenue of provident employment—and I am not niggardly enough in spirit to deny them such desserts. Let them make hay. But could there be any other, societally valuable, reason? Yes, indeed: and a very potent one. It was supplied by the great Joan Robinson who judiciously deployed common sense where economics made no sense at all. Of course, she was passed over for that meretricious Nobel Award, for questioning the specious authority of that *genre* of the Modernist Mantra(s). There is only *one* good reason she said to an Indian student in the Sixties (who shall remain anonymous) when asked why anyone should study the subject, given her scathing lampoons against economics. *It is to protect oneself from the dissimulations of Economists, she said, simply.*

Other than the employment argument I have mentioned, I can still think of no better answer than that. It is certainly the only reason that I still peruse it.

11

On Capitalism (and Latter-day Debacles)

A long time ago, I broke with the routinized 'left' and 'right' posturing(s) of Modernist thinking. That sort of 'politics,' I think, is *passé*. Besides, they both derive from a Euro-Modernist discourse of '*progressivism*' that I reject as the very bane that holds us all in deleterious thrall. Instead, it is preferable to view all policy issues with a sense only of their real histories and current contexts. No idea, or *praxis,* is privileged, *a priori, per definitionem.* This may well be the only way of bypassing the *ennui* of the Tweedledum-Tweedledee choice-binaries one is usually confronted with.

Besides, any '*ism*' is only as good as the quality of its real 'human' governors. At any rate, we know that the Anglo-American variant of Capitalism became the dominant *modus* of that *genre,* within Euro-Modernism, for some obvious reasons. *Pax Britannica* and *Pax Americana* saw to that. It is that model that will likely dissolve as these times continue to *devolve.* There are more quiescent Capitalisms that may yet endure, if only in the mode of firm regulatory, societally mindful, regimes such as evidenced in Denmark, Iceland, and Switzerland.

The materialist viewpoint that saturates 'social science,' in its 'universalist' guise, has all but excised *culture,* to the point that we conceive of such entities—such as capitalism—as '*culture-free.*' They are not. Much like 'Economics,' Capitalism is not '*universal,*' despite its high pretences. Interestingly, and not coincidentally, we follow Anglo-American variants of both Capitalism and Economics as the 'norm' today. *Both are culturally derived, culturally bound, and culturally located.* And, as such, these notions can, and must be rescued from their limited provenances.

The Anglo-Norma formations, for the most part, let *greed run amok*, being— apparently—willing to let society, and ecology, go under. Less so the Danes, or the Swiss: similarly, very recently, the Icelanders were gravely tempted—but walked away.

Why?

These are *cultural* differences: the Danes and the Swiss are both deeply self-conscious *tribal* societies who value their *cultural endowment* at least as much as the huckstering creed—and are quite reluctant to let the latter wholly subsume the former (the US and the UK, *au contraire,* are long past their '*gemeinscahft*' traits, given their fateful descent into empire). The '*Steppenwolf*' quasi-Germanic soul couldn't quite stomach such excess, even in the past: little wonder that their most sensitive geniuses suffered debilitating moral turmoil at the gathering pre- dations of Modernism, like Nietzsche and Kierkegaard. Japan is also similar—as were virtually all *traditional* formations not wholly overrun by *Euro-Colonialism.* But the Anglo-Norman is made of far sterner stuff, and stands, ever-ready, and all insouciant, to pawn away the planet for a mess of pottage.

It has been said that Modern Capitalism is an amalgam of English Econom- ics, French Politics, and German Philosophy. I could parse that, more accurately, as *English greed, French romanticism about 'rights,' and German religiosity.* The Ger- mans, so to speak (with only a touch of hyperbole) do it all out of a Protestant *Ethic,* not irrefragable greed. And the French will take anything (be it War, or the Working day) only as far as bright lights and *vin rouge* allow (and I am only partially joking).

Therein, the difference(s).

They are all 'capitalist' societies, but diverge in important ways: and it is Culture that holds the key to 'difference.' It is the vital, constitutive essence that defines a soci- ety (which is a far cry from the 'social contract' ideas of society dating from the so-called 'Enlightenment'): *stated succinctly, human society is a balance of affections, not a balance of interests. As I have written elsewhere, to understand (modernist) politics you have to know (real) economics: and to know economics, you have to know anthropology (of course, to know only 'economics' is to know less than nothing).*

It also helps if one deploys what I have termed '*reverse anthropology,*' i.e., *returning the compliment of critically studying European institutions*—as *They,* for centuries, studied All *Others.* But, this is clearly not how Modernist social sciences are organized, to their lasting detriment. It is high time *real* social science, *i.e.*, scientific scrutiny, were applied to the so-called social sciences. Their original epistemologies are somewhat haphazardly situated, to put it mildly.

In economics, *par exemple*, one presumes an *individualist* standpoint, in sociology a *collectivist* one. So, Economics 101 and Sociology 101 cheerfully deny each other's first principles. Even within Economics there's a split: Micro-economics being individually oriented, and Macro (of the Keynesian kind) being aggregative. Then the two, to compound the confusion, are 'combined,' to form a syncretic synthesis—*i.e.*, a right royal mess—that is mutually destabilizing.

From Smith onward, a 'deductivist' line of argument constituted economic theorizing. Ricardo actually elevated this *a priorism* into what he termed 'inspired introspection.' O what ingenuously insightful 'guesswork'! For example, the so-called '*propensity to truck and barter*' was not an inference from any meticulous anthropology of human societies, but a light deduction from a complacent look, in equable self-scrutiny, into dear old Adam's stoutly Glasgovian soul. *But the real is not so easily apprehended: it can only be patiently derived from careful observation. As Marx had it, if appearance and reality coincided, there would be no need for Science.* But, as I have written, it is *Policy*—i.e., *motivated pleading*—that drove Classical Economics, not '*theory*': that latter was merely a *post-factum* rationalization. And that truth has not changed, to this day.

Micro-economics is an 'ideal' *instruction manual* to specify the various 'rationalities' necessary for Capitalism to function: *i.e.*, for workers, consumers, and capital-owners to' know their place.' You know the litany: *maximize this, minimize that, etc*; and, when one is not so engaged, in modern economics, one is busy importing mathematical models from the natural sciences to underscore the '*physics-envy*' of the discipline, and ensure its suitability for that coveted Nobel Prize. *Stated bluntly, Economics has not made one single, significant, 'advance' in any direction, other than obfuscation, since the nineteenth century.* Macro-economics, a late addition, was not Economics at all, but only a *policy-laden management tool* to help tame the 'instabilities' that Capitalism is prone to.

Marx was right, like some others before him, about the basis of Capitalism (*i.e.*, *accumulation via expropriation*), though tragically wrong about the 'communism' he thought would set it all right. *He overlooked Lord Acton's simple axiom about Power (and its fatal attraction for the Tribe of Men).* Instead, folks like Milovan Djilas and Robert Michels were right: that a Collectivist order, still operating under materialist norms, would only create a 'new class' that would 'manage' it all, for the 'people'—*neither at their behest, nor on their behalf.*

I will sum it very shortly: no Grouping(s) of Men (gender intended) within Modernism, can—ever—be trusted with Power: it is this facet of 'Masculinity 'that subverts all Utopias. It is also the basis of all Dystopias. This is not to say that relatively benign societal forms cannot, and do not, exist: but they cannot be built to modernist, i.e., materialist, specifications.

Now, *exploitation* is at the heart of all Capitalisms: be that of wage-labor, women's work, nature's bounty, *etc. The difference between what the real toilers make and what they get paid is the basis, in all such 'extractive' societies, of the 'surpluses' that rulers retain/expend as per their discretion. Labor produces, Capital appropriates*—an idea that would have been acceptable as trivially true by both Smith and Ricardo: of course, modern economics, cravenly, flees from such home truths.

Europe did not become prodigiously rich because of a 'free market': it became rich via piracy, plunder, and pillage added on to 'markets' it forcibly created, monopolized, and militarily managed. Instead of the standard bromide of 'free trade' and 'competition,' think of African slaves, Indian ryots /coolies, Chinese opium-addicts, at one remove; and then picture the systemic looting—of India via 'taxation,' and the willful destruction of its manufactures; of the gold mines of South Africa, of the silver mines of Latin America; the produce of Central America; the slave trade, the sugar trade, the spice trade, and all such glorious momenta of that great bloody orgy of European mastery over the world. Then tack on the genocide(s), and the ecocides: O what an enthralling tale of primal, accumulative, despotism!

I could sum it all up, allegorically, in but one baseline Query. Where are the 2000 Native American nations that flourished on the North American Continent, but yesterday? That is the Alpha and the Omega of Capitalism, Euro-style, not the wretched nursery pap that is taught in those glossy Economics texts gobbled up by hapless students, today, globally.

And yet how quickly is it all forgotten, excised—nay, made respectable! To think that such unrivalled Conquistadores are now become piously devout civilization-mongers and banner-bearers of democracy and rights. And that hoary process is still grimly afoot, today, under the new-fangled guise of *'globalisation.'* Instead of the Merchant Adventurers and the East India Company, of yore, we now have J.P. Morgan and Goldman Sachs.

Now that's *Progress.*

So, no: regrettably, it wasn't 'Yankee ingenuity' that 'built' America: it was, originally, outright theft: of lands, labors, and resources, belonging to *Others.* It is these artifacts that were, accordingly, their earliest 'capital.' The 'ingenuity,' such as it was, lay in the initial organization/execution of that theft, later to be supplemented amply by annexation, war profits, and empire. *Commercial* Capitalism looted the world in its wide, long, mercantile, sweep. *Industrial* Capitalism, that succeeded the former, ran through the Colonies for raw materials and labor, then markets. Today, Finance is the preferred *Tool of Exploitation* with *imposed,* inexorable *debt-peonage* the lot of the vast majority of humankind. Adapting Elizabeth Browning, one might well intone a fit caption for this process, as: '*How can I fleece thee?; let me count the Ways*'—which would make for a diverting account of 'how the West was won.'

More seriously, the roots of this rabid *Financialisation* were thoughtfully fabricated a long time ago, at Bretton Woods, with the dollar replacing sterling as the new instrument of mass despoliation. The World Bank and the IMF made it their business to go about forging the coiled chains of indebtedness in a world that lay prostrate at the feet of the real victors of the Second Inter-Imperial War of the twentieth century. The Soviets 'won' the ground war, at horrific human cost, but the US-UK reaped the riches thereafter. However, the Wheel, as it will, Turns. Today, it is Anglo-American Capitalism that teeters on the verge of disorder: not struck down by the evil plans of anarchists and communists, as antic cold war propaganda would have had us believe not so very long ago, but by its own chosen ilk: red-blooded, USDA prime, pin-striped, grey-suited Captains Courageous of Capitalism, the fly-by-night derivative-wielding, latte-swigging, techno-cowboys (it is still largely a male preserve) of Wall Street.

Sic transit gloria mundi. An empire of greed undermined by its very own Midas mania. The *Empire Strikes Out!:* there is a certain poetic justice to it. Today, the system consumes more than it produces, borrows more than it saves, owes more than it could ever pay back.

The QE voodoo attempts to foil the inevitable dollar collapse by keeping interest rates at zero, even negative rates. But that only, and far from inadvertently, sets off a merry asset-price boom that will certainly, in time, crash the two markets that bestride the world (the real 'economy' has long since given up the ghost): in securities and real estate. *But, of course, the Game Masters know all this.* It is a 'desired' collapse that will, happily, take matters out of their hands (to everyone's relief, not least their own. And, believe me, you wouldn't want to know their Plan B). So, the only *curiosum* now is: which of them will go first?

Well, we may not have long to wait. And what's next? Well we may have to rescind most of the great, consecrated Myths of Capitalism: it 'works' only when fresh, gratis, *spoils—lands, labor, resources*—are freely available for the taking. Besides, its monistic *materialism* becomes its own self-immolating scourge. Take contemporary America, as a good exemplar: after having, with profits in mind, heedlessly dismantled its industry, laid off its skilled labor force, decimated its

middle classes, ravished its great natural endowments, unsettled baseline societal norms, militarized its civic culture, corrupted governance and undermined
its legitimacy, and bankrupted its finances—*what's left?* Only the two ancient,
humble, standbys: *Land and Community.* It will need to embrace both in a new
philosophy of *sharing and co-operation, setting aside all Neanderthal notions of
'private property,' in any and all societal resources vital to the general welfare.*

Ditto with its *asocial* individualism, and its Social Darwinism. Yes, let our
'free marketeers' frolic feely—in cautiously limited spheres of little import to the
public weal. But, in all else, *let the real stakeholders, i.e., the Community, hold Corporations to strict canons of societal accountability. And let that footloose 'profit motive'
be held in rein by the higher 'community service motive':* can you now imagine the
coming *genre* of Economics texts?

And abroad? It could well be the Age of the BRICS setting up, quietly, a new,
(more pacific) world order. Well, can you blame them? They had to do *something*
whilst we were frenetically busy tunneling our frenzied way under, into an apocalyptic, Financial, China Syndrome. And, all extant probabilities indicate that
European capitalist societies, who have thrived for four centuries, soaring high
above all others, *via* force, fraud, and double-standards, will now have to make the
humble descent into the corrective demos of the humdrum realities of a Planet
Earth that can easily accommodate human *needs*—but not runaway, demonic,
werewolf *greed.*

Recalling Gandhi's famous quip, maybe it is time, now, for a little '*Western
Civilisation.*' Who knows?: there could be a season, a purpose, 'under heaven,'
even for that obviously rare felicity, as per the old Psalm from *Ecclesiastes.* Of
course, even a stout heart might well feel a pang—at witnessing that long-standing oxymoron wither away.

12

On Singaporeanisation

Or, Some Bitter Fruits
of Globalization

In these times, it is necessary to begin with some caveats. The reference to Singapore is not to its people who, like people everywhere, try to live as best as they can under given constraints, but rather to the uniqueness of its modular structure only. It may also not be gratuitous to add /emphasize that Singapore is, in Euro-Capitalist terms, a ringing success story whose materialist indices/underpinnings are not under challenge in this Paper. The critique is posed on quite other grounds, which are not often deployed in mainstream discussions of the successes (or failures) of Globalization. Finally, I pen such vignettes as Notes for Reflection only.

Globalization has its uses and abuses, and its critics and trumpeters—who have covered much of both. But there is one concern that may not have received the attention it needs to. I call it—what's in a name!—*Singaporeanisation.*

Now Singapore, in its Western usage is a miracle, colonial, City-State (that Empire and Finance lovingly built) that the World Bank, and Wall Street, dearly cherish. In fact, this darling of the West gets routine raves from its sponsors: the Economist Intelligence Unit ranked it as #1 in the *Quality of Life* (more on this, later) in Asia, aside from its being fondly seen, by many, as the most 'globalized' country in the world.

Yes: for some 5 decades it has been, much like Hong Kong, the one *Non-European* space (other than Japan, S. Korea, and much later, contemporary China) where, *voila!*, almost all things (and their owners) function just like they do in the 'Mother Countries.' Buses, trains, run on time, the bustling malls stay open, and luxury cars cruise—albeit, at lawful speeds—any time of day. Commercial hub, Financial centre, Trading port, its GDP, thanks to banks, and other Global Trans-nationals based there, stands tall. Really Tall.

'Law and order' is proverbially secure, the Polity suitably 'managed,' like the Press, and the streets are safe—even for women (this last quite unmatched in many major Western metropolitan settings). Everything, if somewhat mechanically, 'functions'—including an education system that turns out cadres of the technically competent, if quiescent, professionals.

In fact, Singapoean elites are proud of their *'First World'* (now a somewhat quaint term, given that we are all supposedly living in *One World*) status: even air quality, pollution, and suitably 'advanced' diseases are, if dubiously, on par with their US counterparts—though, in areas like crime and public safety, standards are arguably far better. If all this is seen as 'miraculous'—for being extant in a *non-European* context—it follows that, like Hong Kong, *Singapore is an early 'success' in the advent of Globalized Capitalism* (the rise of China, of course, has quite eclipsed their success, much like that of Hong Kong, given sheer scale factors alone). So, it all sounds, *viewed in Western, Modernist terms* (*btw: in this short note, the terms European, Modernist, Western, and Capitalist, are all used 'structurally' and synonymously*) highly satisfactory—so what could possibly be wrong with this 'success' story?

Well: let's probe further. The City-State-Country is ethnically dominated by Chinese, with Indians, Malays, and hundreds of thousands of European expatriates as secondary communities. Indeed, a staggering 42% of the population are 'foreigners.' So, is Singapore *Chinese?* Well, if one checked the family names of the dominant elites, it might appear so.

But a hint of paradox emerges if one examined some of the *given* names which are blandly western/'Christian': Sarahs, Susans, and Rogers, proliferate. Are they all *Christian?* No, they just happen to like *Western* names. There was a faculty member at the National University who changed his name to John Wayne (*sic*). Why?, he was asked: so Westerners can pronounce it more easily than his Chinese name. This is trivial, of course, in itself, except for what it suggests.

But is there any serious sense in which Singapore is *Chinese* at all, *culturally*. Or Indian? Or Malay? Many of the maids working in Singapore, a few years ago, came from Mainland China. They themselves were sure, and many locals agreed, that *they* were far more Chinese *culturally*, and that Singapore itself was really quite *culture-free.* Yes, all stamps of *real ethnicity* have been virtually purged by Capitalism, and Modernism. *In fact, a telling index may well be the one short paragraph that Singapore gets under the header of 'Culture' in Wikipedia. Multi-Culturalism?* Not really, though many religious affiliations exist, and 3 or 4 languages spoken. Nor is it *'Multi-Party,'* politically, as also suggested by Wikipedia. A Secular ideal? The End-point of Globalization? No.

It's more a case of the old observation about the early Ford automobile: *you can buy any color you wish so long as it is black. Producers and Consumers only, with no tradition, heritage, or values, that are at all dysfunctional to the requirements of Capital Accumulation.* A museum of Singaporean 'culture,' alas, would not have many artifacts in it. Indeed, is Singapore even *Asian?* It could easily be fitted in as yet another (except, far safer) borough of New York, without either the host or the guests noticing much difference. However, *compare Singapore to Bali, and one understands the real difference between the presence and absence of a living culture.* It must give one pause.

Now, there is a serious sense in which the US, unlike, say, Denmark, Japan, or China, is also *culture-free,* despite the fact that all its institutional artifacts are of Anglo-Norman derivation. The US is now a Giant Conglomerate of Little Communities inventing/disinventing *sub-cultures* generationally, but where great, long-lived traditions, and heritage, have no serious purchase on Everyday Life (contrast that with the real, solid, culture-bound traditions of a genuine community, like the Amish, and you understand *ersatz* for what it is). For America is not an *anthropic society (i.e., founded on shared, reciprocal affective relations of care)* but a modernist, contractual, settler nation-state where *'civil society'* is but the impersonal means to the personal gratification of the egoistical wants of mutually autonomous individuals.

Is Singapore, therefore, but a Modernized, Americanised, Mechanised, Island of Consumerism? Japan, of course, after its defeat by the US, had to put away much of its Japaneseness, in cold storage, but it never really evaporated. China, after the Revolution, similarly shed some of its traditional past, but the rural countryside is/was still 'governed' by traditional Chinese norms, as prevail in China's many regions, *at least for now*: of course, it may well be that China will, one day, 'modernize' itself wholly out of its own millennially cumulated cultural skin.

How about India? Well, the British *'modernized' (i.e.,* transplanted their own systems) much of India by force, in their Reorganisation of the Indian economy (to favor their own needs). But the Brits, stolidly mercenary, aimed mainly at *tribute*: so all their *'reforms,'* from land tenure, to administration, to postal, educational, and communications/transportation systems, were pointedly *functional* (not dissimilar to the far more 'native' Mughal Empire who also engaged similarly, *leaving village cultures unravaged*, if far less efficient at it). *Stated differently, traditional Indian village-cultures survived, despite the British Holocaust* (and their planned destruction of its native industry).

But today's Global Corporates, are far more *werewolfish* than the sluggish East India Company: and they threaten to uproot all of traditional India, inside-out, within just one generation, if unchecked. *It takes eons to build Civilization: it takes, I think, perhaps less than two generations to dismantle it.*

Now the US, being *culture-free* itself, can only approach the globe in a *culture-blind* way. So, US Corps have no willful *agenda* of cultural havoc, but simply achieve that result mechanically, *via Walmartization,* where the *rural Retail* sector, the living veins of sub-regional cultures, and outlet for a myriad peasant arts and crafts, the creative/cultivated genius of the land, is entirely expunged. In fact, this ground-level process is more lethal, and insidious, than the fact of encroaching foreign ownership, and the rising dominance of foreign banks and credit, whose effects are principally Metropolitan, and Eco/Political, at the *national* level. But *Walmartization* itself is incomplete without a titanic media-blitz, saturated with all-powerful images of rabid consumerism: and India's latter-day media, affiliated with their foreign networks, have performed this task with admirable passion.

And Contemporary Bollywood, taking unacknowledged cue from its Great Guru, Hollywood, has delivered the *coup de grace*, with its new thrust of R or X rated, and sustained, *debasement of language added on to the more conventional and routine depiction of women as sex-objects*, virtually assuring *the catastrophic withering away of the very basis of culture and morality.* Indeed, the horrific rash of attacks on women, in India, as mar daily news headlines, are but one direct result of this.

To enunciate the norm of today's dominant force of Modernism, A-morality is what makes A-mericans of all of us. After all, as Oscar Wilde has it, America plunged directly from barbarism to decadence, bypassing the phase of civilization. I would have to, perforce, add to Wilde: it is now rewound straight back from decadence to barbarism again!

So, what Globalization can achieve in India, now, is far more dramatic than the two long centuries of lazy British despotism. What is at issue? Economic 'Growth' will take place, in that quintessentially destabilizing, uneven way: and Consumerism will continue to gain root as an overarching *societal norm.* This is vital: *Capitalist Greed is a necessary, but not a sufficient condition, for the explosive expansion of Capitalism, American style*—the required complement, for the latter, is the wholesale adoption of *Consumerism* by the populace. Both these adjuncts require a large, salaried, middle-class, and a vast working population, cut adrift from traditional/peasant access to subsistence. In effect, workers are the prime *producers* and, collectively, the prime *consumers*.

As life, and livelihoods, begin to resemble a lottery, and family/social structures crumble, rootlessness and dehumanization, in particular in metropolitan milieus, advance; illness and disease rise, and Grand Corruption, Mafia-style increases. Las Vegas is a good example of the bland nature of this form of corruption that does not spill over on to the street (though today the US, *as a whole*, is similarly made over, by the unquestionable supremacy of Finance, in that very same image). When the Mafia owned it, street crime was zero, and law and order near-tight (Big Crooks don't favor petty crooks on their beat). Now that Wall Street has bought Vegas, the streets are still much the same: financial machinations continue, as before, at the top, and peace is yet kept on the street.

Just like Singapore.

Interesting: corruption at the *Apex* (*i.e.*, at the level of the ruling oligarchy of elites where it is endemic*), i.e.,* in Anglo-Am *epicenters*, is rarely seen, or reported, as corruption: but, when a pathetically deprived *native* clerk, in the far periphery of the globe, asks for a petty bribe, then the Western/Modernist public Chorus shrieks corruption, thereby transferring attention deftly away from the much larger phenomenon of *Legalized Corporate Thuggery*, which is the *modal* form of the Globalized State today, in many parts of the world. As ever, it's the small fry that get fried.

Telescoped over time, all GDP and no Culture will soon make of India a rather dull Nation. Just like Singapore (where shopping may have to substitute for any other form of solace). And its ancient, rich and prodigious, *Traditions of Conviviality*, arts, crafts, and rituals, will be all but extinguished (a process extant in Mexico where, after NAFTA, a third of its huge *Campesino* populace were displaced from agriculture and crafts, to beg, steal, purvey minor artifacts, or to labor, in serf-like conditions, in the Maqiladoras by the border). And, in time, shall we all Mount the Great Wheel, and work the mill all day for that choice GMO bit of desiccated, BGH cheese. *'Course, it ain't just Cheese:* for those with purchasing power, there'll be plentiful sex, TV, and food (religion will be wisely 'managed,' to stay within modernist limits) as well.

Just Like Singapore.

It will be a Big Jump Forward for Profits, and the Grim Regimes of Globalized Materialism. But a giant leap backwards, a Great Regression, wherever culture and civilization still abound. In fact, this has always been a signal issue in European Colonialism and Empire. *In synoptically compressed terms, human*

Civilization is built on a rejection of materialism; barbarism, on its worship (stated differently, Materialism is 'bounded' in traditional society: in *Euro-Capitalism*, it is wholly 'unbounded').

So, when Capitalist/Modernist elites speak blithely of the 'Quality of Life,' they are speaking, unknowingly, of Quantities, at base. The 'Quality' of societal life is *not* achieved by legal and constitutional structures, nor by creating an asocially 'free' individualism, nor by the institutionalization of wage-labor, production for private profit, and the celebration of a casino economy, *but by the preservation of the organic processes of affective reciprocities* as they pertain, *par exemple*, within *familial* relations.

So-called '*Equality*,' '*Freedom*,' and '*Democracy*,' the tendentious *slogans* of the emergent bourgeois in Modern Europe, as they sought to wrest space from their feudal governors, are also *not* necessary conditions for the life convivial. *The human family is not built upon equality, nor freedom, nor democracy: yet it offers a haven, a sanctuary, to all who gratefully dwell within it.*

The human family is both natural and social simultaneously: it offers the human, heat-seeking mammal, what s/he craves the most—warmth, reciprocity, caring, and love. At the nuclear base of this are the *labors/activities of women*, as they pertain to the '*paradigm of femininity*' and nurturance. Tribal societies elevate this idea of the centrality of *kinship* to cover the entire society as a species of extended kin. And Civilization is achieved when this '*paradigm of femininity*' restrains *masculinist* drives for domination and violence, within the limits of the *gender-struggles* extant.

Class struggles are about Power, and are masculinist in essence: gender-struggles are about the Moral boundaries essential to Civilization. In effect, Civilization is about the *pacification* of *human existence* (within a continuous Sysiphian struggle), *rather than about turning the latter into a mine-ridden battleground of permanent, and encroaching, insecurities, and generalized discontent and disaffection, such as Globalization has achieved everywhere it has visited.* It has nothing to do with material artifacts, possessions, or advancement of national, or societal, wealth. In fact, it is profoundly *Anti-materialist*, though far from being Utopian *Indeed, being real, it is anything but 'utopian.'*

The Modernist West lost sight of this simple truth centuries ago, in its triumphalist spate of Modernist Revolutions. *In fact, all its Utopian cravings thereafter, from More to Marx, were a species of a pathetic cri de cœur: to rediscover what it had itself first wantonly self-destroyed. Its existential despair is, also, similarly located. Now, you can fathom the great despair of a Nietzsche, or a Kierkegaarde: they 'felt' the Loss, keenly, but could not name it* (ironically, but not at all atypically, Nietzsche—who was nursed unto the end by his caring sister after losing his mind—fulminated, much like Schopenhaeur, against the *deficiencies of women*, whenever opportunity allowed: *thus do the unenlightened bite the hand that nurtures).*

As such, India and Japan both were overrun by rampant *barbarism*: *for Capitalism, European-style, is Barbarism Unbound,* in terms of anthropic values (one must *not* mistake double-entry book-keeping, or the compounding of interest, as artifacts of *civilization).* The destruction of traditional culture/society by barbarism has been either dramatic and explicit as in the willful genocide committed against Native Americans, Carribs, Latin American Native populations, Australian Aboriginals, Africans, *etc.,* by European Powers, or it is far more carefully planned and institutionally provisioned, as in the case of modern Japan and modern India.

Myanmar is the newest, hapless, chosen target: under the guise of the 'modernist creed' of 'human rights' and 'democracy' it is, perforce, being brought under the sway of the global, corporatist scramble for resources, far beyond what the British rulers managed/intended during their unholy tenure there (a fate not dissimilar to that of equally unfortunate Tibet at the hands of modern China).

So, the real issue of *Singaporeanisation* can now be stated.

The West, once capitulated to *predatory Capitalism,* ran amok in the non-European world, dismantling/destroying living, *organic cultures* that largely lived within the matrix of family and kinship—and so posing no impossibly permanent threat to either Nature, or to contemporaneous social formations. India and China, albeit *Empires,* nonetheless enjoyed largely peaceable relations for millennia: one might compare this to the internecine wars of European nations/states from its modernizing beginnings, to glean some aspects of the difference. This is not to suggest that Modernism is more war-like than traditional societies; for, in both cases it is Men, and their *'paradigm of masculinity,'* bristling with violence, which carry the seeds of aggression: rather, it is that *Modernism generalizes a permanent climate of ineradicable insecurity that makes conflict an ever-present aspect of reality in all domains.*

Anthropic society is about *stability within contentment,* Modernism generates its antipode—perpetual *restlessness and discontent.* Today, that process is *globalized* with all barriers to its advancement, save a few, under grave threat of atrophy. *Culture in such a globalized world is, or becomes, Resistance:* not because it 'chooses' confrontation, but because globalized forces compel it to, on pain of extinction. *Religion, as Lewis Namier wrote (in the European Context of religious wars) is another name for Nationalism.* It is very timely to remember this simple fact so the process of *cultural revolt* extant today, is not misunderstood (*as usual, when the finger points to the moon, the uncritical moon over the finger).* Anthropic culture, often *via* its religious arm, is the repository of a society's deep moral sensitivities: Modernist expansionism, of the Globalizing kind, rubs against its grain—and provokes a predictably knee-jerk response.

Globalization, today, apparently, has no other force that is so irrevocably committed to opposing it, since Modernist Sectors everywhere are ambivalent in their critique of it: those who welcome '*civil society*'—the province of '*universal egoism*,' as Hegel noted—as a 'progressive' step, are ignorant of its true nature. *It is the guaranteed breeding ground for the capitalist ethos*, and the latter's fig leaf of civic respectability, masking all its predations.

Important, perhaps also to note here that Marx wished for the *abolition of civil society, not its consecration.* I have named this struggle, in other writings, metaphorically, the struggle between the *Mammals and the Reptiles (i.e.,* the warm-blooded *and* the cold-blooded). *It is the struggle between Tradition and Modernity, everywhere.*

But it is also, ultimately, the struggle between Barbarism and Civilization, Materialism and Culture (interestingly, *scientific materialism*, after quantum physics, is on the decline everywhere: with a *probabilistic* universe replacing the older notion of *deterministic* one. There is a form of liberation here that may well spread to *philosophical materialism* as well, thereby undermining much of the *intellectual* scaffolding of the Classical, Materialist world-view, stemming from the European Enlightenment. Clearly, we are on the threshold of another Great Revolution in modes of thought).

All we *need* is love, sang the Beatles, not so very long ago: and yet by perverse Modernist inversion, *all (we think) we want is money*—the latter standing as the proxy for the death-dealing, soul-benumbing, and debilitating, *Regime of Things* as oppresses us all today.

Let us hope, therefore, that a *citywide wall-to-wall-street-to-street shopping mall, or Singapore,* will *not* be the sordid face of the future for the newly emergent world. To amend the insightful Oliver Goldsmith: *Ill fares the land, to hastening ills a prey—where Wealth accumulates and Cultures (and Civilizations, I might add) decay.*

Part III

The State of Being

13

Anthropic Dualism

A Tale of Two (Sub)-Species—A Comment on 'La Condition Humaine'

For at least the last 35 years, I have felt that the solution to ALL the ills of human-kind vest with Women: there is no societal ill—from capitalism, to militarism, to despotism—that is not Male-inspired, directed, and enshrined. Both greed and dom-ination have been male preserves for millennia (it is these twin traits that undermine every 'emancipatory' movement, sooner or later). Women have largely 'looked the other way', leaving such madness(es) to men, whilst they built the life convivial 'in the shadows,' in the domain(s) of domesticity. Now, it is time that they 'stepped out,' and said NO. I rather think they are, today, 'on the move.' I think they will succeed. And all men have to do is to 'step aside,' so to speak (voluntarily, or involuntarily). The only partial exception to the 'rule' I enunciate above is the many tribal societies that have successfully 'imprisoned' the predatory drives of men within the healing matrix of kinship (this does not eliminate the drives but places restraints on them). And we cannot hope to do much better than that (unless genetic engineering discovers a way). Note that this is not 'utopian': since such 'states of social being' have already been achieved in human history.

In my 2007 Festschrift Lecture, I call this 'gender struggle' the clash of the 'para-digm of masculinity' with the 'paradigm of femininity,' each being viewed as a 'cluster of traits' (Kanth, 2007).

[N.B. *This rumination, above, I circulated to a few colleagues, recently: understandably, the males in that group declined direct comment, but a few women responded skeptically, pointing to the postures of some of the 'big name' women out in politics, currently, as not presenting much hope. This somewhat extended Comment, below, in response, might help situate some important matters: or so I would like to imagine*].

❅

Some truths can be so trivial, as to escape notice. To participate (effectively) in the exclusively *male* domain of power, the few *women* who do, are,—whether aware or not—*'self-selected'* by mainly male criteria: the vast majority of women, of course, don't make that choice, and remain outside of such processes.

When I suggested women will/could now assert themselves, it will *not* be the likes of Hillary Clintons or the Queens of England: *i.e. to 'rule' like men*—but to fundamentally *'feminize'* societal goals, *in toto*, by dismantling/defusing male institutions/approaches by simply approaching them *qua* women.

Yes (providentially), Women Are Not Like Men.

To state this simple truth, I am aware, is to court a near knee-jerk Critique from all variants of *Modernist Ideology* (left, right, and center: I have devoted a book length study to the delusions of that latter named, in my work entitled *Against Eurocentrism*). This fact, far from being vitiated by the charge of *'essentialism'* (the ideological bugaboo defined by Euro-Modernism) illustrates a very plain, and widely understood, *existential truth: i.e.*, it is verifiable by the empirical record; let's score, for example, of necessity very quickly!, *all the Females who have built Empires that committed genocide, raped men en masse, looted, plundered, and planned and dropped nuclear devices on hapless civilians.* Ok: so the list is about as long as a book on the wit and wisdom of George W. Bush.

No wonder, no self-aware woman seeks 'equality' with men (in a very different vein, it has been well said that women who actually seek such equality simply lack ambition…). *It is also indefeasible realism*: it is in their *instincts* that men and women differ. *Yes, Virginia, we 'humans' are natural creatures vested with natural propensities—which is why 'human nature' is such a distorted phrase.*

The so-called 'Enlightenment,' that made governing European males think of themselves as near-gods, was to carry on, but now in amended secular vein, the hoary *anthropic* Judeo-Christian tradition (not alone in this presumption) of seeing humans as apart from, and *'above,'* animals. Modernism, the broad intellectual seeding-ground for Capitalism (and its twin, Socialism) *fears* 'instincts': they are contrary to its *'rationalist'* (if misanthropic) postulates. *So it is that animals are allowed 'instincts,' but we can't have them*—for: (a) in the JC view *we are not of their order*, and (b) also, we must, as modernists be *'rationalist'*: if not, then we fail prescribed capitalist criteria as, say, in the premises *of economics e.g., where to be 'rational' is to be, inescapably, materialist i.e.*, we must *'want more'* by *theoretical fiat* (so, as an aside—a Buddhist, or a Jain, could not pass a micro-econ exam: note how a *philosophy of materialism* is insouciantly tagged on to the *metaphysic of rationalism*).

To be 'rational' is to be *materialist: yes, we are All Pigs*—figure of speech only, no offense to that inoffensive animal, in modernist economic theory, as we join hands to reach for that 'higher' indifference curve—*ex hypothesi*. One can now imagine the shock waves that the great Darwin set off by his works, to such *creative pseudo-anthropology*: yet, modernist social science was to survive it all, unfazed, in its ignoble stride.

Now instincts controvert such pathetically tendentious parables. But Nature is what nature is: so we can't invent ourselves as a new species, *sui generis. Of course, Modernist 'social science'—where the adjective is far more telling than the noun—is an eclectic jumble of ill-fitting ideas and epistemologies: e.g.,* in social anthropology, *the study of non-Europeans by Europeans*, we seek and find *'difference,'* usually to elevate European societies on some or other scale; yet, in Economics, we assume a *'homogenous,' universalized, 'rational' economic man*.

Or, take Micro and Macro in Economics: Micro 'assumes' *individual* actors/behaviors, which 'add-up' to the economy, obviating any social (*inter*)dependencies. Macro, suddenly, morphs these intrepid individuals into near-Class categories (lumps) of *collective* behaviors. No wonder, the average freshman student finds it all beyond him/her, and, resorts, resignedly, to committing it all to rote.

So, instincts still crop up, if randomly: they are 'ok' in variants of psychoanalytical theory *e.g., via* Freud (where we are gratuitously gifted largely phony 'instincts' such as *'Oedipal'* cravings—and, similarly, Keynes, for his part, can speak, quite seriously, of *'animal spirits'*: boy, did he get that phrase right!). And Levi-Strauss, we might recall, in heroic modernist vein, attacked Freud—saying, more or less that *'instincts explain nothing: they are that need to be explained.' Really, instincts explain nothing?* Let's parse this notion a bit: this heroic European male would have to be quite a god, in his own right, is he not? Yes, of course: for HE is the *enlightenment-powered-rationalist-bearer-of-emancipatory-tidings-and-civilizing-missions-for-all-humankind*, such as *liberté, egalité,* (*except, alas, for*

Women and non-Europeans who had to fight HIM: for exactly those rights), and (my own, humble, addition)—*banalité. He is sans anything so contemptible, and lowly, as mere 'nature.'*

Robert Solow, Nobel Economics laureate, is supposed to have said, more or less, in a talk that *'we can do without nature'* (if true, what a barking example of the unabashedly conquistadorean approach to our universal, generative matrix!): and, naturally, his fellow travelers are now seeing to that as a *realizable empirical goal* in the very near future—except, *au contraire*, the real truth might well be that *'nature can do without us.'*

Father 'Science,' one notes, is not very respectful of 'Mother' Nature, in the Modernist idiom. One has only to watch the public antics of our current scientist-heroes—Dawkins, Krauss, *et al.*—to see how they strut, congratulating themselves on what they take to be their thundering *anthropic* achievements. After all, *they are no part of this 'nature' that they are subjecting to inquisition*—and better still, *they have done it all with no assistance from nature, such as, just possibly, that gracious, evolutionary 'gift': of grey matter.*

Yet 'nature,' banished from the salons and boudoirs, is invited back in when it is serviceable, *e.g.,* in justifying oppressions. Possibly why, despite all of the above protestations, *both women and so-called 'primitives' were seen at one time, by the same lineage of Law-Givers as, no less, 'naturvolk,'* belonging to the 'lower' domain of the, yes, *'instinctual.'*

Or, take the term *'human nature'* (a bit oxymoronic: or is it just plain moronic?) which was such a heuristic template in the construction of the *'Social Contract'* schools of speculation. How easefully were 'men and women' conflated within *One,* single, *Monist* 'human nature,' *in particular when amplifying its pejorative traits, such that Women, implicitly, were absorbed into the gross catalog of the egregious sins of Men.*

The German Enlightenment (Nietzsche, Schopenheur, *et al., not least influenced by Ancient Indian Vedic texts)* went far in this regard, where the presumed 'nobility' of men, in contrast to the craven natures of women was seen as virtually axiomatic. Even where extremism was absent, the privileging of men as *'rational'* (though dispassionate *calculation* is what they were getting at), and the disparagement of women as *'emotional'* was/is a common binary. It never occurred to these worthies that they might actually be viewing it all in a contorted *mirror image—i.e., the wrong way around:* that they might be capturing, but 'falsely,' *a real, even critical, division between men and women,* that is rarely allowed to intrude into social theory. Of course, this ideology was not at all inconsistent with hoary Biblical wisdom where *sin falls upon the human race by virtue of error on the part of the eternally vulnerable female* ('frailty, thy name is woman,' echoes Shakespeare, faithfully).

In fact, the telling phrase *'women and children'* is eloquence itself, in its patriarchal coupling: and so, amongst a host of even more vital disabilities, women in supposedly 'advanced' European republics like Denmark and Switzerland, *had to wait far longer than some European Colonies,* for the right merely to have the franchise extended to them (the domestic 'shrew' had to be tamed first, presumably). After all, why would such 'enlightened' *preux chevaliers* give the vote to 'children'?

But, to return to context. I have cited my Festschrift *Lectures,* in the preamble to this Comment, where a fuller explanation can be found, so let me, in desperate brevity, now define this important male/female dyad. *Men are vested with the 'instinct' to kill (it's an entire set of traits constituting what I term the 'paradigm of masculinity') and women with the 'instinct' to nurture (which I term the 'paradigm of femininity).* Now, note that I speak, necessarily, of *instincts: this is not to say that either sex cannot 'mindfully' depart from text—but it does constitute a departure, 'going against the grain' so to speak.*

Essentialism? Really? Let us now address that issue. Firstly, if an empirical fact is confirmed *ad nauseam,* across millennia it is (or becomes) an *existential fact: and there can be no gainsaying the grim record in the history of humankind of wholly masculine predations (I have already noted but a few choice headers in that grim litany: mass rapes, slaughters/extirpations, genocides, and so on.)* Secondly, leaving such humbly demotic empirics aside, what superior, *'prior knowledge'* of Creation/ Evolution does Modernism possess, to, *a priori, and ex cathedra, deny the existence of what are termed 'essences'?* There is not, nor can be, any such *epistemic 'foreknowledge' of absence*: only *Argument ex Hypothesi. And, assertion is not proof.*

Besides, are there no instincts vested in men and women that are at all recognizable across history and cultures (despite some of the more facile fabrications of Margaret Mead), *via* their empirical expression(s)/(wo)manifestations? I believe the evidence is overwhelming. Let me argue now, by analogy: does Nature not possess 'essential' properties? *Consider: isn't gravity an 'essential' property of matter?* If so, why is it a surprise to discover similar *'essences'* (or instincts) in humans: *especially when we grant their existence in animals, with whom we share so much of our genetic make-up?* Because we are 'enlightened,' and therefore have 'left nature behind'? Or because we are, divinely, 'made' in the image of Jesus?

So, it's time we put to rest the old shibboleths. There is not *one* but *TWO* *'human natures': men and women are two distinct sub-species of the human race.*

And, unmistakably, men have ruled over women, in collective terms: *there is no historical instance of any female 'ruling class' returning that 'favor.'*

✳

Now, to extend the Argument. There are some powerful analogs here to be noted: *men have oppressed women, much as Europeans have oppressed Non-Europeans, and property-owning and/or power-wielding classes have oppressed the sans-culotte.* What happens when the oppressed orders, as they oft-times do, begin to challenge their oppressors? The rulers respond either by outright suppression or, more cleverly, by favoring a few of the *sans-cullotte* to move up to ranks of 'leadership'—so long as they 'play by the rules.' This has been the case, *e.g.,* with the long history of anti-Colonial revolts.

Indeed, in the case of British India, Lord Macaulay decreed a *Minute on Education* (which, fatefully, shapes the educational system in India to this day), which carefully laid out the need to create a cadre of Indians that were *'native in color, but English in tastes.'* But, given propitious circumstances, such a loyal 'Fifth Column' is/was eventually routed by others far more authentically representative of the suppressed orders. This is what is at work today: *there are more women in 'leadership' roles in politics than ever before in modernist history (the present US Senate has 20 women, the largest admittance of its kind: and, the world over, more women Chief Executives than ever before).*

Yet these women are by no means, necessarily, representing *women,* in the first, or even the last, instance: they are simply 'playing by the rules' (and winning). *But the Story does not end there.* In much the same way as workers need to (and often do) acquire a full 'consciousness' of their condition, and natives similarly of their own servitude, *women have to: (a) come to recognize their own conditions of existence, and (b) recognize also the need to do something about it. This is a process—that takes time and evolution (learning by doing, and undoing).*

And the process faces formidable odds: the powerful Ideology of Patriarchy has been around for millennia, so a Simone de Beauvoir here, or a Gloria Steinem there are insufficient, though important in themselves, to occasion such transformations. As US elections demonstrate, a skillfully managed media will not let women *'play the woman card'* any more than they let Obama 'play the race card' (even had he wished to, which he quite obviously didn't, because he didn't have to: in fact the *only* card on the table, in such races, is the Capitalist-Empire card, a well-worn card, which is played by All, more or less).

As such, the Candidates that are allowed to gain any notice are those that: (a) are handpicked by the governors, and/or (b) have already cloned themselves in light of prevailing norms. *So, it might be expected that a whole slew of women in leadership are, likely, but token-women, male alter-egos, molded by Patriarchy.* This is not at all to trivialize their roles or achievements, but merely to point to the limits within which they can, and might be expected to, function. *Despite the caveats, they are yet a visible symbol to millions (of men and women) that women can do what men do: and like the wily Indira Gandhi, of India, sometimes beat men at their own (nefarious) game(s).* And that last holds out the possibility that, given the right circumstances, even 'token' women may be prompted to break ranks. And that is far from being trivial.

But all this, thus far, is commonplace. *What is of much larger moment is the conjecture that women, being 'different,' may pursue their 'politics,' also, differently.* Our very understanding of political power, let alone the means used to acquire it, and the use to which it is put, might well alter fundamentally, if this be true. A few thought experiments might help elucidate that.

Can one imagine a political party that is solely of *women, by women, and for women*? What might it aim to achieve, *i.e.,* what might be its Agenda? How would it go about trying to implement that Agenda? How would it relate to other 'mainstream' (or '*man*-stream') institutions? Or, consider further: how would standard *policing* functions and practices alter, in society, if *All* police were constituted by women? Ditto, for Armies? And Parliaments? Even more interestingly: would they retain Police, Armies, and Parliaments, at all?

What Political/Societal priorities would women espouse, if they were 'in charge'? And how might women, *left to themselves,* solve perennial conflicts such as Israel-Palestine, or India-Pakistan (*here's a clue: what if droves of Israeli and Palestinian women, one fine day, frenzied by the relentless violence, just walked across their respective borders to join hands, hug, and cry out: Enough!*)?

What would their notions of 'Justice' be? Or War? Or Empire? Or Science? Or the State? If such queries seem 'odd,' perhaps one might reflect: *is there nothing, similarly, 'odd' about gender-singularity when that gender happens to be men, as it has, in all history? In effect, could it not be true that ALL our ideas about 'human society'—philosophical, scientific, and cultural—have been shaped, or rather, 'warped,' by the outright, monist, and exclusivist Male Domination of it.*

Women have been, undeniably, the perennially, omitted, nay *shunned, Other,* in the grand societal game played by men. *And so we are ALL, men and women, reared virtually indelibly in a Man's World, believing HIS dreams, delusions, and dysfunctions, to be eternally 'human' and 'universal,' and, even worse,* '*inevitable*'! So it is that *it is Men who have defined our standards* of '*normalcy*,' and all manner of Appropriate/Inappropriate conduct(s), including, most importantly, Morality and Religion. How would world religions be different if Women were their inspirations, and not men? Indeed, would 'religion,' as we know it, even exist?

Would a woman Buddha have forsaken family and loved ones to seek an arid, abstract 'enlightenment' abroad? Would a *Jane* Christ let herself—even as scriptural fantasy—suffer crucifixion in that ultimate trope of the male ego, or might she have, intelligently, 'compromised' with the 'enemy' and called for a truce? Would 'enemies' exist, even epistemologically, in their discourse? Would their philosophers have moaned on in paroxysms of existential despair, or drown themselves in a swamp of misanthropic nihilism? Would Capitalism exist, as we know it today, if women had to make that choice? Would they have built the Bomb, and used it?

Further, would they have beshrouded the living planet with unscalable means of instant nuclear annihilation? Would they have, for good measure, let the 'profit motive' destroy the environment, let entire species disappear, patented life-forms, and experimented with biological weapons of warfare? Would they have fought Two Global Wars, not to mention a quadrillion smaller ones, and prepared for a Third one, to 'protect' ethnic, national, or economic, supremacy? Would they have, cheerfully, practiced genocide, or enslaved entire peoples? In sum, could it be that a *woman's world*, if *she* were permitted to wish it into existence, would be somewhat different than ours?

If so, can the question, therefore, not be asked: *do we, thereby, really live in a 'human' society, or merely in its 'worst case scenario'—of Patriarchy?* And so we can, thereby, also ask: *can the world not be better than it is if we could somehow break with its current Masculinist monism?*

✳

I have argued elsewhere (notably in my *Against Eurocentrism, op. cit.*) that all of European Utopian cravings from the sixteenth century on, More to Marx, were an extended, passionate *crie de cœur*, lamenting a 'paradise lost': of the *social affections*. Stated simply, the expansionary drives of Modernist-Capitalist-Patriarchy had put the Big Chill upon the 'life-convivial,' as monetization, commerce, and industry leveled 'organic society' and its many, if simple, hospitalities.

Real *anthropic* societies, good or bad, are not '*contractual*,' but *Affectual*—which is why *modernist* 'society' is *society rent with conflict/dissension, dysfunction, and anomie, and therefore is not a society at all*. And at the heart of affective society is the *familial* principle, upon which template women have, across time and space, built the foundations of conviviality and civilization.

Notice that the *'family'* is a *natural* entity (it exists amongst many animals, too), despite its many societal/cultural forms. *Notice, also, it is neither democratic, egalitarian* (in contrast with the wretched dissimulations of Modernist propaganda), *free, individualist, nor contractual*: but it still gives the human animal, male or female, what it (apparently) craves most—*care, warmth, love, and affection.*

We, as mammals, are *heat-seeking* (not *light-seeking*: navel contemplation has been a singularly male hobby) animals: at our fondest, we *huddle.* It may be the only 'paradise' that is possible within the rather desperate anthropic condition. *And it is Women who, for millennia, have helped constitute it. And it is men, who, out of touch with their own feelings, and (mis)led by their unbridled egos, 'step outside' that magic circle, and begin that free-falling descent into alienation from their own species-being that has, over centuries of devolution, produced the turbid turbulence of Modernism.*

So, *male-articulated Utopias* ('Socialism,' 'Garden of Eden') were simply heart-felt, wished-for extensions of that *modus* of 'hearth and home,' whose warmth/felicity was being corroded/corrupted by the fell forces of greed and commerce. One has only to read Oliver Goldsmith's *The Deserted Village,* to glean their pathos, or some of Marx's earlier writings (before he succumbed to the very masculinist temptation of *'scientific socialism'*).

Thus, it is in the domain of *kinship* that the *'feminine principle'* has been most active in history (tribal societies are all species of *extended kin*), and women have an *'instinctive'* affinity for it. Why? *Because they are, then and now (barring some new genetic/social engineering, part of our incipient Trans-Human future, that may alter this), the bearers, and first nurturers, of new life.* Further, this new life, in the human animal, is more vulnerable than many in the animal world, and requires years of intensive caring *(that can only be assured if a modicum of relative peace prevails: that being also the locus, in society, of all societal morality).*

So, women are/have been the virtual founders of the convivial order of family and domesticity: and these 'values' are not 'free choices,' but imposed by the 'natural-social' requirements of child rearing. *In effect, women are, and have to be, the original peacemakers.* Now there, in radically encapsulated form, one has both the *essentialist and the existentialist* basis for the *'difference'* I have argued is fundamental to understanding the male/female dyad.

❄

It is ironic that our wildest dreams never wander too far from reality, for we, apparently, know so very little other than ourselves (and sometimes not even that). Indeed, the paucity of the human imagination is far more striking than its alleged sweep (consider the laughable limits of science-fiction when visualizing 'other' forms of life, for instance). So, to imagine a *woman's world* may be startling at first, especially to the bigoted. But, it is—if nothing else—*necessary*. Indeed, therein may lie our only hope for a real, permanent salve, given the depletingly repetitive pattern of masculinist conflicts/tensions in world history. And women's powers lie girdling us all like a vast ocean of uncharted possibilities, so we would be foolhardy to think that they are only effective when curbing, say, drunk driving *a la* MADD. However, this latter example may, possibly, hold a clue.

What would it take to get the vast body of women to care deeply enough about the ills of the world (which, sooner or later, are visited upon them) to wish to become pro-actively involved in changing the world? *Could it be, perhaps, only when their very last refuge from the wasteland of male madness is threatened with extinction?* In India, for example, the unbelievable rash of brutal, public, daylight attacks upon women has fomented a rising tide of ire of a kind that has not existed since antic Gandhian times of anti-British agitation.

But such a *logos* may, I think, yet be mistaken—perhaps *it is MEN who now have to realize the enormous potential of women in all the regards* discussed above, and thereby: (a) begin to learn from women, and alter/restrain their own ways, or (b) 'step aside,' and let women 'manage' the public household, or (c), adopt both (a) and (b).

By the way, (a) is no leap of fancy—it has already been achieved, typically without homage to its inspiration: *Gandhi's Satyagraha, and Thoreau's Civil Dis-obedience, are but variants of the art of passive resistance that women have deployed, universally, with some effectiveness, if mostly within the domestic household.* It may not be merely in the *kind/quality of means* deployed that women have much to teach us all: it may be, far more importantly, in the wider, 'higher' charter of *human-societal Ends and Goals.* Of course, I am 'only' speculating: *but is there any truth that has been gained/gleaned in science or philosophy that did not first commence with a speculative query?*

Indeed, *en générale*, might it not be a revelation for us all to learn that Women may afford the 'natural' *solution(s)* to all Male (inspired) *problems?* There is a certain poetic justice to it. And if so: would that register another evolutionary triumph for Nature, or be just more evidence for an inspired 'Design'?

The Question abides.

14

Querying the Cosmos

The common sway of Euro-Philosophies, by convention, can be filed, in a brevity of convenience, in one of two hoary genres: *idealism, and materialism.* The former ascribes primacy to consciousness, the latter to 'existence.' Loosely speaking, it is about the primacy of mind, or matter. It is also about Origins.

In one view, we 'begin' with atoms, then ascend, howsoever inexplicably, to 'consciousness.' In the other, the origin is in some universal *geist*, which then 'devolves' into more mundane stuff. At least since Newton, materialism (and its progeny, empiricism) has been the dominant spirit (!) of European, and Modernist, science. By virtue of that, and for other reasons, it also became the vogue, via '*physics-envy,*' of the so-called social sciences, and metaphysics. Durkheim (consider 'social facts' as 'things,' *e.g.*) and Marx ('it is not the consciousness of men that determines their existence, but their social existence that determines their consciousness') are but late-entrants into that ilk, that included the great Canonicals: Bacon, Smith, Hume, Mandeville, Locke, and Hobbes.

Scientific and philosophical materialism was the dominant idiom at the level of the elite intelligentsia, whereas a more crass form of 'materialism' *i.e.,* the glutinous embrace of greed and gluttony, became the mainstay of the governing classes, with the expansion of markets and the 'profit motive' (their conjunction giving birth to the pseudo-science of modern 'Economics'), after the Crusades, and along the grand route(s) of global Colonization.

The Church was fatefully dualistic: its theology was ineluctably 'idealist,' but its science (and few would under-estimate the contribution of the Church of Rome to the study of the sciences, despite Galileo and all that) maintained a 'relative autonomy' from it—with the so-called 'Reformation,' and the 'Enlightenment,' further removing it from dependency on dogma, as in the work of Descartes or Kant (which sustained the dualism, nonetheless). However, the 'essential tension' between the two views remained, and still remains, extant throughout. *In the beginning was the Word, says One: in the beginning was the Deed, says the Other.* Each school, idealist or materialist, is further segmented into multiple variants: monistic, dualistic, dialectical, and so on.

In the natural sciences, the advent of 'field physics' upset the notion of matter as *'prima materia.'* Relativity ideas suggested that matter itself was 'exchangeable' with its *dual: energy.* Thus 'energy' replaced 'matter,' so to speak: but with further evolution, 'quantum field theory' overshadowed prior notions, with the *'field'* as *datum*—and both matter and energy subsumed within it.

Bell's Theorem seemed to defy the Classical notion of the Sovereign Absolute: the speed of light. Quantum ideas, apparently, brought human *subjectivity* back to the center of things (with their varied notions of the Observer effect, Heisenberg Uncertainties, Quantum indeterminacies, *etc.*), after a long, historical, hiatus. To quote Heisenberg: 'the ontology of materialism rested upon the illusion that the kind of existence, the direct 'actuality' of the world around us, can be extrapolated into the atomic range. This extrapolation, however, is impossible… atoms are not things.'

In the so-called *'Copenhagen Interpretation,'* the objective perilously depended on the subjective, apparently confirming ancient Vedic ideas. Of course, the religiously inclined saw in all this an opportunity for a 'counter-Reformation,' renewing a moribund theology on a *nouvelle*, quantum basis (*par example*, P.C.W. Davies' idea of a 'finite theism'; or, as with F. Capra, 'for the modern physicist, then, Shiva's dance is the dance of subatomic matter').

A new, evangelical crusade (prominently, in the US) erupted against Darwinian evolutionary ideas, and the idea of an empty, meaningless, universe (*via* Hawking's suggestion of 'God as the Edge of the Universe'). But, many scientists also felt 'liberated' from the 'iron cage' of scientific materialism, inspired by what appeared, at the sub-atomic level, as a *'self-aware universe'* (Amit Goswami, David Bohm, *et al.*). To quote Planck: 'as a man who has devoted his whole life to the most clear headed science, to the study of matter, I can tell you as a result of my research about atoms this much: There is no matter as such. All matter originates and exists only by virtue of a force that brings the particle of an atom to vibration, and holds this most minute solar system of the atom together. We must assume behind this force the existence of a conscious and intelligent Mind. This Mind is the matrix of all matter.' There is even the suggestion, in this perceptual scheme, that 'nature' itself is only a construction of mind. As Niels Bohr put it, 'There is no world of quantum, there is only a quantum mechanical description.' So it could be that the 'mind' is the knot that joins consciousness to matter.

Our current Orthodoxy, the 'Lambda-CDM' framework, of today, suggests that very little (perhaps only 5%) of the universe is governed by our traditional matter-energy *dyad*, with the vast unknown, being given dubious names such as *'dark'* (meaning, of course, unknown) matter and energy. But this new 'data,' inherently, supports neither school—so that the Question of *Origin* remains unaffected by it.

❄

Now I have, thus far, made reference to European, or Modernist, Science—to the neglect of all else. This should elicit no surprise: today, *all* of us, East and West, are Avid Consumers of the Euro-Modernist Version of Everything. Their hegemony is near-complete. However, a trek backwards in time to Antiquity makes short work of the content of this present hegemony.

I am referring to the multi-faceted insights of *Vedic* science and philosophy that have left no field of knowledge untouched, though still largely unacknowledged: a casual peruse of the literature reveals the egregious omission(s)—*there is not one major idea in science or philosophy that does not originate in some, or other, text of Vedic antiquity.* Yet Modernist science—even when cursorily acknowledging lineage—stolidly begins with either the 'Greeks,' or with the 'Enlightenment.' Why should it matter, in other words, that the so-called 'Pythagorean theorem' preceded Pythagoras by centuries? Maybe it doesn't: or does it?

The dating of this achievement, of course, remains problematic. European accounts of Non-Europeans, generally articulated during their suzerainty over the Other as Imperial Powers, have to be heavily discounted, as with the concocted Myth of the '*Aryan Invasions*' that, supposedly brought civilization (not to mention Europid traits) to the sub-continent (that was to be rudely, and tragically, rent, during/after grant of 'independence,' both by Colonial Design and by Nativist Infighting). Ditto with the feint that Sanskrit was preceded by some nameless 'Indo-European' mother ancestor.

There is a broad analogy there to the same worthies, high priests of academe no less, who once suggested that an in-migrating, Caucasian tribe occupied Egypt and built the Pyramids (to deny Black Africa its own claim to splendor). Unfortunately, some Nativist extremes, in the opposite direction, in understandable reaction, are also somewhat intemperate, in this regard. Suffice it to say, for the limited purposes here, that thousands of years before the European 'Enlightenment,' Vedic scholars were debating such issues with a profundity rarely equaled since. The noble Siddhartha himself was no mean scholar: and his legacy, much as that of Jainism, is still richly relevant today.

I want to introduce here the Sanskrit word *Pratityasamutpada*, which is relevant to this quick *précis* of the Idea of Origins. It may be translated as 'co-dependent origination,' or 'interdependent co-causation.' Nagarjuna, the great Buddhist savant, codified many of the tenets of the Buddha: here, in desperate summary, is the notion (*via* Thich Nhat Hanh):

This is, because that is. This is not, because that is not. This ceases to be, because that ceases to be.

The implication for ideas about origins couldn't be clearer. Instead of the simple either/or of 'idealism *vs* materialism,' it is the notion of their 'co-dependency': the world, as it is—or the worlds as they are—has a multiplicity of causes. Jain science, similarly, stresses, *in extremis,* our one-sided interpretive tendencies in the face of a universe gifted with the inscrutable 'suchness' of things (the 'Blind Men and the Elephant' is, not accidentally, a Jain tale). The Buddha's skepticism, similarly, refused/disdained answers—in eloquent reticence!—to no less than *Fourteen Questions* about the ultimate nature of things.

In the *Upanishads*, the iteration of *'neti, neti'* (Sanskrit for 'not this, not this'), in similar vein, negates all (self-assured) descriptions about the Ultimate Reality, if not the Reality itself. Even earlier than that was the equally irrefutable Vedic notion of '*Maya*' or 'dependent-reality' (*i.e.,* data contingent upon sense-perceptions).

Here, again, Nagarjuna, in his classic *Mulamadhyamakakarika* (or, Fundamental Verses on the Middle Way) argues: 'Things do not arise out of themselves, they do not exist absolutely, their permanent being is not to be found, they are not independent, but they are dependently arising.' It will be found that many schools of contemporary philosophy are negated in those few words.

And, despite the current reign of the 'Big Bang' theory, I predict that cosmic physics will, perhaps sooner than later, shedding its inescapable Modernist arrogance, arrive at this subtle, if ancient, and Vedic, *quietus* of realization. A more pedestrian way of making this point is perhaps *via* the Jain story of a patient cured after eating a bunch of herbs, not knowing which herb was actually medicinal. The moral: just as the patient was restored, despite ignorance as to which herb really 'worked,' so is there *wisdom in supporting all traditions*, given uncertainty as to the real distribution of their truth values. Pascal's wager? No: millennia after Jain deliberations, Pascal was offering a utilitarian gamble only—rather than *scientific caution in the face of uncertainty in a pluralist world*, which is the Buddhist-Jain message.

But, to extend matters even further: is this 'plural world' itself real, or a delusion (*i.e.,* a world of appearances only)? The *Vedanta*, to bring in another venerable Vedic tradition, is clear: we are deceived by Maya, the creative power of the universe, into believing in the Plural. Its binding forces are *Ahamkara* (ego), and *Karma* (volitional action), which tie us to the Wheel of *Samsara* (the material world). This Maya can be 'seen through' by *Darsana* (epiphany). So, it is *Avidya* (ignorance) that leads to *Mithya* (error) that can be overcome by *Gnana* (knowledge).

But, to what effect? The realization that 'experienced reality,' much as the experiencing Self, is hollow and empty (*Sunya*), and lacks a Self-Nature (*Svabhava*). *The World, in other words, is Empty.* Modern-day Quantum scientists and Existential philosophers alike could, easily, perhaps, take cue from that. As C.T. Kohl has it: 'there is a surprising parallelism between the philosophical concept of reality articulated by Nagarjuna and the physical concept of reality implied by quantum physics. For neither is there a fundamental core to reality, rather reality consists of systems of interacting objects. Such concepts of reality cannot be reconciled with the substantial, subjective, holistic or instrumentalistic concepts of reality which underlie modern modes of thought.'

Surprising? The real surprise is why Our European scholar is 'surprised' that, five thousand years apart, our best minds see the world, bare, bleak, and beautiful—similarly. Of course, one may have to set aside the *Euromyth of 'progress'* to glean such insights.

❄

The high priests of Modernist science, despite the quantum revolution, have been, and remain still, draped over with the patina of dogmatism and determinism, the very mirror image of the Church dogma it was once contending with. And Modernist Science still overlords it over *All* (proscribing this—acupuncture, *e.g.,* at one time—or ridiculing that, and partnering with the State in Dr. Strangelove fashion) much the same way as the European titan—of commerce, industry, or government—strides across the globe today, altogether cocksure of his imperial mastery over it.

Let me sum up: *we live in the best of times, and the worst of times.*

Best, because a panoramic penumbra of human possibilities is now become visible to the insightful, the world over: worst, because the old North Atlantic

Hegemons are still preventing universal access to its gamut of gifts, based on their apparently incorrigible, if time-honored, practices of extortion, monopoly, and expropriation. Be that as it may, it is become increasingly clear that the only certainty about the larger universe may well be *uncertainty*. Neither materialism nor idealism, of the classic *genre,* that so dominated Modernist social science and philosophy—can be sustained: they are both *passé*.

In the case of both social science and philosophy, such broad cosmologies—borrowed, admiringly, if unwisely, from physics—are neither of relevance nor meaning. To understand our *species-being*, we have to know the real anthropology of our kind. That has been made impossible by the Euro-Modernist to the extent that all but unconscious Judeo-Christian premises have, for the most part, driven its 'Protestant' discourse: with 'humans' elevated above 'animal traits,' and 'instinctual drives,' and with 'progress' being but a secular mirror image of the 'pilgrim's progress' so dear to evangelism (unquestionably, Marxian visions of a communist utopia are but a 'materialist' rendering of that very Christian heaven, much as Marx's early writings are a lyrical paean to *Christian* humanism).

EuroModernism adopts the astounding feint of assuming that we can, as a species, invent ourselves, willy-nilly (*via* Universal Declarations, forsooth!), any way we wish, with no mind to our societal and natural drives. Millions have paid, dearly, even with their lives, for the *simpliste naïveté* of such 'epistemic' errors.

Regrettably, Darwinian ideas, albeit closer to reality, do not, by any stretch, amount to a fully specified anthropology (as evidenced in Herbert Spencer who adapted them valiantly, if quite uncritically, to his 'synthetic' philosophy). I do provide such a non-Modernist anthropology, in my *Festschrift Lectures* (*op. cit.*) that centers on the differential roles of male and female: it may, or may not, be 'preliminary'—but it is a first attempt, of sorts, to rectify one of the Great *Elisions* of Modernism.

As I have repeatedly suggested, it is many *genres* of *matrilineal Tribal Societies* that have largely domesticated, *via* the affective matrix of kinship, the otherwise inexorable 'paradigm of masculinity' whose predatorial proclivities have sundered the planet, repeatedly. So, a realist, *anthropic Utopia*, as distinct from unrequitable Modernist fantasies, far from being futuristic, may have already been achieved in human history. At any rate, returning to cosmologial ephemera: *'God' not only plays dice (so Einstein was being just a mite presumptuous, in, as Niels Bohr had it, 'telling God what to do'), but all manner of games, many of which we have no clue about.*

Given that, what is most undeniable, perhaps, is our own, rather pathetic, fallibility. True, we may know much more than what was known: but we also, *ipso facto,* learn, as we go—*that there is even more now that we don't know. The ratio of the known to the unknown, thereby, appears to be an ever-diminishing one.* Stated differently, we may know more and more, over time, but still lag behind not merely what is to be known, but, more importantly, what *needs* to be known The proper scientific posture then, in the face of this ontic revelation of the limits of our epistemic quests, is *modesty*—nay, humility—itself undergirding a pluralist regard for the 'multiplicity of causes' that, *en générale,* confound our investigations.

Turns out, Hegemonic aptitudes and inclinations are as pernicious in High Science as they are in the mundane world. It would appear the Buddhists and the Jains have, after millennia, still a lot to teach us—if only we let them: and not merely in the arts of knowing. For knowledge maybe a necessary condition, for a meaningful existence, but it is, surely, far from sufficient. For the latter, we may have need of *wisdom*: and, in that area, *Euroscience* is, still, pitiably, a non-starter. Until we do advance, and soon, in that rarefied realm, the Modernist armies of the willfully ignorant will continue to lay waste, and irreparably ravage, this ruggedly bountiful planet, hurtling blindly as it is through an empty universe—be it, as the case may be, illusion or reality.

15

The (*Sub*)Human Condition

(Euro)Modernism is a Bell Jar, inside an Iron Cage, within a Gated Gulag. Yet, in tragic paradox, it comes meretriciously wrapped, within the exalted drapery of 'freedom.'

Freedom! What a mind-benumbing, hallucinogenic, inchoate, daydream! What an ideally devised sop for the millions! It has been the 'discourse' (another term to beware of) of Europe, for at least four centuries. The very (shallow, conniving) largesse of language of Modernism should inspire an instant, and very grave, caution. O those *Universal* Declaration of Rights!

My—anyone would think they *(i.e.,* the good folk that own and control everything) were just giving it away, for sheer goodness' sake! Has one (almost) reaching for musical instruments, and marching boots. If I had a penny for every soul who has believed in such tripe—only to stumble grievously upon the cold, hard rock of societal reality—I would be more opulent than kings.

The Myths—fables, fictions, and folklore—of Modernism are quite innumerable: and there are few of us, even within the charmed circle of the 'intelligentsia' who are not—even in these apocalyptic, latter-days—susceptible to their lures. Let me put it, perhaps, more effectively: *if Modernism were Dorian Gray, its hidden Portrait would be one sorry mess of an addled, distending, putrefaction.*

The conceit of Europe (amongst many) continues to be that it has 'discovered' (or is it 'invented'?)—if not quite *delivered*!—'freedom' as the desirable, if not even ideal, anthropic condition. Even a noted 'realist' philosopher found it edifying to sub-title his work *'the pulse of freedom'*—regrettably, echoing all those Anglo-Am demagogues who deploy it to cover up unseemly intentions and deeds. *Freedom: for what? From what? For whom? Against whom?*

These latter queries abide, as they have for eons, in a dead zone of deafening silence. Yet, the paradoxes have always been there, plainly to be seen. *'We hold these truths to be self-evident,'* wrote one set of their ilk, *that 'all men are created equal,'* whilst entire colonies of African slaves languished in their backyards. *And what about Women?* Ah, well…

Their petty, patriarchal, property-owning dream of a pacific 'equality' with one another—*bespeaking fraternity 'twixt fellow-governors*—as a 'band of brothers' might, within a racist and sexist frame, at a time of crisis, squaring off against a larger force: that may be all that is 'self-evident' in that high snatch of prose. Yet, the drivel still drones on.

The above is, admittedly, a true, but trite, example. Less shallow is the fact that *'freedom'* was the dissembling, populist slogan of the emergent Modernist Captains of Commerce and Industry, as they battled the sires and seigneurs of the *ancien regime*, seeking the support of the mass of the *sans-cullottes,* who were stirred up to serve as the ill-fated cannon fodder of their rank ambitions. And, heavens, did they 'deliver' oodles of 'freedom,' in lordly fashion—*first, and foremost, to themselves!* Peasants, serfs, laboring orders, 'freed' from their customary rights, dispensations, farms, foraging lands, commons, and related means of subsistence.

All that these wretched of the earth lost filled the bloated bellies, coffers, and ambitions of these New Titans. Yes, the serf was 'freed': and for two or more centuries, entered that abundantly 'free' state of destitute vagabondage before rampant industry corralled them all, *via* whip, workhouse, and gunshot, into those 'dark, satanic mills' (that vulgar apologists, of both 'left' and 'right' saw—and perhaps still see—as the necessary stepping-stones to their versions of Utopia). It should give one pause, for the simple error of mistaking *ideology*—in the sense of tendentious fabrications—with *reality.*

✳

Ignorance of societal structures and anthropic realities assisted the success of this propaganda whose most tragic consequence was perhaps the ease with which the very victims of its noxious effects embraced it, seeing in it, astonishingly, a salve for their impossible situation.

Hope is indeed given as a sop to the hopeless!

The fulsome tragedy of uncountable millions, over generations, viciously severed from their secure moorings in the womb of a tightly integrated *societal compact* was forgotten: and, adding further offense to injury, the rootless victims of that *Great Severance* were now to be celebrated henceforth as the heroic 'individuals' of our epoch, 'free to choose,' and free to embrace, and experience, every random and planned, evil of a sordid, materialist, unrequiting, hell.

Hell is 'other people,' wrote Sartre: yes, *Hell is Us,* the disaffected zombies that dwell in the living cemeteries of Modernist society. And, yes, utter wretchedness and *angst* can produce such magnificent *cri de cœur* compositions in art, music, writing, philosophy, *etc.*, can they not? Even if, like Van Gogh, they killed themselves, in so doing: or, went mad, like Nietzsche. *Yes, the contented rarely exert themselves to the point of genius—or dementia.*

Society was reduced to but *Two* functions necessary for the accumulation of wealth: *producers* and *consumers*—with workers and owners the two major classes of the New Order. Society, compressed to a giant mill grinding out the gaudy means to assuage the greed and gluttony of a few, and (a part portion of) the basic needs of the vast multitude. What a grotesque devaluation of the real riches of anthropic life!

Individuation, now a mark of European superiority, instead of being seen as the misbegotten *Niflheim* of social perdition, was to be celebrated as the highest canon of the human condition, despite its all too obvious affinity to the *Slough of Despond*: of alienation, despair, and anomie.

So now we add 'freedom' (*i.e., from* social obligation, responsibility, caring) to a self-seeking 'individuation,' and we create the *Ideal Modernist Wasteland*: that vaunted 'civil society' of *universal egoism* where each exerts against the other, in a competitive struggle for survival, one-upmanship, advancement, achievement, enrichment, *etc.*

I once asked the time of a corporate executive, a stereotypical New England Yankee, striding up a Boston street in that 'hurry' that bespeaks the personage of importance: 'buy yourself a watch,' came the laconic retort. In short, *Modernism exalts the model of a society of beggar-thy-neighbor, and the devil-take-the-hindmost. Being* was buried, forgotten: *Doing,* blindly, endlessly, was enshrined as the 'Protestant Ethic' with the celebration of 'labor' (preferably performed by *Others*: women, underclasses, Non-Europeans, *et al.)* not as a lamentable, Post-Lapsarian doom, but indeed as a higher-order *Virtue. What Modernism destroys, in its depravity, is the very possibility of an Anthropic Civilization, considered not as some far-fetched utopia, but as a very realized, and hence realizable, historical entity going back even prior to Antiquity.*

In my metaphorical usage, Modernism destroys real, anthropic humans, tied to teach other by close-knit, affective ties, and turns them into *Post-Human* Reptiles: cold, canny, uncaring, and calculating. In contrast, our traditional forbears were all simple, tribalist Mammals, warm-blooded, emotive, and familial. As a *First Strike*, Modernism sunders the delicate tapestry of the reciprocal 'social economy of affections' which is the hallmark of anthropic *Being*, and substitutes the cold, concrete, implacable jungle of vested, asocial, amoral, *self-interest*.

As I have writ elsewhere, the European *hegemon*, thereby, is not yet ascended to civilization: indeed, he has not reached the ladder yet. In fact, *He* (the male voice is inescapable: it is the 'paradigm of masculinity' that informs the Modernist straitjacket) went, catapulting, straight *from barbarism to decadence*.

❊

The traits of anthropic life are rudely, even absurdly, simple. There are no ideals to be realized. There are no propositions to be proved. There are no goals to be attained. And the only ethics are societally—*i.e.*, *naturally*—derived ones, not the products of extended navel-contemplation. No surprise, really; for we are but *hominids*, self-conscious apes, driven by innate and powerful instincts. Part of the art of social *being* is to tame or sublimate these drives (*in point of fact, the 'degree of civilization' attained, rests on how far the 'paradigm of masculinity' has been tamed/ trumped by the modus of femininity*: and it is in this regard that Matrilineal tribes with *matrilocal* residence are far more 'evolved' than Modernist societies) so society can perform *nature's* prime requirement: *propagation*. Yes, it would appear that 'god' did not place us on earth, after all, to 'realize' some noble theological expectation worthy of those 'created in His image.' Our 'values,' especially *morality*, stem from that 'necessity.' The human infant is perilously vulnerable, arguably for a longer stretch of time than others in the animal world. So, the prime rationale for '*Order' Within* is to secure the infant's safety (the requirement of provisioning food is far less stringent, and needs far less effort, *en générale*).

Women, owing to nature's quirk, as progenitors, and the first food-providers for infants, are the original, and prime custodians, of this vital function. 'Security' simply means taming the innate violence of men, or submitting the 'paradigm of masculinity' (violence, domination, aggression) to the gentler, but yet firm regime of the 'paradigm of femininity' (nurturance). This is achieved, historically, by ensnaring masculine dispositions within the matrix of the affective ties of kinship, which is the familial basis of the natural unit of our species: *the Tribe.* This does not wholly subdue male proclivities, but distracts them, alters their sights, be it for short or long periods of time, from *Within to Without.* In a very similar fashion, tribes 'make peace' with each other by entering into affinal, marital, relations: with kinship again serving as the binding cement.

Morality is the base coding of kinship: at its root is simply the 'rule' of whom you can harm, with impunity, and whom you cannot, which helps define the 'tribe.' It is similar to the coding of *incest,* which prescribes whom you can marry, and whom you cannot, which helps define the 'family,' or the extended family, or 'group.' Matrilineal tribal societies are likely our earliest, viably functioning, societal entities: and their achievement has arguably never been exceeded, once one deploys non-Modernist criteria, by any other societal form. Real Anthropic values are perhaps best learnt from their example.

Kinship confers contentment—it is our *natural* state (*i.e., the social and natural are one*). 'Happiness,' *au contraire*, is another wild, undefinable, hyperbolic, Modernist feint. It is within the 'family' that the wayward, restive, instincts of men find some temporary repose, and that is satisfaction enough (for all). Yet the achieved 'armistice' is not necessarily permanent: and men, can and do, 'break' with tribal codes—*i.e.,* they break away from the 'paradigm of femininity'—to found feuding groups that go on to become *empires.*

Back to Modernism.

The modern University is amongst its prime *tools of containment.* In fact, the Governors of Modernist societies have *two* tasks that often run against each other: to promote the accumulation of wealth, and also to serve (in appearance, or reality) the demands of 'justice' from the downtrodden orders (*i.e.,* to 'legitimize' the order). The University reflects the self-same mission. For the *farm* and the *factory* to hum along, subject to the (altering) wishes of the commanding Lords of the Realm, the University has to be a hybrid of the two. It, too, performs *two* vital functions (and several ancillary ones). One, its scientific labs farm the Technologies that drive its great, Productive Machine. Two, its ideological cells complement, and help manufacture, the desired *stasis* of mind and disposition, that nurture, in turn, the passive consumer, the meek elector, and the atomized citizen. These two functions approximate, more or less, the ontological split between the natural and social sciences. Now, the fact that debates, within the second platform, often exceed the bounds of mainstream 'requirements' should not obfuscate their real function.

Look at the plethora of flag-waving 'rebellious' outlooks that have come and gone: Marxism, feminism, deconstruction, structuralism, post-colonialism, environmentalism, *et.al*, that have all had their 15 minutes in the spotlight—only to end up in harmless ghettos, far from the action. When women, within the educated, protested—and could not be silenced—they were granted a fief: *Women's Studies*. When enough Blacks resisted, they got the *satrapy* of African or Ethnic Studies—to lull their best minds into more realizable dreams: of tenure. Needless to add, neither form of protest had any lasting influence upon actual *public policy*, save in exceptional outlier instances that actually prove the rule (Chomsky, in one of his early works, called mainstream academic elites, more generally, the 'New Mandarins').

For all the manifold tribes of 'dissenters,' Racism and Sexism remain the alpha and omega of all European formations, everywhere, regardless of their (mild) protestations to the contrary. One swallow does not a summer make: and yet the election of Obama, or the (likely) coming election of Hillary, is (and will be) used to convince us that those pernicious ideas and practices are a thing of the past. If you can bring yourself to believe it, the Good Society has already been achieved.

But, to return to the University. Under today's globalization, the universalization of this institution, especially in its North-Atlantic, Anglo-Am patent, on a sound (or is it, rather, the *unsound?*) Modernist basis, presages the universal adoption of this 'Standard Model' of economic, social, and political existence demanded of peoples the world over. *One Piper, One Tune;* and 7+ billion are, with or without consent, accepting the *Rules of Engagement* of Modernism.

Indeed, no Hegemon in world history has expected, nay demanded, more. So, clearly, it is De-schooling, rather than schooling, that is the order of the day. Let me state it baldly: the species is doomed to the extent that Non-European worlds are imprinted indelibly, as they are by the day, with this Modernist daguerreotype.

❋

I have said that Modernism was the *First Strike* against the conventional norms of Anthropic society (one must thus honor Europe's claim to priority in all things). In one swoop, the time-honored 'compact' that yet subsisted even within the unequal, hierarchical, violent, morass of feudal society, was obliterated. Henceforth, the Modern sector would leech off all other sectors, heedless of any countervailing obligations, both domestically and internationally.

However, the North Atlantic had even more destiny to achieve. In the Eighties, came the *Second Strike*, this time of *Late Modernism*. Whom the gods wish to destroy, it is said, they first make mad. Late Modernism, in euphoria at its global success, turned *cannibalistic,* and began to feed upon itself. Whilst continuing to fleece the world, *willy-nilly,* it let the most parasitic of economic activities-*Finance*- despoil its own productive capabilities, thereby effectively, and possibly irrevocably, commencing the process of self-subversion.

Never in the history of Modernism has Unproductive activity so mortally threatened more productive spheres. In all irony, therefore, the 'Second' strike might also be its, if somewhat dubious, Last Huzzah. So, the question is posed: who is to save EuroModernism from its own Himalayan follies? Well, it may well be, howsoever unexpectedly, its *Non-European* clones as they are, and as they are being engendered, in Asia, Africa, and South America. China has the *mantra* pat, by now, and present-day India appears eager to chant it: Russia with an ever-fading memory of its near-extinct socialist inclinations, remains, as yet, half-and-half.

So the chance remains, for late Modernism to be revived—or is it resuscitated?—by these *Emergent Powers.* However, their own dependence on the on-going viability of EU, Japan, S. Korea, and the North Atlantic—all of whom are technically bankrupt—may not be wholly conducive to their role as Rescuers of the Modernist World.

❊

I rail against the European variant of Modernism, which is not only the *Original Template,* but also the one that triumphed globally, *via* the antic means of fraud and force. Do I claim it is devoid of all, or any, merit? *Look at it this way: I can burn my house down in order to cook my dinner—and claim the latter effect to be undeniably meritorious.* But the *cost?* There's the rub. *The benefits of Modernism are numerous*—my personal favorite is flushing toilets—but they come at too frightfully unaffordable a cost for the species, and perhaps even our planet.

It is the European, Modernist, Governors that have brought the ecological world to the very brink of existence, the societal world to breakdown, and the economic world to collapse.

The world is suicidally *nuclear* today because of *Their* venomous invention(s) (no African, Asian, or *Other,* could even dream of such cataclysmic technologies of barbarism). Worse, *They* have force-tutored the globe, on pain of punitive destruction, to follow in their ruinous footsteps, in all domains.

The Soviets were busy, for decades, quietly undermining their own achievements, but nonetheless the West forced them to abandon their frame of *self-exploitation,* to join in the *Great Game.* Similarly, Maoist China was headed no place in particular, and yet had to be bribed and goaded to give up its own form of quiescence. And so on. As such, it is the European Modernist- in particular the

Anglo-Am set of forces—that is squarely responsible for where we are today: *in the Greatest Crisis in the History of Our Species.*

As a species, we don't need much to be content. This is not idle philosophy: but an amply attested fact. Tribes yet exist that are contented, if 'proof' were needed. It is a Modernist travesty that, prior to its advent, the world was steeped in '*poverty.*' Firstly, poverty is a *relative* notion, and has no content. If the intended meaning is *deprivation*, then that is always the willful creation of those who privatize, and monopolize, resources vital to the welfare of the many. In effect it is a *policy creation,* and not a natural state at all. It is also the goad to involuntary labor, within Capitalism, so no governor would ever dream of abolishing it. EuroModernism has, in fact, specialized in that manner of enforced *deprivation,* domestically and externally, for centuries—exacerbating inequalities, globally.

No tribe we know of ever starved to death unless it was under dire compulsion—of conquest or natural disaster.

We do not need a 'GDP' to grow every period, unto eternity. We do not need satellites, microwave ovens, nor even hi-powered computing machines as personal household items. Nor do we need to transport ourselves, at the spur of the moment, from sea to shining sea, across the globe. Nor do we need to dream (and this will one day be a tidal wave) of a *Transhuman, extropian* world of robotized humans, literally *internalizing* new technologies. *Nor do we need, even more tellingly, to labor all our lives, and against our inclinations, for people we don't care for, making products we may not approve of, and under conditions we are not enamored of.*

From the mines of Potosi, to the slave plantations of the American South, and the latter-day, corporate-funded sweatshops of Bangladesh: such has been the real sway of the implacable EuroModernist *Impulse of Exaction.* So, the query is moot: what manner of 'freedom' is the Modernist really celebrating? One would hope it is not the earthshaking 'choice' between Coke and Pepsi.

At any rate, the freedoms that matter are not 'freedoms' at all, but ordinary anthropic *needs: to be sheltered from want, indignity, and insecurity.* Such manner of benefice has only been possible in small face-to-face communities, of a *gemeinschaft* nature. The Tribe is exactly that. *It is one big, Extended family.* Its ties are *Affective.* They are not rent by competitive disaffections. Nation and State belong to a very different order. They are organized from above, and are not based on affective *empathy*: they are formal and impersonal. They run on bribery and/or intimidation.

In fact, the Modern Nation-State is a European '*fait accompli*' innovation dating from the Treaty of Westphalia. Few peoples in our *Pre-Modernist* past 'chose' to be self-organized in that manner. If it happened, it is because it was imposed by on them—*by force*. The dilemma of Modernism is clarified—we as humans crave satisfaction of anthropic needs that a nation state cannot deliver: quite literally, it doesn't 'care.' Yet a tribe delivers such wherewithal without asking.

A social economy of affections differs vastly from a political economy of interests. It is the difference between a moral economy and a material economy. Better still, it is the difference between (anthropic) civilization and (Modernist) barbarism.

Now we should comprehend the spectacular failure of 'Communism' (those that reap delight from that failure need to recall that the latter *tried to build a better society for all,* and failed—*aided, generously, in their failure by the global machinations of the West.* Yet the latter has failed, too, and quite miserably at that, *but without trying anything even remotely meritorious*). They tried, unfortunately, to create the former (fraternity, sorority), but based on the latter (bureaucracy, dictatorship).

That circle simply cannot be squared. *Gemeinschaft is gemeinschaft and gesellschaft is gesellchaft—and never the Twain shall meet.* As I have remarked elsewhere, a little anthropology goes a long way in avoiding terrible blunders in policy. I do not 'idealize' tribal society any more than I disparage Modernism— uncritically. Yet, it is clear to any thinking person that the antic tribe embodies values that are worth emulating. *No tribal society has ever poisoned the air, made waters toxic, and threatened the planet with mass-species extinction (including our own).* Those values are, arguably, important to reclaim, especially in these times of large-scale distress and disaffection with the present climate of drift. The (Euro) Modernist needs to consider: look at the twentieth century, the century of *High Modernism.* Look at its capacity for slaughter and war: is there any precedent for the sheer scale of the mass-murder in any other form of society?

Has drudgery, homelessness, unemployment, insecurity, stress, and tension, vanished? Have those resounding, meretricious, 'Declarations' been fulfilled? Look at the current consequences of the long-drawn High-GDP EuroModernist Way: in ecology, in social cohesion, in economical viability, in morality, both public and private.

Are we, perchance, happier for it? The *Happy Planet Index* is not found cor- related, *en générale,* with GDP, except perhaps negatively. Look at the stupefying stockpilings of nuclear warheads, biological weapons, *et al.* Look to the disasters that, actually and potentially, accompany accidents—even in peaceful nuclear facilities. Look at the current setting of the Doomsday Clock.

Add them all up. *Is the EuroModernist Way one big, grand, success story?* Regardless of how one answers that question, the reality of our tribal natures yet asserts itself, quite naturally, in the 'last instance.' As the crisis deepens, communities rediscover lost commonalities, the commons itself being reclaimed *en route.* Today's impecunious young are now discovering the boons of the succoring 'green, green, grass of home.'

Family, as the *First Benevolent Society*, is again being recognized. And cryptocurrencies, co-ops, and mini-barter-economies are emerging, spontaneously, worldwide. And so, it appears, the process of revitalization begins afresh. It is, perhaps, an opportunity—to *rethink* all things. *'Progress,' that term so dear to Modernism, sometimes, may mean no more than a (welcome) return to our Anthropic Roots.*

The 'Garden of Eden' may not be an idle myth: Marx built his own utopia on the basis of what he understood (at a time when Europe studied the 'Other,' after first subduing it) as *'primitive communism'*—which is none other than the tribal society form(s) I have been referring to in these passages.

16

Nostalgia, for the Future

It may be comforting to know that these are the *bad old days* (more on this, at the end). I mean, we don't have to '*look back in anger*,' join a retro film club, or wax nostalgic for such gallant memories any more: they drench us every day, if we dare catch even just the headlines at the top of any news hour. Of course, not for nothing are they called news '*stories.*' Yes: *stories* are what they are—tall ones, bald ones, new ones, old ones, fake ones, opaque ones.

There are so many genres to choose from (yes, we wouldn't be who we are if we didn't have at least 36 flavors, in all things—I'm surprised we accept, for the most part, just the *two* sexes on offer: surely, god owed us, *in his own country*!, a couple of dozen?—to get well and truly bored). It becomes quite fuzzy to determine who is deceiving whom, anymore.

Deceit? Lies? That's old hat. *No, savvy folks prefer to call it 'spin'*: they spit on their hands, put a little spin, and pass it on—to others, who do much the same, and so on. Yet are they everywhere: lies, near-lies, crypto-lies, proto-lies, nano-lies, black lies, white lies, in-lies, out-lies. Lies to get you to pay more, expect less, fear this, hate that, eat this, shun that, believe this, doubt that. It's a wonder anyone can keep up. Governments lie to people, Corporations lie to Government Agencies lie to each other, each lies to every other: and all that when they are not, simply, lying around.

O, what a tangled web it all is. Beats me how children, still new to this sort of thing, cope with it. They are led to at home, at school, on TV, at every turn. No wonder they turn, increasingly, to things that make them *feel* good, rather than *being* good. *In fact, bad faith may be the only non-depreciating currency around.* Now, I am not talking about *little lies* at all. I am talking about *Great Big Systemic Lies:* like democracy, legality, accountability, justice, equity, rights, peace on earth, *etc.* Partly, this is not new, it's part of the rubric of *Modernism,* everywhere. But it is far, far more obvious than ever before. It's a *Crisis of Faith,* before it's any other kind of crisis. So it behooves us to ask where/when did this *last phase* (yes, it is over, or will be, soon) of real decline set in. I think it dates from when Reagan and Thatcher took office. Before that, it was all sort of predictably boring. From cars to movies to music to unions to governments: they were all ho-hum. After that, it became excitedly, dangerously, *unpredictable.*

An odd *mélange*—of Ayn Rand, Rambo, and Milton Friedman (that last worthy recalls the *economics:* of that era: remember the *Laffer Curve?* It's still worth a laugh. You know the adage—'Lies, Damned lies, and Statistics?': *well, think—Economics begins where Statistics leaves off.* I don't even trust the *word*: there's probably, a con in it, somewhere...). Suddenly, the sky was the limit, there were no-holds barred, *and amorality became a national idiom.* The Old Order was being scuttled, top-down, by the new Masters of the System. Down-sizing, out-sourcing, union-busting, vote-rigging, regime-changing, war-mongering, sort of a general *melee* of a *Stasi*-fication of public life. Hitler was on the same road, but—a mere novice!—he never got very far. We did: to the point of being irrecoverably out of control. *No one can stop us now, except us.* It's a scary thought.

Reagan and Thatcher. I muse, at times, at what might have transpired had the two, in a fit of mutual adoration, turned to romance: and, say, got married. Would Britain have become another State of the Union? Or, would Reagan have been crowned the new King of England—and America? Oh, it was all very *possible*, don't doubt that for a minute. After all, a Mr. Obama, from someplace, got elected President (oodles of learning in just that). *Believe in fairy tales. It's a fairy tale we are in* (*albeit a cannily scripted one, no less*), in a wildly careening orbit that is headed straight to Outer Space. Orwell could have written a very quick, powerful sequel to his *magnum opus.* Of course, it would be quite unnecessary: since *they*, ingenuously, (mis)took his original work to be a mandatory scripture-cum-instruction-manual.

Now that newspeak, double-speak, and forked-speak, are all part of everyday *patois,* I await the coming *rewriting of Fairy-Tales.* The possibilities are, divertingly, endless. Grandma could first eat the Wolf, then Little Hood could put her down, swipe her teacakes, take title to her house and possessions: and issue derivatives on it leveraged at 100 to 1. Or, Dorothy could team up with the Wicked Witch: dropping Toto off by the nearest junkyard, placing the Tin-Man in the Recycle Bin, the Lion in a circus, the Scarecrow by a passing forest fire, and grandma up for a short sale on E-bay, banishing the Wizard from Kansas to Afghanistan: and then grow GMO crops for export.

My personal favorite: when the Duke of Nottingham waterboards Robin, accuses him of WMD (weapons of mass destruction), and has him, and his merry men, removed to Guantanamo—after they have all been betrayed by Maid Marian, his new secretary of state and secret admirer. Of course, King Henry, meanwhile, would get himself duly elected President, in a run-off against Richard, after his Ecclesiastical Courts halt the mandatory Recount. And then they could merrily work on how to engineer a *bail-in* of the resident population of Sherwood.

And you didn't think it's possible to live in a time when fairy tales come true! Believe your eyes. How will it all turn out? *The End will be pretty banal, even hum-drum: It will All Collapse* (at which point they will all scapegoat each other in high protestations of innocence). No—no big bangs at all: just a pathetic set of whimpers. For, though Caligulas may run riot for a while, they don't finish up too well. *Karma* catches up. Ok: for now, their nominated horses may be running wild. But how far, and how long, can they run? You see, the *Commoners* (remember them? *They still exist*, in burrows, beneath the radar) are fed and done with all the tyrannical '*isms,*' and 'ocracies' of this wretched age: with communism, capitalism, cronyism, terrorism; with democracy, plutocracy, theocracy, and bureaucracy—and all the grandiose systems that require the blessings of priests, politicians, presidents, and *politbureaus*.

Yes, a quiet collapse might be a boon: where it all winds down, and just plain *stops*. For a really, *long*, decent, interval. So we can all catch our breath: and, very, very slowly, mindfully, and ever so patiently, *rebuild*, from the bottom up, our indelicately torn and twisted lives. And, who knows? We may once again, someday soon, take time out to hear the early birds twitter, come early dawn—and look upon ensuing day, minds unwarped, hearts unjaded, without desperation. See?: Utopia, at base, is really quite simple.

And now to let on why I think it is comforting to know that these are the bad old days: *because that's the only way we know, for certain, that the coming future will be really good.* And, tell you what: we'll be big about it—we'll let them keep their MTV, if they leave us our indolence.

17

A God That Failed?

Over 50% in the US, lucky enough to be employed, earn either $30K or less. The labor share of income has never been lower, since WWII, though productivity has not declined. Yet US Corporate after-tax profits are at their highest in years.

Locally, Detroit is bankrupt (who's next?); and most of the G7 are close(r) to insolvency. According to the OECD, the Poverty Rate for Children in the US is above 17%, an incredible 21% of those surveyed saying they were unable to feed their families. Income (not to mention wealth) Inequality data is so skewed that we might have invented a new *genre:* the *Occidental Satrapy.* 4.5 million homes are on, or close to, foreclosure: and the Fed has already taken over a trillion dollars worth of Mortgage Backed Securities. And now a new Bill might have US Tax-payers foot 90% of the costs of such toxic MBS's. Yet QE succeeds QE: and Debt ceilings are, still insouciantly, raised every year (now at $17.2 trillion through 2015). So, where does all the 'easing' end up?

By now, we all know where: in big bank coffers, stock and hi-end real estate markets. Whilst the real economy (remember that?) hobbles on, dismally. Food prices rose above 12% this year (capping a steady, perceptible, increase annu-ally).Yet, *official* Inflation figures—at slightly above 1%—keep us mollified (the CPI scales in rising rents, but *not* rising home prices). Items made abroad, and returned to the US, at slave/serf wages, also help keep price indices down.

Unemployment is said to be under 7%, but is more likely above 10% (over 5 million are estimated as 'missing' *i.e.*, as having dropped out of a grudging market): and more so for minorities, and other underprivileged. At this rate— high Unemployment, Poverty, Hunger, *etc.*,—the US may well end up not a leader of the 'Free World' but, rather, of the (erstwhile) 'Third World.' How art the mighty fallen!

GDP growth is projected at 2%, or even above: but it is doubtful if it is even positive. Of course, property values and stock markets still keep up their merry, if zig-zag, climb. The reward for savings is virtually nil: ten-year securities yield no more than 2%. And any reasonable link between risk and reward was snapped over a decade ago.

Egged on by textbook economists (raised on hoary ideas stashed in ivory towers, far from the madding realities of real life), deficits and debts, public and private, are being raised year to year. No, Standard and Poor will likely not downgrade the US Credit Rating a second time, after being sued on the first try. *In similar vein, ex post facto legislation can now legalize illegal activities* (you see, 'democracy' has its uses: as Santayana said it, eons ago—'*democracy is the paradise that unscrupulous financiers dream of*': how's that for prescience?), whence the distinction between regulators and the regulated quite vanishes.

Indeed US-EU plans are afoot (called the TPP) to place Transnationals above government lawsuits, whilst allowing *them* to sue governments for obstructing 'free trade.' And so it goes. Our overseas saviors are losing patience: up until now their income from US bond purchases (apart from the purchases) was plugged back into the US, enabling it to consume and invest beyond its means. This is abating now. The BRICS are, day by day, changing their minds about the dollar.

We can handle a bond sell off, on their part, by further credit creation. But not if they start selling dollars. That would be the definitive end of the line. Prices at Walmart and the ubiquitous Dollar Stores—significant indices of so-called 'social cohesion'—would, then, have to be seen to be believed. And who, perchance, is virtually pushing them (*i.e.,* the BRICS) to do exactly that? Take a really wild guess! We could stave off even that hazard, for a while, if we had any gold reserves to boast of. Do we? Anybody's guess: except Germany, recently, guessed wrongly.

Now India's timeless *Vedas* suggest that *samsara (*the material world) is born of error. And error, of ignorance. *Well, the ultimate sinkhole of error and ignorance is achieved when Neo-Libs run the world's economies, and Neo-Cons its politics.* That equation is more powerful, in its toxicity, than *e=mc squared*, when put to (ab)use. So the 'crisis' of today may only presage further disaster. You see: up until now, the Monetary Authorities engineered a little recession, every so, to keep wages down and profits up. The Economists covered them by quickly manufacturing complex 'theories' supporting (in 'models,' of course) the idea of repetitive cycles (Oh those creative gales of destruction!: that was just *progress* we were told) as 'natural' to the economy.

Never mind that many statistical series exhibit that penchant quite independently. Which brings us to, perhaps, the biggest, and best-kept, secret of all. If we ask who, or what, is responsible for the so-called 'recovery', and/or the 'long recession,' here is what we might normally hear *(i.e.,* the usual players): Wall Street, State Street, and Main Street—meaning Bank Fraud, Government Error, or Corporate Mismanagement. Everyone has had a merry go at the First: Conservatives pick the Second, and Liberals, the Third, in dependable, knee-jerk fashion. Of course, for those wanting to pin the blame on 'foreigners,' there's always the whipping-boy of China (odd, given that they have kept us alive for quite a while).

The notion that something larger may be at issue, is never entertained, for being well beyond their intellectual horizon(s). *Could it be that it is really Laissez-Faire Capitalism that has failed, not any of the above taken singly, or even together?* Bears (re)thinking. You see once you let the *Profit-Motive* take over all affairs, you can't expect 'social responsibility' to be waiting in the wings like some friendly, neighborhood overdraft-protection plan. Mr. Friedman, who actively urged Corporations, in his puff, to go out and maximize their hearts out, had many obvious talents; but deep thinking (on the social implications of private prepossessions) was perhaps not his *forte.* He did not see it fit to add: 'b*ut do it responsibly.*'

No, for that would be *'paternalism':* right (and, *no*: we also do *not* tell people to work for a pittance, consume, obey, and be silent…)? Or, maybe he thought that the Old, Rhetorical Stand-by—the *'invisible hand'*—would collar the errants, in time, and subject them to sanctions. If so, it may not be Friedman's error, leastways in the first instance: it redounds, instead, perhaps, to our *Great Scottish Source.* Of course, it could also be that *Smith said it was 'invisible,' because it simply didn't exist!*

So, there: even in Economics, gods have clay feet. And they are, providentially (!), not too big to fail!

18

The Knowledge Game

There might have been only one, consolidated, 'social science,' had the project, *ab initio,* and over time, not been mediated by various vested interests. It would have had to be a *realist* Anthropology, the science of *humans*: in their *totality. Stated simply, a science exists anywhere where one can identify regularities—the degree of 'hardness' of the science resting upon how strong, or weak, these regularities are. So, prima facie,* a science of humans is, at least, *possible.* But is it *necessary?* I will return to that, later.

As it transpired, of course, the so-called 'social sciences' developed *willy-nilly.* Each branch challenges the other's basics: in Economics, Micro 101, *e.g.,* you learn of *individuals* as constituent elements, in Anthropology 101 you learn that *aggregate* units are primary. In fact, it gets even thornier when *sub-parts* of the same 'science' defy each other, as Micro and Macro in Economics.

Modernist social science, for the most part, is a European, *Post-Enlightenment* project, carrying with it all the societal stresses of *Modernist* Europe. It was a 'reactive' entity from the beginning: profoundly influenced by the Revolutionary epoch—late eighteenth century—in France, and America. Auguste Comte and Emile Durkheim would exemplify that 'precautionary' mood.

The nineteenth century added even more *anxiety* to its 'social science,' with the rise of overtly democratic and socialist movements: Max Weber would serve as a very late, mature, representative of that tendency. Economics was also spawned in this general *milieu*, but was necessarily more nuanced, being little other than the *necessary ideology of emergent capitalism* ('economic liberalism'): as such, it was initially *opposed* to the extant *status quo* of mercantile-aristocratic rule, as with Smith in Scotland and Quesnay ('laissez-faire, laissez-passer') in France. So, the discourse began with a 'critical' pose that swiftly waned, once Capital had replaced Land—as the dominant demi-urge.

Then Economics went quickly from *Critique* to *Apology* (compare Smith and Ricardo to Claude Bastiat [France] and Henry Carey [America], *e.g.*), and today it is, with vengeance, *the vulgar lingua franca of the Modernist Epoch: i.e.*, it can be deployed to justify *any* policy required by the powers that be—by simple alteration, at will, of its axiomatic assumptions. That is what it serves as today: either a *post-factum* rationalising calculator—or, an *a priori* policy abacus. And its 'predictive' value? Amateur astrologers could do better, even by flipping a Bitcoin (many IMF predictions could serve as sound examples, even when they are being, uncharacteristically, ingenuous).

In effect, it could have been a real, *empirical* science, if the will existed: but axiomatics are so much easier for propaganda!! Ricardo, instructively, claimed 'inspired introspection' as the basis for his ideas: indeed. It is a 'science' only of assumptions, truisms, and tautology: I have called it a *'self-referential language game with zero representational efficacy'* in my *Against Economics* work (*op. cit.*).

Today, it takes the hoary, baseline truisms of supply-and-demand (known to all engaged in trade for aeons) as far as well-financed ingenuity allows. In fact, it is no more than a *policy* science: and so, perhaps, not science at all. 'Micro'-economics is a series of tautological narratives, full of pseudo 'laws,' told from the vantage point of the Employer, and specifying the 'proper,' *i.e.*, the 'ideal' roles of entrepreneur, worker and consumer, in an atomizing, individualist ontology, predicated upon laissez-faire. It is none other than an 'ideal' *Capitalist Manifesto*.

Its lineage (in the British tradition) would run, Smith-Ricardo, Jevons-Marshall, *et al.* So-called 'Macro'-economics is the more 'open-ended' *Policy* Manifest-Toolbook tasked with the proper 'ordering' of a mature capitalist economy, albeit with an aggregative, totalizing, ontology. Anything can happen 'out there,' in the real economy: so Policy needs be ready to do/say anything. The Fed, today, in these times of near-chaos in economic policy, illustrates that very bold Macro spirit of 'Leninist' *adventurism*: like Napoleon, it first acts ('engages'), and then, when pressed, invents plausible, *post-factum*, scenarios of 'explanation.'

It can't help it: it has to make it up—there is no fount of 'economic wisdom' to draw on. Yes, 'rules-of-thumb' (where available) are what work, in practice: if not, there's always guesswork. Had they read Ricardo (or even knew who he was) they might have also termed it, gleefully, 'inspired introspection.' *Where Policy goes, thither Theory follows: that is the secret of all Economics.* Its (Brit) lineage would be Lauderdale-Malthus-Keynes, *et al.*

Now, taking in the two variants: *Micro is, gushingly, enamored of 'freedom,' Macro is stern of command and control.* So, in many regards, the two 'systems,' in desultory fashion, challenge-contradict each other's assumptions, but they are merrily 'merged' anyway in the very smooth, and creamy, *mélange* that Paul Samuelson lovingly crafted (to be called the *Keynes/Neo-Classical Synthesis*), in the early Post-War period of the establishment of *Pax Americana.*

Want Laissez-faire (in normal conditions)? There are helpful formulae available of either Classical or Neo-Classical vintage. Want Intervention (when War, or economic calamity attends)? Try a Malthus, or Keynes.

Yes, you can have your 'theory' cake, and eat it too. Mind, it's always about 'intervention' and/or 'laissez-faire,' as policy options, *within* the capitalist economy- not *against* it. And everyone is happy so long as no one is *gauche* enough to cry out: socialism! Give away loaves and fishes? It'd be more 'rational,' in economics, to try and walk on water!

Now, to return to 'social science.' *Who needs it?* Well, with the 'professionalization' (no I did *not* say *prostitution*: though, about the tenure system within the academy, it has been remarked that if you've been a whore for a full stretch of seven years, then…) of the rank, within the sprawling university system of today, we can guess at the answer.

Ah yes, 'tis the legions of our venerable academic tribes who have taken us so far along the road to *scientism* (Chomsky termed them the 'New Mandarins'). No, I will not stoop so low as to refer to the infamous Sokal affair, or the indiscretions of Margaret Mead, or of Hans Eysenck, because they are simply individual instances: my commentary is on the entire *Enterprise,* instead. But, long before such a stratum of 'yea-sayers' were firmly ensconced, what prompted such an institutionalized artifact?

Here, we need to refer to the rudiments of power and domination. Modernist rule requires a beholden intelligentsia, much as Pre-Modernist empires relied upon priests and soothsayers. So now we can fathom the issue of its 'necessity.'

Here's a little thought experiment. What if a plague affecting only economists were to hit the planet and eradicate the species? Would the economy stop? Hardly: as it is, the engine runs on, higgledy-piggledy, when it runs at all (fired by those proverbial 'animal spirits' of the investing order), free of economic, or any other, nostrums. But Policy makers will, surely, be stumped: with Panglosses all departed, who will now defend their errors and extortions?

Who will argue, *e.g.,* that raising minimum wages will hurt workers? Or, who will say that full employment is to be avoided since it spurs 'inflation'? Or, that to tax capital gains is ruinous to the 'inducement to invest'? Or, that unions are a 'monopolistic' contravention of a 'free market' in labor? Or that a welfare dole for drudges, being an unsustainable, demoralizing, 'paternalistic,' intervention, needs be held down to the severe maxim of 'less eligibility'? Or, that usury is just another 'efficient' market-clearing mechanism? Or, that income inequality robustly promotes incentives to work hard, and to take risks? Or, in sum, that capitalism for the poor, and socialism for the rich, is the very 'best of all possible worlds.'

In the nineteenth century, Economist and Counselor to Whig governments, Nassau Senior, sagely argued against reducing the Workday—from Twelve to Ten hours—saying that the move would cripple capitalists: since *profits were made in the last hour*! His contemporary, Robert Malthus, was even more reprobate as he argued against allowances for the poor—since they 'allowed' them, in the long run, *via* implications of his so-called 'Law of Population,' to further 'multiply'—presumably like bacteria in a *petrie* dish (implication: more humane to let them die! Marie Antoinette should have studied with economists: she could have topped that 'let them eat cake' crack, after the very first lesson). You get the picture. 'Science' can come in very handy. But rarely is such *modus* of social science on the side of 'We, the People.'

And I don't mean just Economics: *e.g.,* Political Science is not far behind. In the Sixties, Robert Dahl argued against the very existence of a power elite or a ruling class. *Who Governs?*—that was the book's interrogatory title (never mind that the title is itself self-shorting. Governors and Rulers don't necessarily coincide: *the Monkey is often visible, but the Organ Grinders, though occasionally audible, can remain quite invisible*). His Answer: *no one, really*; just particular coalitions, built around topical issues, who crop up randomly—and vanish. So, power is, quite ineffectually, 'dispersed': thereby, the placebo of Pluralism and Democracy is pleasantly confirmed. Concentration of power in *America?* What a canard!

Take that line, and why, next thing you know, we'll all go looking, globally, for meaningful links between Bilderberg Clubs, Trilateral Commissions, World Economic Forums, the Bank of International Settlements, the Rothschilds, *et al.,* under the bed! So, let me sum up. The governors have obvious 'need' of such manner of 'sciences,' both to secure order and to maintain legitimacy. And, for a few, they are a provident source of income and employ. *But ordinary people 'need' it as much as they need to be lied to, spied on, or coerced to go to war for 'king and country.'*

But there is more. There is an arresting feature of Modernist social science, *viz.*, its 'sub-division' of the 'sciences' into multiple entities. So we have economics, political science, sociology, *etc.* It appears, at first blush, to be no more than a heuristic, a device to make it all more 'manageable.' It also appears to be a North European philosophical penchant: *to 'atomise' all phenomena as a means of contemplation* (the Greeks, *e.g.*, *whom I place as part of a larger Mediterranean Civilization, unrelated to a North Europe that eventually annexed their ideas, au contraire, were never more comfortable than when engaged in what might be termed 'holistic' theorizing).* In contrast, ancient Indian thought always spoke in terms of large, cosmic, wholes, and very rarely failed to 'totalize' in their speculations, even about micro phenomena. *But is it just that?*

Let me first present an analog, well aware that analogies are always less than perfect. If I split an Entity into multiple parts and then hand them over to a tribe of analysts who work on the parts quite independently of each other—much like academe where the social sciences are split into various domains that barely communicate (I have had editors turn articles down simply because they went 'beyond' the scope of the 'discipline')—who is there, at some point, to resurrect the original Entity under scrutiny?

And how can Society—our original *corpus*—be fully understood as an organic being, with a creature-specific *logos,* with a specific history of evolution, if such a 'Comprehensive Viewer,' by definition, is not allowed to exist? Indeed, it cannot be. Of course, the philosopher often totalizes, but (s)he is based in the Humanities and is, normally, not 'required' to know the social sciences: nor are such sciences obliged to take his/her ideas seriously. So, the 'heuristic' of a 'division of labor,' amongst the social and behavioral sciences, negates, *prima facie*, the possibility of recognizing society as a *totality.*

And that is the Primal Default, much like Original Sin, of Modernist Social Science(s). It's almost as if society itself is only permitted to be understood, by scientists, in the various disciplines, on a 'need to know' basis: much like the scientists who worked on the Manhattan Project—and, like many of the latter, *they too don't know, or don't wish to know, what the Game is all about.* Worse, the very 'separation' *within* the social sciences is question-begging and issue-evading.

One example: if Economics is the 'science' of wealth, and Politics is the 'science' of power, then the fact that they are 'separated,' *ab initio,* carries the latent presumption that wealth and power are *not* inherently linked, and can be studied, 'normally,' apart. *Similarly, to study 'Economics' independently of 'culture' is entirely foolhardy: indeed, Modernist Economics poses as 'universal' and 'culture-free'—until one understands that it is, in embodied form, European, Capitalist, Protestant, Secular, Quasi-Theology.*

Indeed, its role in advancing Modernist ideals is not dissimilar to that of Roman Catholicism in defending European Feudal society. Possibly, it is rewarded with a Nobel Prize, alone amongst the social sciences, for that heroic effort.

At any rate, in sum: society in its totality, and as a totality, cannot be arrived at by scholars engaged, separately, and, hermetically, insulated from one another, in the various sub-disciplines. *The Parts studied partially, if/when added up, cannot constitute the Whole. So, to get a full measure of Anthropic Society one MUST start with the totality: in structure, process, and historical evolution.* There is no other way. So, Modernist social science, as constituted, quite vitiates its own putative objective of the acquisition of coherent, societal, knowledge.

I will withhold comment on whether this is a purely adventitious fact, or not. Of course, I'll grant, a *genuine* social science—much like Western Civilization!— catering purely to curiosity, in the mode of self-knowledge, could be *a really good idea*. As I had said at the outset, there can only be one real science: an *Anthropology of Humans*. But it needs to be *accurately* constituted first. And its merits need to be argued for, in every instance, not assumed. Nor can its insights be imposed upon people, perforce, by simple resort to the notion of the inherently superior claim of science on temporal power. Until then, alas, it is no more than yet another sacral myth of Modernism.

19

Toward *Non*-Centrism

Will the gee-whizzing, and good griefing, never stop? Every day is discovery of a new scam, be it of Government or the Corps., reported by the few (outside the matrix), and ignored by the many (inside the box). And the usual bursts of indignation, sincere or otherwise. It is not that scams have increased *per capita,* as much as the means of unraveling them (largely *via* the medium of the Net, since more conventional channels such as the 'free press,' *e.g.,* have little import today). Truth is that the 'system' has *Always* been run this way, except for the sheer brazenness of iniquity on part of the powers-that-be today.

That last is both novel—and not. It is novel in that it has, in most part, shredded that slender fig-leaf of public trust upon which the legitimacy of modernist governments rests. *Par exemple*, trust in the Congress of the US is now reported to be in single digits. It is not new in the sense that we have reverted to the 'open rule' of pre-democratic times when monarchs and aristocracies did just that— with little fear, for a long time, of reprisal.

So, it should be clear that the difference between the 'bad old days' and the 'bad new days' is simply in the fact that governments invest resources today in the acquisition of legitimacy (by any means!). Power feels 'safer' that way: and it is not at all misguided in that perception. After all, neglect of that simple notion had produced the convulsions that shook the Royals of Europe in its Long Century of Revolution(s).

Guile and cannon sufficed in the past: now it is the cultivated near-delusion of 'participation' in governance, if not actual *rule:* pulling a lever, or stuffing a ballot box once every few years, is seen as 'participation' enough for the 'masses.' The sheep that are to be sheared, *via* taxes, fees, prices, or coerced labor, are, howsoever minimally, 'shepherded' carefully—into safe pastures of ignorance and/or quietism. But, today, the North Atlantic Powers, urged by their financial overlords, have, boldly, rent the veils. Gone is the recent neologism of 'plausible deniability,' or even simple legality: since the laws can always be retroactively altered to suit the occasion. And yet, *We* cling dearly to the great myths of democracy, even as *They* cling to the apparati of power. Who, one wonders, is the more deluded?

Recall the 'embedded reporter' of recent history?: well, today, every organ of government is 'embedded'—in the ever expansive *logos* of reward without effort, and taxation without representation. The Statue of Liberty is now a Statue of Unbridled License: and there is no real sign, anywhere, of even a miniscule bust of *Responsibility*—let alone an entire Statue.

Hell hath no fury like an enlightened liberal, wrote a famous Bolshevik: but where is liberal outrage, today? In fact, Late Tsarist Russia may have had more scope for significant dissent than is possible openly today: which may be why the Tsar was so easily overthrown. Every derogatory epithet Europe had hurled, for eons, at the Non-European 'third world' (crony capitalism, dictatorship, banana republic, police state, *etc.*) is understood now as quite befitting their own situation. There is, likely, an abject lesson in this for all those heady votaries of a linear 'progress' in societal affairs who dominated discourse for much of the twentieth century (as I have written in previous posts: to 'imagine utopia' may be epistemically very satisfying: but is ever an ontic disaster—if we understand the rudimentary basics of human anthropology).

Nations had governors in the past: now governors, public and private, have nations—in their pocket. And neither operates on behalf of, let alone at the behest of, the 'people.' Quite literally, they can take your money and/or your life w/out the quaint notion of 'due process.' The bail-out, or the bail-in, will see to the first: the drone to the other. All right: maybe the entire North Atlantic is not quite like that: but they do adore, and follow, their Leader, so!

Of course, it suited these worthies to wax righteously indignant when such infringements were committed by arch-enemies such as a Hitler, Stalin, or Mao, as they do today, when they strike gallant poses of chivalry *vis-à-vis* the unfortunate nation of Ukraine (or Kosovo, or Iraq, or Libya, or Afghanistan): *fallen first to wolves, then to thieves, then to scavengers—which is the normal trajectory of Modernist European Empire(s).*

First they start a fire, then they yell fire, then they loot the premises—when the terrified populace has either fled, or is in hopeless confusion. How many times has this drama been repeated since the sixteenth century! This is how *They* make, and unmake, 'history'—better termed '*theirstory*' since it is all really their story—prior to writing it all up in their multifarious journals (it is nice to own the world's media!), to be avidly consumed by the next generation of the willing/involuntary *ignorami.*

But not all are so easily duped. Russia, China, Brazil, and South Africa (India is, sort of, half and half), and perhaps a few others, remain just a bit outside this baleful net of mass deception. They have seen it all before. So, where is all this leading? The goal of *sole ownership of the globe* is not a new-fangled North Atlantic dream: it is an antic fantasy. Unfortunately, it is unachievable—at *Any* cost.

Tyrannosaurus can thunder about, crush and terrorize the weak and helpless, and raise up great storms of dust: but, in the long haul, indeed in the none too distant future, we know how it ends (even Hollywood knows that script). This is the way the world, of *European Hegemony*, ends: not with a bang, but a whimper. It is only appropriate.

But the irony runs deeper. The disarray is not owing to the machinations of any 'external,' cunning, vengeful, adversary bent willfully on revenge or destruction. It is more a case of blind, self-propelled, *self-destruction*—where centuries-old high hubris dissolves in the rabid rent-seeking vortex of greed supernal.

Gandhi had said, about the British departure from India, more or less: 'we have come way a long way together: we would like to bid goodbye to them as friends.' Perhaps, in similar, and due protocol, we might all join in simply to say: *'Adieu: and Requiescat in Pace!'*

20

The Bell of Atri*

Is it time to ring it?

Consider. Let's try, at first, a pure thought experiment, with no empirics alluded to, and no resemblance to any society, past or present. Of course, if it begins to feel real, it's just the power of suggestion—no more.

For starters, let's deem this but an exercise in the construct of a 'free society.' Of course, it won't be *equally* free—some will be free-*er* than others Maybe, even a whole lot free-er. Some will be freed of property, income, employment; others of rights, status, and dignity. Some of subsistence, others of liberty, and security.

Yes, all shall be free—of something.

Let it also be driven by, let's pick this one out of the hat, unalloyed *greed*. Why not? Being *modernist,* the system has to '*move*' of some accord. It cannot, nay must not!, stand still: each year, even the humble coat-hanger must be 'new and improved,' each season. So, bluff materialism will do (no, Buddhism is *not* an option), and selfishness will come to be ratified as *rational* behavior. Let it be self-governing in the prudent sense of the *real rulers governing themselves,* peaceably than by resort to arms. For want of a better word, the '*political formula*' could be termed a *democracy.*

Of course, no major institution will actually be democratic: not schools, not bureaucracies, corporations, churches, courts, nor armies. The electors will, in some proportion, simply vote every so (on a pre-selected palette of 'electables' proffered by the powers-that-be): no more is needed in that formula. It won't matter that the elected 'governors' are swiftly purchased, or rented, by some, or other, special interest(s). After all, given that the best of everything is ever up for sale, it follows that the existing government will always be the best, as Twain had it, 'that money can buy.'

The Guardians will show great acuity in ensuring that no one comprehends the difference between the (office-bearing) governors and the (corporate) rulers. *So, whilst 'politicians' serve as made-to-order whipping-boys, the rulers will remain invisible, and exempt.* Legality, of a formal sort, will prevail, if only in part: indeed, as every wannabe dictator knows, why taint a good thing with legality? But, more importantly, an active mass media will instruct the masses to think, or not to think, as needed.

Free, nay virtually compulsory, public schooling will raise the young on a suitably stylized mythology of 'nation.' Indeed, the 'dumbing-down' will begin, humbly, at Grade school. The universities will become fee-charging, revenue-driven, diploma-mills—*tools of accreditation* only. The shadow rulers will show great sagacity in maintaining, publicly, the delusion of *free choice*. There will be (at least) 36 flavors in all items, except politics: *there, One size will have to fit all.* The 'people' will, naturally, fancy a torrentially wild competition exists in industry and economy.

That the very few might be propping the many goods and bads, that are publicly flaunted, will not cross any one's mind. *Amorality* will be churned out as morality; *guided* public conversation as free speech. Slavery and serfdom, of the traditional kind, will be most sanctimoniously outlawed: all will be *wards,* instead, of this Brave New Order. Like good stewards, the Guardians will see to it that these wards know (and keep to) their place. They will be suitably *divided* to prevent any emergent sense of their shared, collective lot: gender, class, ethnicity—anything, real or imaginary, will do that serves the purpose (and so the blue-skins will rail against the purple-collars who will assail the violet-gendered—and so on).

The Guardians will think for them, dream for them, administer for them, pray for them, dispense justice for them, tax and spend for them. The masses will vie with/within each, in all spheres, but never seriously quiz their Overseers. They will all eventually learn the guiding mantras: to *Consume, Obey, Be Silent.* Above all, they will all, regularly, pay annual tribute, in prescribed financial form. Their Financiers will merrily deploy such funds, enhanced by free credit, in their global gambles, behind closed doors. Succeed or fail, in such ventures, they will always win: since the public kitty will always be open to them.

To expand globally, great armies and navies will be raised, the only real reservoirs of anything approaching job-security. Great Multilateral Agencies will be instituted purporting to pertain to global welfare but serving only the topical interest(s) of the 'free society.' *Other Peoples* will be subjugated, financially or militarily, all in the name of 'development,' or 'democracy,' or some such lofty notion drawn from the tendentious lexicon of *progress.*

In the interest of politeness and civility in discourse—to which the Guardians remain ever devoted—no one will mistakenly think it *empire,* nor call the intermittent slaughters *genocide.* Frequent war(s), suitably televised, will divert public attention, stoke jingoism, fund new arms, and help maintain domination. Indeed, there will *always* be a cannily invented, hyped-up '*enemy of the year*' worthy of respect—so resources usable, and necessary, in the civilian economy could be profitably diverted to militarism, and its 'hidden' economy. Of course these 'enemies' will, by pure coincidence, be located near coveted resources.

All major commodities will, sooner or later, be cartelized and monopolized so as to extract rents from the entire planet. The poorer amongst the comity of nations will be robbed of their natural resources: minerals, forests, and fresh water—their farmers driven to suicide, their children perishing of malnutrition, their masses engulfed in vicious chains of poverty.

Nature's bounties, air and water, at the opposite pole, will be rendered toxic and noxious: bio-diversity will dwindle, as species vanish, and the environment degrades—perhaps irreversibly. Maelstroms of self-propelled credit, with its accompanying skullduggery, will drown the real economy with mass indebtedness—a new, and inescapable, condition of commonality. Even sovereign states will be bankrupted to secure real assets at bargain prices. All markets will be fixed, as nearly as possible. The ensuing, chronic depression(s) will not be called that— again out of that admirable sense of propriety—and *recovery* will be the new, receding light at the end of the tunnel. Junk food, gross entertainment, anomie, despair, and ill-health will keep most imprisoned in their cells; those who actively protest will meet more public forms of incarceration and sanction. After all Robespierre was perhaps right (?): *virtue without terror is ineffective*—and the Guardians are nothing if not deeply enamored of their (own) virtue.

A certain measure of *Stasi*-fication of society will ensue, with ever-expanding network(s) of spying, surveillance, and abusive authoritarianism. Stark *survival needs* will keep almost all enchained to that sole, overriding, pre-occupation—

without any mind to any other aspect of civic life. Reduced to fending for baseline animal needs, a callous brutishness will emerge, debasing language, deportment, and human interactions—virtually extinguishing human civility.

A well-tuned movie/TV industry will exceed itself in delivering that exact mix of violence, depravity, and dystopia—day after day. A sick, harsh, banal, and bestial, society will slowly gain ground electing, more and more, for the Darwinian 'laws of the jungle.' *Increasingly, it will be a prison lovingly built by its own inmates, having duly internalized all needed systemic demands.*

At some point, in this 'managed devolution,' time-honored distinctions between good and evil, right and wrong, will vanish and cease to be operative. *It will be a late modernist hell, rational and maximizing, in extremis:* not wrought of fire and brimstone, but of a quiescent amoral wasteland run through by greed and gluttony, restrained only by fear and insecurity—*sans* charity, empathy, good feeling, or good faith.

A society of hopelessly irrefragable zombies. How's that for a wild thought-experiment? It's only fantasy, of course. And don't we all thank goodness that we *don't* live in such a *post*-1984, 1984! *But, to return to the opening query, consider this now: if, perchance, we were to encounter such an impossible state of social being, along the way, would ANY be moved to step out—and ring that bell?*

The fate of humankind may well rest on the answer.

Note

*   A Sicilian folk tale.

Part IV

Decline

21

Rites of Passage

Nietzsche spoke just over a hundred years ago of the 'twilight of the idols.' Idylls, perhaps, is the better term. If it were twilight then, surely it is dusk now. However, his 'idols' were the ones (supposedly) overthrown by Christianity: power, dominance, mastery—indeed, it is tempting to think of these traits as belonging, to the '*Paradigm of Masculinity*'—POM, henceforth- as I define it (and as referenced in my YouTube Talk, previously cited). In fact, he was bemoaning the dispiriting sweep of socialism and democracy across Europe, unlike (the more admirable) ancient Roman ancestry of Conquest and Empire. Weaker, submissive, values, he felt, were triumphing against stronger, '*Steppenwolf*' ideals: morality was but the Argument of the Impotent.

I am speaking, *au contraire*, of the *dissolution*, today, of the very putatively 'Christian' set of ideals that he disparaged: humility, charity, pity, *et al.—i.e.,* the 'Paradi*gm of Femininity*' (POF, henceforth), as I represent it—in the West.

But, first to point to some obvious conceptual errors. The POF is not an expedient strategy to seize power, whereas 'Slave Morality' is (in that sense Christianity is simply the 'ideology of slave revolt,' assisting the latter). Also, to use the term 'morality' for both Master and Slave orientations is erroneous. The Master *qua* Master has no morality, only *stratagems*: the slave, *qua* slave, is driven, *ab initio*, by moral-ethical considerations of equity, justice, *etc.*—even if 'compelled' to seek 'regime change' to achieve them. Finally, one must not confuse ideals with reality: Christianity, for all its apparent meekness, was more successful at sheer conquest than Islam.

But my real point is a little apart from that discussion. I am suggesting that 'democracy' is not an ideal, but a *ruse*—or perhaps it is an *ideal ruse*: *it is the most effective prophylactic against revolution* (Santayana called it 'the paradise that unscrupulous financiers dream of'). Although America did not invent it, it surely perfected it: the masses vote—and then 'special interests' buy out the legislators (as the ever insightful Twain had it, you get, thereby, the 'best government money can buy'). All are served, if unequally: the *illusion of participation for the many, the reality of control for the few.*

Since the late eighteenth century, Western thinking has been ever mindful of the 'revolt of the masses.' In fact, the very birth of so-called 'social science' is connected to that sentiment. From the time of the French and American Revolutions, 'social science' has striven to be the *science of 'mob control,'* or the mind-set of *Counter-Revolution* (clear enough in the work of Comte, *e.g.*). Beyond that, the challenge of emergent radical, and socialist, ideas reinforced that 'mission' with the original 'cold war,' that commenced right after the Bolshevik Revolution, sealing that fate. Of course, inevitably, a few dissenters would always exist, tenuously: but they were easily marginalized, or 'ghettoized'—and reduced to zero impact. Economics is a good example of a discipline banishing dissent straight into the boondocks.

So, most of twentieth century public discourse affirmed the Western rhetoric of 'human rights' and 'democracy' (despite naked Western support for brutish dictatorships and oligarchies. My personal epiphany moment was when Gerald Ford refused to visit India supposedly because Indira Gandhi had, dictatorially, declared a 'state of emergency,' whilst merrily driving in an open jeep in Madrid, but days afterward, with General Franco!). It was needed in the ideological and political struggle against the Socialist East. A trivial illustration: the US passion for 'democracy,' in 'hostile' Syria, is somewhat at odds, to put it mildly, with their gracious omission of such passions *vis-à-vis* 'friendly' Saudi Arabia.

However, the game changed at the close of the century. With the USSR set aside, there was no 'competitive need,' any more, to keep up the prattle (China had been 'won over,' similarly), at least in the Nineties. The gloves came off, and one by one, old grade school 'liberties' were swiftly shed, doffed like old shoes. This is highly instructive to understand Classical Old-Style Euro-Colonialism, Sixteenth century on: *if Empire can be so transparent now, in the twenty-first century, how limpid must it have been in those bad old days!* One can only shudder to think.

Today, the 'freedoms' still available are the technical minimum necessary to keep a private capitalist economy running: *i.e.,* basic economic 'freedoms' persist, whilst political liberties are being steadily eroded. It is easy now to see the conflicts of the European twentieth century, in perspective. Hitler was only trying to achieve for Germany what had already been accomplished by Britain, France and Spain, centuries earlier. Italy and Germany (and Japan, although in a very different sense) were, in effect, late-starters, in the lucrative game of global conquest: and failed. They may actually have succeeded in gaining entry into the Imperial Club, had Germany not made the fatal blunder of attacking the USSR.

But I want to point to even higher-order lessons, about our species. As I have repeatedly written, we anthropic beings are, in essence, *Tribal* entities (the current EU elections are described as bringing to office 'nationalist' parties: this is, of course, standard modernist jargon. Actually, it is our old friend, *European Tribalism* that is, again, showing its ever recurrent face. Ditto, in Ukraine, where ethnicity was played, astutely, against ethnicity. If it were Africa, they would have all screamed 'tribalism,' in loud unison).

And, as tribals, we are richly blessed with creative 'myth-making' aptitude(s). Indeed, it is astonishing for how long myths can be sustained, despite evidence to the contrary. Just one example: Adam Smith had written, unambiguously, that Governments are constituted to 'defend the rich from the poor.' Yes, Adam Smith, *not* Karl Marx. If there were a Nobel Prize for Sociology, he should have gotten it (Economics gets it for simply being the matrix ideology of capitalism, but that's another story). Think of how many Sociology and Political Science Courses, Books, Dissertations. Speeches, and Manifestos, are negated, and tossed into the bin, by reference to that utterly simple fact. Yet, here we all are, tirelessly, trying to virtuously square the vicious political circle, generation after generation—trying, in effect, to get 'democracy' to deliver. Every election, Hope votes, with all its Heart, for some new species of Gamester: with sad, if predictable consequences.

Nor do people fully understand that we vote in but a 'governing class,' *not* the ruling class, which is never elected (I actually happen to believe that, at most, some 200 families effectively run *all* Modernist societies—*i.e.,* are in control of the 'commanding heights'—regardless of the 'political' system). In this regard, studying, perhaps, the pronouncements of the Bildeberg Club, the Trilateral Commission, and the World Economic Forum—where one actually can!—may be far more informative than the endless spirals of Media hype that dominate public discourse. The great *myth* of 'democracy' thus trumps, continuously, the *fact* of Corporate rule.

Mosca, of course, had it right: 'democracy' is yet another '*political formula*,' a device—to secure acquiescence. Power needs to be *legitimized* (as Napoleon had it, *one can do anything with bayonets except sit on them*): in order to be safe from challenge. Shakespeare wrote that 'the evil that men do lives after them, the good is oft interred with their bones.' But, with myths, it appears to be quite the opposite. Most myths actually embody hope, not despair, and are keenly clung to: which is why dictators last as long as they do. And myths can blind critical faculties to the point of a virtual extinguishing.

'*All Men are created Equal*' proclaimed the Declaration of Independence: this bromide was scribed by 'Men' who held captive slave families in their backyard, in the Modern era, and who had, insouciantly, eviscerated *Two Thousand plus Native American Tribes* (or shall I say 'nations'?) on their way to drafting the grandiloquent 'Declaration.' Worse still, think of the millions who yet 'believe' such balderdash, generation after generation. Surely, as David Hannam—rather than his contemporary Barnum to whom it is *en générale* attributed—had it: *there is one born every minute.*

Let me proffer a slightly more complex issue, as another case in point. If the Cosmos—societal and natural—is carefully observed, then the case is almost readymade for a theology that affirms an egregiously ruthless, rather than a benevolent god: and yet religions continue to peddle a kind and just Paragon—and millions gladly buy it. Clearly, Satan gets a raw rap in all this: he's like a biblical Snowden blowing the whistle—except nobody's listening! So, the mythmakers have it easy, for we, as part of a collective anthropic entity, want to, and are programmed to, believe in our *Totemic* gods.

Durkheim suggested that we simply worship 'society' under the guise of worshipping 'god': and it's easy enough to see that generous, *en masse*, suspension of disbelief, at mass rallies, *e.g.*, where societal values are being, ritually, affirmed. Mass hallucination is quite close to the point. So, what does that tell us? What useful learning can we imbibe? A posture of *De Omnibus Dubitandum*, when it comes to societal myths of any society, in particular as they pertain to Power.

In Modernist formations—*and most of this discussion is within that restrictive template*—as Mannheim had it, *Utopia* (or, justice-based movements) struggles against *Ideology* (the propaganda of the system) in continuous fashion. (Successful) Revolutions only invert the specific forces in that equation, temporarily. So, in an important sense, the balance between 'good' and evil,' in macro-societal terms, is near constant. The POM subverts, over time, any system that tries to pacify the fundamentals of societal existence: so, like Sysiphus we are, periodically, compelled to pick up that rock, and start the trek up the hill again. So 'progress' can and does take place, but is always fragile, subject to periodic reversal and regression. And the poor, the powerless, the underprivileged, women, and many kinds of minorities, fare ill.

It may seem trite, but the hoary axioms that 'All Power Corrupts', and that 'Eternal Vigilance' is the price of maintaining any societal gain, have stood the test of time—and remain invaluable guideposts. Isaiah Berlin spoke, a long time ago, of the difference between 'negative' and positive' liberties, but the discussion is vitiated by the *individualist* paradigm of 'choice' being deployed. In Traditionalist tribal formations, patiently arrived-at *'consensus'* achieves a *collective* balance between the two that no 'democratic,' individualist voting rule can hope to achieve.

As such, Modernist societies are ever rent by chaotic economic and political forces, leaving behind a deeply divided, adversarial, system that is permanently at war with itself. And rootless, inchoate systems produce alienated, anomic, asocial, individuals profoundly out of touch with their own *species-being*. To use my own choice of metaphor, *mammals*, thereby, are turned into *reptiles*—to calamitous effect. The *Great Modernist Elision*, common to both Euro-Capitalism and Euro-Socialism, lies in forgetting that *Anthropic Society, is in essence a Moral entity*: by substituting a 'material,' 'contractual,' 'amoral' edifice instead, since the Enlightenment (odd name for egregious error!), Modernism has subverted itself—and is doomed to fail in any, and all, of its forms.

The discoveries of Quantum Physics, so very unsettling to Classical Physics in some regards (for 'god,' *contra* Einstein, does play 'dice,' and other games, on occasion), have now shown materialism to be both bad science and bad philosophy. Interestingly, early Modernist social science, conservative or not, heavily based on Newtonian templates, and out of sheer physics-envy, took this materialism for granted *(e.g.,* both Durkheim and Marx).

So, much remains to be *Undone*.

The failure of Modernism could be simply written off, as an episodic fact of human history, were it not for the critical fact that it has, in these times, a near-complete stranglehold on a Planet that could likely go down with it, *via* its misleading *Mantras*. In this, as in so many related areas, traditional, antic, tribal wisdom still remains the untapped treasure trove of sane ideas for a possible, feasible, and sustainable, amelioration.

22

The Last Train

As I have suggested elsewhere, the *Grand European Transcontinental Express,* in its phase of what I term *EuroModernism,* went streaking straight: from *Barbarism to Decadence.* But one set of bogies, never properly enchained, broke away early. I am referring, of course, to the now dominant *Anglo-Am* formations: ever more energetic, adventurous, and aggressive, than their steadier, parent Locomotive. 'Broke away' is likely an improper figure of speech, because they were always of a *separable* cast than their European cousinages, having asserted their *singularity* as early, perhaps, as Henry VIII's personal schism with the Church of Rome—undertaken for zeal *other* than religious—if not earlier.

Decadence requires cultivation of an ambient, flighty spirit that was ever foreign to their innate, stolid, somewhat hidebound, temperament. The Brits, then as now, are a strong, stoic, empirically grounded, phlegmatic people (I refer, always, in such characterizations, to the *governing Male* of the species). Given that the American Colonies derive from them, I treat them as *one people, divided by a common ethnicity* (we could usefully add the various cousinages as well: Canada, Australia, *etc.*). They are do-ers, not talkers; utilitarians, not romantics. They are also great, even tremendous, thinkers, but in the very down to earth *micro* spirit of careful observation of patiently amassed facts and figures, rather than in the Greek or Indian speculative sense of lofty, even mighty, imaginations.

Modesty forbids. Accordingly, philosophy, or grand literature, or high culture, does not entirely suit them—but *science*, preferably geared to some applied scheme of *engineering*, does. So, decadence, at large, was *not* their thing. Sartrean, or even Kierkegaardian, *existentialism*, let alone *angst,* could simply not take root in England, anymore than it did in America. It was, very much, a European thing. So, whilst Europe, having matured in its own brand of Modernity, slid into decadence, of one or other kind, the Anglo-Ams, finding that Exit from the Old Railroad blocked off by their own inclinations, merrily turned history around—and went hurtling back: to the *ye olde* standbys of Empire and Domination. Back to Barbarism, so to speak.

Their little big electronic engine that could, and would!, streaked here, there, everywhere, led by a rather prosaic 'urge' for: *world domination* (though the phrase may be too grandiloquent for their taste). Here, but a few of Its major stops, outside of its own hinterlands, *after* WWII: Dresden, Hiroshima and Nagasaki, Korea, Vietnam, Central and Southern America, Africa, West Asia, East Europe, *et al.* Inside their own domains, they try but to maintain *order,* always taking what *they* need first, in that drab, colorless, unemotional way. *Joylessness* being a chronic ailment, they derive no apparent *satisfaction* in the effort to hold, or expand, the *greatest Empire ever known,* external, or internal—it's all patient, pedestrian, business-as-usual dynamics. They are not into self-aggrandizement. Stated differently, it is all only a *chore,* and is achieved in all banal grimness: by legal means (that fig-leaf *is* seen as important), if possible: by *any* means, if not.

So, now to understand Ferguson (USA). *It is only one more act, at the humble street-level, vivid only for being caught on camera, of imperial policing of native populations, in a standard, monotonic, centuries-old usage.* Consider, for just a moment, the rich, more antique, mosaic of *history* it is such a small part of: of slavery, of genocide against Native Americans, of annexations of Mexican territories, of Cuba, Hawaii, and the Philippines—*these were not, by any stretch, aberrations.*

The script has not, in these times, altered in scope: only—if at all!—in (a few aspects of) style. What happened in Ferguson happens, daily, someplace on the planet, still under some form or other, of Occupation. The killing Machine never stands idle. *As I have suggested, elsewhere—shifting gears a bit: baldly stated, the most important historical fact of the last Four Hundred Years is the systematic murder of Non-Europeans by Europeans, on one pretext or other.* The Europeans (*sans* France, perhaps) appear to have grown somewhat tired of it—whence the 'decadence'—but the Anglo-Ams stand ready, even striving to energize their aging geographical parent in this unwholesome regard.

Speaking more generally: regrettably, the aficionados of the variegated myths of *EuroModernism,* especially 'democracy,' still don't get it—another measure of the quiet success of this near-perfect system of absolute control. So, in meta-phor—rapt in the propaganda value of Tianenmen Square, we almost lose sight of Kent State.

Yes, the blessed *State of Aphasia*: it surely *is* one of the *Uniting* States. That's the real beauty of the well-greased Myth of (Modernist) Democracy: it gives all *subject populations* recharged faith in the system—even as it grinds them, in all surety, straight into the dust. *Minorities*—not merely of the ethnic kind—and the vast Majorities of the *sans culottes,* who still dream the hallowed dream of 'citizen-ship,' may now need to wake up.

We live today, as a century ago, as *subjects,* under the largesse of a virtually continuous *Empire,* no more no less, the sops of sovereignty and multilateralism notwithstanding: only China and Russia may be said to live, howsoever tenuously for now, appreciably outside of its *Universal Hegemony.* Perhaps, it is still not too late to understand the serene expediency of Anglo-Am 'democracy': apart from its various ancillary benefits—to the governors!: *it is by far the best, most economical, long-lived, and self-sustaining, prophylactic ever devised*—against *revolt.*

23

A World on the Wane

The Wherefore and the Why

It may be moot to dwell, even muse, on the extraordinary state of things today. I mean, behind the veil, the mask—indeed, the *reverie,* of everyday 'normalcy' with which we are all smitten. An irredeemably *Wrong Turn* taken by Europe four centuries ago, pursued to egregious lengths by its Anglo-Am *Avatars,* has the institutional world now teetering on the brink of rank disorder and dissolution.

The infelicities run in crushing overload. Species disappear by the day. Great chunks of the living planet have been despoiled, in some instances irrevocably. *Empire-madness* has led to large-scale regions (like West Asia), with long histories, plunged into churning cauldrons of political chaos—unworthy of their culture and civilization. Entire economies have been shaken-down, ruined, run right through, by a triumphalist financial *gangsterdom* that is the new ruling *demi-urge.* Ecologies are being ravaged with multiples of the force and fury invested, say, in large scale fracking; the seas are choking with the daily swill from the ever cataracting corporate blunders: oil spills, untreated waste-disposals, nuclear dumpings.

Clocks, other than the Doomsday One, have been rudely turned back, mocking the myths of *'progress'* dear to the Modernists, even as we revert to a breathtaking *Neo-feudalism* in regards to the all-out exercise of near-despotic power. Rule of Law, justice, sovereignty, and other such sacred terms of Modernist parlance, have all washed up on shore as no more than empty, dead, archival slogans of the past, with little content remaining. Ditto, with the liturgy of full-employment, peace, and societal amelioration.

Never, in the history of the species, has gross cynicism toward all charity, benevolence, and inter-societal empathy been so abundantly in public display. Antic hostility to the *Other*, and a righteousness wholly at odds with its *actual* conduct—(mis)guided by greed and a 'Viking' spirit of domination—propels NATO to the very gates of Asia, whilst still lisping the old gibber of human rights and democracy. Civic decencies, co-respecting behaviors, approaches of care and consideration—leave aside compassion—are becoming as obsolete, in particular in the Anglo-Am world, as the old soup-and-fish. In contempt of the *facile* fables of Smith and Mandeville, *private vices* now redound, in hypertrophic size and scale, as ginormous 'public vices.'

An *Empire of Unregenerate Lies*—in lineal descent from the old standards of 'perfidious Albion'—is fast dissipating the very last provinces of an almost moribund, dying, *morality*. As the swelling ranks of the super-rich gloat and strut, the impuissant—nations, peoples, tribes, strata, persons—are hunkering down to hold on to the little they have left, in a now hopelessly insecure world. Those who pushed that atomic button once before stand ready to do so again, for yet another mess of pottage—and few would care to doubt their earnestness.

Pandora's box is wide open, and empty; evil genies are out of their smoking lanterns, and evil geniuses plot daily to ransack the planet to its very last iota of expendability. For all but the .001%, the Great Depression of the twenty-first century is well under way. *No one has a Solution: no one has a Clue.* The effete still prattle on, feebly, about corporate responsibility, societal welfare, and 'human rights': but these are no more than ghosts of political formulas past. The pundits cannot see the forest for the trees. It has not occurred to them—indeed, it *couldn't*—that this is a *Civilizational* climacteric, not an 'economic crisis.' *It is no less than the last, unholy, huzzah of the West.* In fact, the species is being forced to *morph,* from the North Atlantic hegemons down.

Robotics are the incoming *Way*: from drones that kill, computers that play in high frequency trades, and machines that draft the myriad messages that flood the media, hour to hour, minute by minute. A *bionic* world is fast being ushered in: *transgenics* have already swept the plant world, and they are now gaining ground in the animal world, inclusive of our own species. The recklessness in this area virtually guarantees a generation of transgenetically-modified humans, within decades. Given corporate blueprints, the new anthropic template will, likely, be a species that will adapt to the key requirements: *to obey, consume, and be silent*—the three imperatives of our epoch.

In some regards, EuroModernism was no more than a rabid intercalation of *Materialism, Mechanization,* and *Violence*: the terms understood in their most completely encompassing sense. The materialism destroys anthropic morality, the mechanization militates against the vital essences of organic society, and the violence makes the world an angry, sullen, inhospitable, moonscape of dug-outs and trenches, with a caricature Hobbesian world of *each-against-all.*

True, some Non-European formations were also '*materialist*,' but with *two* highly significant differences:

a) *They* didn't push materialism to radical, sub-human, Modernist extremes (save under the brief spell of 'communism,' as, *e.g.,* in China)

b) More importantly, this materialism was never sharply double-dosed with a *regressive paradigm* of *aggressive self-interest*: it is this latter (the vaunted '*individualism*') that violently militates against any and all notion of a larger, 'public' or 'societal' interest, as in Anglo-Am societies, which puts them beyond the ramp of redemption.

The nouvelle 3-D printer that, today, prints out guns, on command, will, in the near future, 'print out' even more apocalyptic, Doomsday, notices for us all. Indeed, the very existence of such a printer is such notice in, and of, itself.

How did we get here? Or rather, how did '*they*' get us here? Here is just one 'movement' in this, still-unfolding, tragic opera. One small part of the world, one subset of tribes, a minor part of the larger human family, donned giant, half-league boots four centuries ago, animated by Modernist ideas and practices. Suddenly, enough was not enough. *The passion for accumulation was inexhaustible,* as currently, also, exhibited by Wall Street and its twin: the City of London. A mere nation was not sufficient, a continent wasn't room enough: *the whole world had to be conquered.* Most of the European Titans went for it, lock, stock, and barrel. First, they spent centuries in attempting to destroy each other. Then they went on an international rampage and, in due time, subdued the globe.

The only *non-European* tribe—nation—that came close to emulation of this 'feat,' in Modern times, was Japan: but it is arguably accurate to say that their depredations were largely *defensive*—they were 'stepping out,' to put up a '*cordon sanitaire*' around their little island, having seen most of Asia gobbled up by Europeans and Americans. Even if that were not entirely true, *Japan would still be the exception that proves the rule of the European monopoly in Modernist global Colonization.*

❋

So, Modern Europe—and its North Atlantic partners—went straight-arrow, from Barbarism to Decadence. In fact, that may be something of an overstatement: for its barbarism is still very much intact, and on display. *Its 'forte' has remained unchanged for four hundred years: the organized, cold-blooded murder of non-Europeans, seizure of their assets, and occupation of their lands, on one pretext or another.*

If one spotlights their North Atlantic Hegemon, and Tribal Chief, the barbarism is entirely self-evident: even ignoring their global depredations, *they who cannot get past skin-color, nor give up stocking wholly gratuitous arsenals in favor of maintaining even the most ordinary civic peace, are no more evolved than the ritually vilified 'Mongol Hordes'*—except that the latter were never craven enough to claim the cresting mantle of 'human rights" for themselves, whilst on their marauding rampages.

❋

So: what *really* happened? Now, for the rest of the story. It is our innate, anthropic, *anthropology* that, always, provides *All* answers. Once society was conceived, *not as an anthropic End but as a Means* (and that too, to a privately, even personally, conceived *self-interest*), as with Euromodernist thinkers (of the 'social contract' variety) and policy makers, the inexorable, final doom of the social was already underwritten.

Human morality is wrapped up in the societal-cultural moment, and stems from it: once that integument is rent, it goes to pieces.

The thoughtless destruction of familial, kinship, structures along with their associated 'cultural' matrix of care and provisioning (the struggle over the *Speenhamland Amendment* to the Poor Laws is emblematic of this, in the case of England) *en route* to the new-fangled means/mores of material aggrandizement, was no small event in human history. Enshrined first amongst the ruling orders, it 'permeated' down: with subject orders, inevitably, also pressured, under heavy duress of factory and farm disciplines, to follow that primrose path to perdition.

With societal morality disintegrating, the species suffered severe alienation from its own *species-being*: *the EuroModernist is most lost, nay marooned, exactly when (s)he is celebrating his/her individuated liberty from any and all cultural restraints.* The *Asocial* catch-as-catch-can 'freedom' is but the waste residue, the drab refuse that is left after the willful demolition of the essential *Wholeness* of both person and society. Thencefoth, *angst* and *existential despair*—in one word a coruscating *loneliness*—overtook the *individuated* European, far ahead of any other human species on the planet, enveloping him/her still in a shroud of restless, unrequiting, inconsolable, *anomie*.

The 'god' of Kierkegaard, despite its 'Christian' spin, is none other than the *familial collectivity*, now lost forever. So, howsoever deludedly, as Durkheim fully understood, the very 'god' we worship is our own *Collective Being—for Religion is merely the hypostatized variant of societal Morality, expressing its essences in ritualized cadences of form.* Grandiose delusions of global mastery, the 'reaching for the stars' predispositions, the 'illimitable growth' hallucinations, the 'anything goes' societal ideologies, are all species of a unique pathology stemming from the ensuing dislocation and disorientation, unprecedented in human history.

With morality extinct, the *Amoral* moment begins: and, thereafter, Euro-Modernism sinned against its own species, with a casual insouciance that is all but short of rabid insanity. *Other than European formations, no Other human Tribe has, as yet, collectively passed on to this stage—and hence still retain the vestige of being 'human.'* It is this critical difference I try to capture with my metaphor of the struggle between *mammals vs. reptiles.* I can put it even more starkly, for resonance: *a Kennedy would have pushed that button, during those dog-days of the famous Crisis, a Kruschev simply could not.*

Yes, it's the mammal that 'blinked.'

The infamous 'drop' on Hiroshima and Nagasaki (and the, similar, utterly insensate, destruction of Dresden), similarly, could only be accomplished by 'reptilian' beings, wholly devoid of common, anthropic, humanity.

❄

I return us, ever, to our *Anthropology.* For we are *instinctual* beings, regrettably now laboring under the Modernist delusion *that we can be anything we wish to be.* Yet our anthropic nature is far from being no more than but a sullen prison. Thousands of tribal societies have managed to live in equable states of being, content with themselves, and in 'balance' with nature. Men and women, *though distinct sub-species endowed with differing instincts*, have, over long evolution, found formulas for a relatively benign, co-operative co-existence, situating themselves within 'being' rather than 'becoming,' quite often free of gratuitous 'Protestant' burdenings: of stifling notions of labor, struggle, and redemption.

Yes, valuing, enjoying, shared societal affections, with time to spare, might well be an instinctive clause of human conviviality. When, and where, successful, this *'paradigm of femininity'* has trumped *the 'paradigm of masculinity,'* to the advantage of the community. True, the *second* set of named proclivities frequently breaks this *'social compact,'* and leads off into states of war and empire—but that much is just anthropic reality: for yes, we are not discussing *idylls.* That the contrary has existed—*and still exists*—is reassuring, and indefeasible, proof of the *possibility* of contented states of social existence *sans* the indelibly Modernist hamster-at-the-wheel parameters of accumulation, growth, work, and do-or-die competition.

So, how might we return to Eden? For now, the *Juggernaut* appears unstoppable. Indeed, the only force opposing it, with any degree of seriousness, today, is religion *(qua* morality, and/or *vice versa).* Admittedly, there's fine irony to it: *market fundamentalism* being challenged by *religious fundamentalism.* But a new set of Crusades will not pause the runaway rollercoaster: indeed, might even fuel its further acceleration. So, is there no hope? In point of fact, as it happens, there is. And, again, there is irony. The only force strong enough to stop it is: *Itself.* As I have written, in previous posts, *Late Modernism* is now cannibalizing itself—at a ruinous rate. It is, thereby, entirely, *self-subverting.*

A global financial crisis, even short of a collapse, or some other equivalent catastrophe (war, natural disaster) will, systemically, induce serious economic and political disaffections. At that point—and we might be there right now—our anthropic nature will, of necessity, revive *new* forms of communal relations, quite spontaneously. And rebuild, from scratch, that *nexus of reciprocities* that we should understand now as our very real, *tribal* being. Indeed, it is already happening, in microcosm, all over the world, even if the corporate media are loath to report it.

Let me draw down, then, with Michael Polanyi's lines: (that, despite it all) *'We believe more than we can prove. We know more than we can say.'* And close, by adding my own perception: *that we are (despite imperial design), as ordinary people—whether 'mammalian' or 'reptilian'—a lot nicer, better, than the system 'requires,' or we let on.*

We are being corralled into the realm of the *Post-Human,* only as a short stop *en route* to an even more invidious *Trans-Humanism: but, as for now, we are not yet wholly stripped of our minimal humanoid traits.* Possibly, then, it's a fair presumption that the *Great Breach* of our anthropic essence bequeathed by Modernism will get, if slowly, and over time, mended.

We can only hope it won't be a case of too little, too late.

Note

1. I confess to a minor contretemps: located in the European cosmos, as I am, my readership is, almost entirely, of that lineage. I wish I could, to allay discomfort/disquiet, depart from facts to mitigate chagrin: but there's the self-evident, rub. All I can say is, therefore: the world has been Their very own personal oyster for centuries—for better or for worse. Perhaps that signal achievement might serve as its own form of psychic compensation, for the unavoidable, ensuing, pain of this inevitable, entirely consequent, and contingent, Critique.

24

Endgame?

I think so.

    A certain kind of Socialism capitulated (rather than collapsed), if unexpectedly, decades ago, to the great glee of capitalist votaries the world over. Of course it had never really worked very well. But they that celebrate its demise would have clapped even louder at its Fall *had it actually worked as per its own socialist ideals.* It is the way with such folk. But they are in for an Unwelcome Awakening. The Capitalism they adore so much, despite its obvious vagaries, is about to suffer a similar fate, though in slow(er) motion.

    It is now simply ungovernable: and is indeed, at this stage, in a free fall, in a spiral dance of dissolution. Of course, rather than 'crash' loudly, it will indecorously decompose, even as desperate new props by way of bail-ins, bail-outs, and other such inspired confiscations, are being arranged. *Then, finally, after a Two-century run, the great myth of the magic of the free market will be laid to rest.* So where will the world be when these Two Great Avatars of *Euromodernism,* that have had such an *unscalable impact,* disappear into the void of history?

    Western Capitalism promised (an individuated) 'freedom,' and material welfare (though they never did suggest it would be for *all*), and came close to delivery (for *some*), albeit at impossible societal cost. Eastern Socialism promised moral and material welfare for all—and *failed* at both. So, their departure is unlikely to be greatly missed by the many, in either instance.

I suggest that the ensuing world to be, is well rid of both. *Isms* that are imposed by the few on the many are, or should be, *prima facie,* suspect: so their age is, very justly, over. Besides, much of great utility, has been learnt, by those capable of learning, precisely in the failure of the two demi-urges. So where does this leave us? In a happy place, perhaps, such as likely existed long prior to their domination. And that is the living world of plural *cultures,* such as animated the social scape before the onset of the Tweedledum-Tweedledee modernisms of capitalism and socialism.

In effect, culture was the supreme consumption and producer good of pre-Modernist times, universally, before European materialism drowned all imagination in a morass of commodity fetishism. We know now that neither capitalism nor socialism were 'happy' societies, regardless of their degree of material success (and this in their own self-assessments; the US, *e.g.,* ranked 105th on the *Happy Planet Index,* last time I checked).

That teaches us that humans derive contentment less from the hyper-consumption of material goods, and more from the enjoyment of *moral and non-material values* such as available to all *homo sapiens* from the dawn of human history. It also tells us that *'progress',* as defined in Euromodernist terms, is bunk: a ruse, a ploy, and a red herring. It also suggests that we need to understand our *'species being'* well, before constructing utopias out of thin air. In effect, knowledge of a real anthropology of humans is necessarily prior to any gratuitous form of philosophical, or political, day-dreaming.

But the modernists, in their zealous haste, had no time for such serious, indefinite contemplation. Siddhartha spent years trying to discover who we were, who he was. The Ancients of all antiquities tried similarly: and, for the most part, they placed moral above material values.

Classical Christianity, which Europe made its own (not without some canny bowdlerization), deriving from Buddhist ideas, was also not dissimilar. However, the European 'Enlightenment,' sudden and unexpected as it was, cried 'Eureka' far too quickly, and went about, tendentiously, 'changing the world'—with predictable consequences. The Enlightenment onward, the European 'crusader,' of one sort or other, has vandalized the socio-cultural world bringing it today to the verge, also, of a natural extinction. *The most dangerous kind of error in human society is a philosophical one: it is the seed-mother of all subsequent errors.*

Yes, I know the European Modernist has given us microwave ovens and motorcars (the same arts involved also gifted us the sure means of a certain *self-annihilation*), but those conveniences have been purchased at impossible human and non-human, costs. It is time that such a hollow ideology of inexorable greed were rolled back. This will transpire, across the world: but, *After the Fall.* Cultures will yet again evolve their own institutions, *sui generis.*

Capitalism, or a for-profit market, can still be retained, by the archaic, in the minor sector of frivolities, the effete pleasures of the few: but never again will/should the means of mass survival be tied to markets manipulated by monopolizing, private owners of the means of employment. Money need not be used universally: and none of it needs be issued in the current form of interest- bearing debt, so very dear, and provident, to bankers. Paper money—scrip—can be issued directly by federations of Local Authorities (*i.e.,* 'Govt.'), with no bankers involved.

Banks themselves can be stripped of 'fractional reserves,' and credit creation beyond actual reserves. Corporates can be limited by charter: in size, scope, scale, and duration—much as unconscionable incomes and wealth by suitable tax codes. *The best things in life can be allocated freely*—now here's a platter of 'human rights' that is, quite obviously, not pushed by the ideologues of capitalism, for obvious reasons. Indeed, the real freedoms requisite to our species are not innumerable: *freedom from want, indignity, and insecurity.*

There is no compelling reason why basic nutrition, mass transit, education, health, housing, media, and internet access, should not be freely provisioned to all, albeit in programmed phases. No, this is not some late 'communist' plot (as might be imagined by those still steeped in hoary cold war propaganda): impeccably capitalist Switzerland has recently pushed for legislation toward a similar end.

Perhaps even 'nation-states' (a late modernist European 'gift') can quietly devolve into local authorities. We know, of course, that *Centers* do not hold: but, why are they needed at all? And, consequently, standing armies can be, incrementally, dissolved—with a local constabulary keeping the peace, as has been the rule rather than the exception in human history. Small, even simple changes, as indicated, can alter our welfare, significantly. *Jefferson, wisely, wanted the Constitution revised/revisited every generation to incorporate evolving wisdom.* So, a motivated populace can yet ask for such changes.

In the first analysis, societies are moral entities held together by shared values, i.e., by mutual 'affections'.

The European Modernist invented a '*contractual society*' (of '*universal egoism*' in Hegel's delectable phrase) where we are manacled together by mutual 'interests.' Whence was born the notion of Society as but a '*means,*' and not a *necessary* human *end. Hell is 'other people'* (Sartre) only in a societal frame where others are viewed as obstacles and/or means to one's own advancement. It is this infelicitous *modus,* forcibly generalized by the European conquest of the planet, that accounts for the *angst,* the *anomie,* and anguished extinction of contentment, that is now spread, like a pall, across the world.

No, 'Post-Modernism' is not quite the appropriate term: I call it the *Post-Human* Society. But, to comprehend that last term, one has to know, remember, what it is to be 'human'—to begin with. Tribal societies that we have not yet torched still retain that primal humanity: so they are the 'labs' that we can still learn from.

It is not that the all-conquering Modernists, in the First Wave, were all unaware of what they were destroying. Idylls of the 'noble savage,' or the more prosaic 'honest injun,' incongruously accompanied the brutal process: 'Ill fares the land' lamented Goldsmith, 'to hastening ills a prey—where wealth accumulates, and men decay.' Tonnies' notions of *Gemeinschaft* and *Gesellschaft* noted the radical rupture between the old and the new: likewise, Durkheim's 'mechanical and organic solidarity.' Kierkegaard and Nietzsche, in tortured genius, tried to come to terms with the debasement of morality and conscience affected by the transformation. They also 'felt' the pain of that rank dissolution: Durkheim, rightly, called the socialist impulse, born of this involution, '*a crie de cœur*,' which also suitably characterizes all the 'utopian' hankerings, from More to Marx.

Yes, the 'Garden of Eden' is first destroyed, before it is, once again, re-sacralized.

We Late Modernists have gone well beyond that original crossing of the Rubicon: we now threaten our own collective existence much as the fate of our fellow flora and fauna. Modernism need not have taken such an invidious form, were it not for its wholly European genesis. *Europe holds prime responsibility for this unwholesome set of 'black swan' outcomes*, having, perforce, led the world to embrace its own historical intemperances, and iniquities, across four centuries of unbridled piracy, pillage, and expropriation.

But it will not lead us out of it: that is likely the prerogative of societies not wholly immured in the acid-bath of *materialism* for generations (despite having acquired an inescapable veneer of it), and hence capable, eventually, of resuscitation of the *desiderata* of civilization. *The Life Convivial has little to do with the hypertrophic paraphernalia of material affluence, devoid of societal meaning:* human felicity still lies in the affective domains, of kinship, community, fellowship, and tribe (it may be instructive to remember that Marx got his own putative '*communist*' ideal from his study of the '*primitive communism*' of humbler, tribal forms).

And, if *instrumental reason*, the Pride of the Enlightenment, will not return us to our *roots*, our irrefragable human essence will: for, as (Euro)modernists we have lived miserably, and, for far too long, in stark denial of it.

25

The Eclipse

In recent blogs, I may have been guilty of suggesting that 'collapse' is 'imminent.' In point of fact, *Anglo-Am Laissez-fare(!) Capitalism has collapsed*: and we are living through only a sort of an elongated *interregnum*. Of course, if you are waiting for CNN to announce it, you might remain in the dark for a while longer. As I have written earlier, the 'crisis' is not scattered 'here' or 'there,' in some or other sector of the economy, polity or society, as you might imagine—if you read and refer to our prime-time pundits.

Nor is its 'cause' to be found in mistake, mismanagement, and malfeasance (though it is inclusive of *all* of them). In the first instance, it is '*deregulated capitalism*' that has failed (indeed, the sheer audacity of that move, taken, Eighties on, is breathtaking. *Take the cop off the beat and what do you get on the street, come nightfall?* That is what America got, societally). One can usefully reduce the causal factor to the 'behavioral,' unalloyed, '*profit motive*' that has been venerated for some three centuries by its European custodians. But, it runs even deeper. It would be correct to say that the eighteenth century '*Enlightenment,*' consecrated an emergent set of mores—constituting 'deregulation'—building on ideas of a century earlier.

Firstly and vitally, real, anthropic society was seen as a 'contractual' affair (*vide* some social contract theories), as a '*balance of interests*': in particular, as but a means to *individualist* ends (*vide* Hegel's correct rendition of '*civil society*' as one of 'universal egoism'). *It marked the fusion of Protestantism, Utilitarianism, and Materialist philosophy.* This step marked, indelibly, the *Fall.*

It also, fatefully, separated West Europeans from their human cousinages, in time and space. The older, '*organic*' view of society, as the mother matrix of all of our joys and sorrows, was given up in favor of a *mechanistic* view, paralleling paradigms in the natural sciences: whence radical 'surgeries' could be performed on social organisms, much as on human/animal ones.

The therapies were all in the direction of '*individuation*' of the human animal, sought to be sundered from societal ties that were presumed to be obstacular to his/her personal advancement. Politically, this was perceived as advancing '*liberty.*' Economically, as enhancing the accumulation of *things.* Religiously, as divesting the individual from a mandatory, social tax on conscience, as Catholicism demanded, in favor of a purely voluntary, 'self-assessed' gratuity. In other words, taken together, in this artificial universe, 'one' is 'free' to pursue 'gain'—with little or no societal, i.e., moral, obstruction. With no 'binding cement' to it, the social world could be swiftly 'disenchanted,' stripped of its epistemic legitimations. Such a universe can only appear vacuously *monist.*

The stolid Bentham, exemplifies this in his famous remark: 'Prejudice apart, the game of push-pin is of equal value with the arts and sciences of music and poetry. If the game of push-pin furnish more pleasure, it is more valuable than either.' The softer J.S. Mill's (godson to Bentham) later remonstrance would have fallen on increasingly dull ears: 'It is better to be a human being dissatisfied than a pig satisfied; better to be Socrates dissatisfied than a fool satisfied.' Evaluations of a *moral* kind had become, quite abruptly, *passé.*

This is vital to understand. *Anthropic society, is a moral entity—before it is anything else.*

Tribal forms, i.e., our earliest societal forms, were mere extensions of kinship; and kinship rests on the family—and family is, ineluctably, a moral, affective, entity. So real, anthropic society is a 'balance of affections,' not a 'balance of interests.'

The Modernizing European had, suddenly, stood society on its head. Small wonder the early resisters, dismissed as 'romantics,' were stupefied—even driven to distraction. I often mention Nietzsche and Kierkegaard, on the continent, as exemplars, but they were really part of a very large tribe. I could also name Carlyle and Ruskin in England, *e.g.* Indeed, the early Socialists, *i.e.,* the *Younger* Marx, and William Morris, were also smitten by the same pain.

And there was not a society on earth, upon which the Modernist European paid his unwelcome visit(s), that was not, similarly, daunted. The world, until then, had known both morality and immorality: *but Amorality was the unique contributory addition of modern Europe to the trove of human artifacts.* It is this that America eagerly adopted, and made its own, being free-er of historical encumbrances—that might have checked and retarded such impulses—than the modernizing European. At its philosophical base, it is this stance that has brought the world to its current impasse.

Now Capitalism can yet co-exist with the moral (*tribal*) restraints of a more traditional society: take Denmark or Switzerland, *e.g.*, or Cambodia, and Nepal. It is somewhat less extirpationist in such contexts. The '*profit motive*' is checked, stringently or loosely, depending on circs, in these societies, by a prudential "*social responsibility*' motive (now you know what it takes to be an elite card-carrying member of the 'First World': and, likewise, why the Bushmen or the Aboriginals may not be entirely unhappy being the so-called 'Third World'). In America, the only check, if at all, is 'legal accountability.' Regrettably, when the Law is itself become a co-opted handmaiden of the financial interest—well, you get what we see today.

It is this, mutant, 'Unbridled' Capitalism, of the 'New World' that is now giving up the ghost (one might hazard to say, perhaps, *that the more morbid modes of both Modernist progeny, i.e.,* Capitalism and Socialism, are now hard by the Exit ramp of history). Born of (philosophical) *Error*, conceived in (moral) *Ignorance*: it now inescapably goes the way of all '*samsara*' (the material world) in *Vedic* philosophy.

Let me put it bluntly: a philosophy of materialism is incompatible with civilization—one, or the other, has to capitulate.

I wrote a book titled '*The Post-Human Society,*' in 1992, outlining the structure of this fateful innovation in human affairs: I finally published it in 2015 (Kanth, 2015). Far from being rendered obsolete by the passage of time, it yet retains a modest validity.

Part V

Modernism

26

On Civilization

Imagine if a troop of monkeys were to be let loose in a room full of live nuclear devices. How long would it be before...? Well, that *is* our reality. We are a troop, nay several tribes of, monkeys—with many more such incendiary devices than imaginable by the plebeian mind. So how long before...? Anybody's guess.

But this post is about *Civilization*. A bit comical, the notion. Apes, playing at civilization...! It likely amuses the Higher Extra-Terrestrials: if, when, and where, they exist. But the matter is earnest, and real, and admits of an arguably logical explanation. I have written oodles of pages on Modernity and Tradition, Eurocentrism, and the *Other*. All of that took as its premise a very strong definition of civilization: *as the pacification of the conditions of our existence on this planet.* Now, that may seem a 'materialist' definition. But it is, in fact, its exact opposite.

You see *One Way*, the *European Way*, of such a possible 'pacification' is to aggressively compel peoples and nature to yield up their troves to the irresistible demands of *Acquisitive Man.* That has been the penchant of Euro-Modernism for at least four hundred years. The Other Way, or the *Way of the Other*, goes far back into Antiquity. There, the 'objective' was actually a 'subjective': *to design ways and means of sustaining convivial societal relations,* if often within Patriarchal limits.

Largely, this effort was 'led' by Women, *spontaneously*, within the matrix of family and kinship. So, the first canons of 'sociability' were built around the highly vulnerable human newborn, ever in jeopardy in the wake of sporadic masculine depredations. Indeed, our first *species-'morality'* also springs from that provenance, that of 'cradling' the very young within a slim cordon of affective security. *So it is Women who initiate, and secure, the vital architectonics of Civilization.*

In the '*Post-Human Society*' of the US today, this 'primal' morality may be the only morality left standing, with all other forms having capitulated to the steady encroachment of cumulative drives. It perhaps explains why we don't sell our mothers, as yet, on eBay, *en masse*. When that 'principle' is enlarged, we get a full-fledged kin-based tribe, which functions as an 'extended family.' In essence, kin-based conviviality is the 'secret' of the relative 'easefulness' of all traditional /tribal societal forms, of which the outstanding, if tristful, 'remnants' are the Bushmen and the Aboriginals. In contrast, Modernist Europe took the *Other Road: that of compelling the forcible extraction of resources, globally,* to build a strictly material haven, first for the few, then for the many (today, it's yet again retreating into catering to the Select).

This provided a modicum of peaceable shelter within 'civil society,' for many, whilst letting the latter yet run rife with mutually destructive competitive, anti-social, drives, machinations, and gambits. However, a fatal flaw lay at its root: of having *no* anthropically based morality to guide its evolution. Pushed willy-nilly by unquenchable *greed*, and its related yen for illimitable conquest, it was only a matter of time before it would run aground, and implode—for the sheer penury of its own atomization, individualization, and *anomie*. It fell, in effect, into a deep, dark pit of its own creation.

Stated differently, the Conquering European—and I speak of Europe's pashas and potentates not the *hoi polloi*—'convinced' the world, *via* chicanery and cannon, that double-entry bookkeeping and compound interest were the very *alpha and omega* of anthropic civilization. Alas, no. And the hollowness of that claim reverberates unmistakably today in the graceless wastelands of internecine strife, breakdown, cynicism and decay, that are all about us within *Late Modernism*—if only we had the interest, and the acuity, to observe, and learn. The error was an epistemic one—of seriously misreading *human ontology.*

No we are *not*—save for a few thousand incorrigible ghouls, as appropriately dwell within the dark sanctums of Wall Street, in grim parody of the 'rational economic man' prattle of generations of 'economists'—the streaking, shooting stars of a cumulating, consumptive, hysteria, the system would like us to be, and believe.

Instead we are, within Modernism today, *a distractedly lost tribe of anthropic hominids* succumbing daily, if indecisively, to the stupefying clash between deeply vested instincts and the superficially embedded ideology of the system. European Capitalism quenched the very founts of feeling instilled in our tribal nature, requiring us to refashion ourselves as modernist *avatars* responding only, and perpetually, to the engaging stimuli of net advantages.

However, Tribalism, like Murder, will Out.

The pathos of this all but unconscious search for tribal affinities, howsoever temporarily, within the potholed, pockmarked, minefield of our out-of-control farm-factory-force complex, is the story of the stultifying contradictions and counter-indications, of everyday life, within Modernism. Free speech, with nothing to say. Education, without cultivation. Passion, without affection. Order, without empathy. Life, without *elan*. Peace, without tranquility. Gluttony, without satiety. Rest, without repose.

Whence the daily scramble for refuge, to mask embittering, eviscerating loss: benumbing addictions, wild autisms of belief and thought, unrelenting misanthropy and misogyny. Armed with this '*charade of vanities,*' the European bestrides the globe today, intruding his scatter of pathologies, fanning the flames of discord and discontent, wherever space permits.

Look about: his indefeasible stamp sweeps from pole to pole. Fracking here, droning there, unbuilding the covenants of antic civility everywhere. Not content with the Planet *He* has so insouciantly despoiled (yes, the *masculine voice* is ever due), he now sets his sights on Other Planets. Can you, seriously, wait—to see, with the naked eye, corporate logos blanching the moon? Worse, actually, may be in store.

And so it goes.

In the imposturous name of 'liberté, egalité,' and even more egregious nostrums of breathtaking vanilla, our blue-green planetary idyll of an inscrutable evolution, has been brought, in these desperate times, to the very margins of survivability. *Irony, piggy-backing on Tragedy. For, All Euro-Modernist Roads are the same: they lead Nowhere.*

Every Modernist step, taken from its sterile beginnings four centuries ago, moves *His* demesne—and drags us *All* as hapless vassals—further and further away from the very *possibility* of civilization, from the host of benign amities that lace the cradle of our familial instincts and inclinations. So far is *He* along this *Road to Nihilism* that he thinks nothing of casually threatening planetary existence itself, including his own peripatetic Self, with Extinction: thus were innumerable innocent human lives snuffed out in a heinous flash, in the infamy of Hiroshima and Nagasaki. *Thus does a brooding sociopath turn into a bristling psychopath.*

Let me sum up: *contra* all the vacuous propaganda of Modernism, the innate *species-being* of us anthropic denizens, is *not* served, in the first instance, by the likes of *freedom, democracy, or equality*—which, in reality, are little more than the tendentiously specious slogans, only, of Modernist dissembling. *Au contraire*, it is instantly manifest, like the sun at dawn, in the heavenly 'tribal,' 'familial' boons of caring, conviviality, love, warmth, reciprocity, and mutual affections—as abound within the matrix of our tribal being.

I have written repeatedly that we must learn, about ourselves, from the *universal* institution of the *anthropic family*, this irrefragable artifact, at once natural and societal, *before it is too late.* Unlike the shibboleths of Modernist jibber, it is *not* built on 'freedom, equality, and democracy,' but, rather on love, caring, warmth, and affective reciprocities.

Anthropic Society is not a 'contract,' an *ad interim* armistice within a tenuous balance of *interests*: but, rather, an enduring balance of *affections.* The Former path clones only a new horde of ever more recreant *Reptiles*, deadly to all species: the Latter radiates, howsoever blandly, the light of, our original, *Mammalian* heat-seeking, essence(s). The *One* pitchforks us to the virtual certainty of Ultimate Nuclear Fission, and guaranteed species extinction: the *Other* urges us on but to amble on to the amiable patio of *Small Felicities*—upon which the languid afternoons of amity are built.

If a touch of nature makes us all kin, a touch of kinship makes us all natuurvolk. And the best we can ever do to ourselves, for ourselves, is huddle.

The Modernist Adventurers who have had us, perforce, 'climb every mountain, ford every sea' not for the pleasure of it, but to help build their own, overflowing balance sheets, have never—and perhaps *will* never!—quite grasp that simple, but ineluctable, fact.

Odd, since our worthy ape cousins have had no problem, ever, with that species of benefice.

27

On Philosophy

The 'problem of philosophy,' a recurring theme of navel-gazers in various eras, is philosophy itself. Any, and all, philosophy, that lacks awareness of a true hominid anthropology, fails, simply, and almost *a priori,* for being *speculative, in extremis.* As such, a 'pure' *philosophy* of humankind, *per se,* be it a Buddha or a Plato, is, effectively, a non-starter. And yet how has the field engaged human attentions, high and low—and for how long!

In European society, the *Reformation* rendered orthodox Religion, the precursor of its 'enlightened' Metaphysics, quite toothless. The Church of Rome, stripped of its various monopolies, was quickly delegitimized, principally in Northern Europe. And this funneled droves of the tribe of *'other-worldly'* thinkers into Philosophy, when not enamored of—or perhaps capable of—the Sciences.

The issue undergirding the vacuity of philosophical speculation is so commonsensical that it is a wonder that philosophy, as a set of high, hypothetical, *abstractions,* even survives scrutiny today. *If we as, Hominids, do not know who we are, and what our innate drives are, how can a realist (whence reliable) epistemology be, thence, constituted by us?* Logically, therefore, the *societal ontology* of the *Species* needs be understood: only then can our various epistemologies be placed, in context, relative to it. The aspiring 'understander' must be, of necessity, 'self-understood' first.

Europe had it almost too easy, in one sense: the powerful legacy of *Judeo-Christian* ideology gave it a ready-made pseudo-ontology that dominated official ideas virtually all the way until the great Darwin rent its veils in sudden, dramatic, and summary, fashion. Of course, the prior Reformation had already weakened its potency, centuries earlier: but the new, 'secular' thinking simply retained its *Trans-epochal* Myths, albeit in altered fashion. The notion of 'Socialism,' *par exemple*, like Morris' *News from Nowhere*, lay, evocatively, in that very same tradition: a secular Paradise, complete with prior 'stages' of a scripted evolution, and the final purgatory of Revolution. Indeed, Marx's *Early Writings* are replete with the intoxicating ideals of J/C evangelism.

The (linear) notion of '*Progress*,' which may well be the most baneful of European gifts to the peoples it conquered—since it has since provided a catchall justification of all manner of depredations—was quite akin to, and derived from, the idea of the '*Pilgrim's Progress*' in Christian idealism. Little wonder that Marxists, until recently, nurtured a passion of intense religiosity, about their sacred Mentor, not unlike that of the Christian martyrs—any questioning of Marx being seen as blasphemy, rather than libel.

The unexpected capitulation of the Soviet Union marked their own grudging 'Reformation,' the final acceptance that their putative 'god' had, finally, failed. Of course, this was gratuitous: there was never any such 'god' to begin with, and one must also resist the temptation of viewing that great relinquishment as the permanent template of either right or wrong in human affairs.

Revolutions fail for far simpler reasons, better understood by reference to Lord Acton's famous *dictum*, the Michelsian '*Iron Law of Oligarchy*,' the Mannheimian struggles between 'Ideology and Utopia,' and my own suggestion of a '*Paradigm of Masculinity*' that, based on instinct, yet contingently depending on specific circumstances that are easy enough to detail, drives the human ape toward the lure of societal domination (as referenced in my own Festchrift *Lectures*).

The important issue is why, after the Reformation, which was an obvious fillip to the sciences, Europe did not develop an adequate anthropology based on readily verifiable *instincts* (late in the day, Nietzsche and Freud recruited instincts into discourse: but haphazardly, and in offhand, even obscurantist, fashion). I have pointed out that the reason is simple. *Animals* were thought to be '*instinct-driven*,' but not '*Man*': since the latter was assumed to have evolved from 'god,' to use a Marxian phrase, as an awe-inspiring '*sovereign of creation*.' So, an *anthropocentric* J/C ideology effectively barred the '*homo sapien*' (itself a very telling choice of phraseology) from the vulgar quagmire of instincts.

HE (and I capitalize it to indicate its import within the ideology of *Patriarchy)* had to be driven, at his best, by 'reason'—and the higher (*i.e.,* Christian) emotions (pity, compassion, and such). Of course, Women and non-Europeans (characterized as 'child-like,' 'emotive,' and 'irrational') could easily be derogated into the animal domain, as *naturvolk*—but not *European Man* who was above such taints.

All this is but trivially true.

The important point I am making is that *speculative* philosophy, of which there is an inordinate quantum innocent of a *realist* anthropology, is but a series of brilliantly colored fantasy balloons let loose from vivid human imagination— with no basis in anything other than the hot air which, for a while, keeps them afloat. The multiple realities of anthropic, societal life are, by contrast, easily ascertainable: and its 'structures' are visible in any and all human societal formations, simple or complex, given careful observation (here, the relatively lowly 'ethnographers' have served us better than the more ideologically driven theoretical anthropologists).

But they are only so ascertainable when we approach them *sans a priori presumptions,* whether drawn from religious or secular myths, much as Darwin approached the botanical and zoological worlds. Anthropology is, or can be, an *empirical* science (not a *'rationalist'* one *a la* Levi Strauss, nor a *normative* one as in the case of a Smith, or Rousseau). Its truths, such as they are, are thereby, to use a telling phrase of Nietzsche—*'Beyond Good and Evil.'*

On such grounds, many other related 'sciences,' such as 'Economics' (or 'Psychology') fail, virtually *a priori*—it's 'assumptions' are, societally speaking, and for the most part, simply nonsensical. Similar strictures apply to the concoction of 'utopias' that are no better than a form of idle mythology: and that have, in European, and similar 'copycat' versions outside of Europe, driven millions to despair and worse—under the iron heel of ideology-driven despotism(s).

The mythical claims for the 'Free-Market' stand, in this respect on the same plane as the *a priori* eulogies extant in erstwhile Europe to the fanciful idylls of 'communism.' In each case, the error is in *inappropriate specification of societal structures and processes, i.e.,* in not anticipating Hegelian *caveats* as to 'unintended,' and unforeseen, consequences.

Philosophical speculation, of course, will likely fare even less well in its traditional haunt of Cosmology, as our scientific knowledge in the area becomes, slowly, more and more definitive. So, its final abode might remain the old stand-by: the everlasting anthropic despair at the unavoidable fate of *mortality*—but even here, it has to, necessarily, share turf with religion; but it has very little direct relevance to serious, societal studies.

As an example, *Existentialism* which, in one form or other, has dominated Modernism for almost Two centuries is (other than its near-relative, *nihilism*) the server-successor ideology to religion (whilst dealing with a Kierkegaardian set of themes): but it cannot be used to define, as with Sartre ('hell is other people') and others, the societal state of being itself, as is often the case, without a radical misapprehension of issues. Indeed, even Levi-Strauss famously cautioned Sartre, in this regard, in a well publicized debate, to avoid engaging in 'three-legged excursions' into anthropology (to little avail). Three-legged? Perhaps 'one-legged' makes the point better.

We are, as *hominids*, primarily *tribal* entities, cut loose from our safe moorings in history by the frequent ravages of *Empire* (itself a frequent 'masculinist' devolution from tribal norms), the latest, and most profound, being the long, climactic, reign of EuroModernism. The *Age of Discontent*, which bears down upon us all like a fetid miasma, effectively begins with that Fateful Transformation. Today, that impulse to *Empire* is quite run amok. So, the break with the Enlightenment I called for in my 1997 work (Kanth, 1997b)—in this, as in so many other areas—is really long, long, overdue. *EuroModernism* (as part of the dominant paradigm of *Eurocentrism)* has already deracinated the economy, society, ecology, and human habitat—for most of us.

The Human Condition is anything but idyllic, even at its best: so, to embrace the transparent ravages of *greed-driven capital accumulation* (the unadorned economic essence of the ruling variant of European Modernism), which is the inexorable holocaust that razes the planet today, inching us all closer to Doomsday, would seem to be but little less than a defining, apocalyptic, species of a 'Fatal Error.'

History repeats itself twice, said Hegel. To which Marx added the rider: first time as tragedy, second time as farce. And a final *third time*, I fear, as *wholesale Extinction*—which is a prospect on the horizon today. To contextualize, but not without some hyperbole: one kind of 'Communism' failed, first, as *tragedy*; next, on its heels, a certain *genre* of 'Capitalism,' as *farce;* now we all wait, with bated breath, to see how the third, and Last, Great, Modernist, European, Gambit: *i.e., Empire,* will fare.

Absit Omen.

Evolution, itself, in a sense, might be said to be on pause.

28

Beyond Late Modernism

What comes after?

First, to quickly (re)evaluate. EuroModernism, a North European innovation, was set off by the early experience of, and exposure to, antic Mediterranean Civilization, gained in the centuries of the Crusades. A taste for, and finally some knowledge of, Commerce, Trade, and Luxuries (not to mention modes and implements of *War*) was, thereby, indelibly attained. The follow-up, and even more lucrative and educational, adventurism in the Americas, and Indies, simply sealed the emergent scapes of the incipient new order. Rome could, apparently, live with both Commerce and classical Christianity for eons; but North Europe, equally apparently, couldn't: whence the impatient break with the restraints of Catholicism, and the construction of a new, far less cumbrous, and profoundly *individuated, 'faith.'*

Society was swiftly, and suitably, 'freed up'—for the accumulation of wealth, mainly amongst the upper echelons. That 'freeing' process, which disabled many, and enabled a few, was trumpeted *via* thunderous proclamations of a new, heroic, schemata of 'emancipation.' The more ignoble the means deployed to secure wealth (piracy, plunder, slavery), the more the rhetorical bombast that enveloped the aerial visions of 'progress.' What were canny formulas for the rulers became, as such things go, solemn undertakings for the lower orders, who took up their own struggles under that same banner, paying, often, a grievous price for their delusions.

It took centuries for common laboring peoples to separate their struggles, organizationally, though they yet retained, anomalously, and all but unconsciously, the meretricious *'ideals'* of their oppressors. So, the new system broke all past, pre-existing, mirrors, signs, and guideposts—and helped separate all from the anthropic roots of their own social existence. *Entropy* and *alienation* increased; kinship, communal, and tribal ties collapsed—and the tyrant's hand lay firm upon factory and farm. Social *compacts* were rent, social *contracts* were fabricated. *Convivial* institutions were undermined/abandoned, replaced by commercial fiats 'legalized' by the newly developing unit of market-cum-administration: the *'nation-state.'* Peasant properties were seized, their traditional rights abrogated, their commons confiscated.

Anthropic evolution was *arrested*, and a mutant direction was taken, tragically, and paradoxically, under the name of a new-fangled jargon, replete with tenet, maxim, and edict—of *'humanism.'* Antique conceptions/ordinances of societal means and ends were warped: affective, emotive, ties devalued, and trivialized—and a 'brave new,' and 'rational' order, was forcibly imposed. Speaking in metaphor, *mammals were smoothly morphing into reptiles*, with the EM governors reveling in it.

The New Philosophers rationalized this novel monstrosity, distancing all from the now disparaged, quasi-religiously ordained, *'ancien régime.'* A system of 'universal egoism' with devil-take-the-hindmost mores—*i.e., civil society*—was unleashed, catapulting the rabid ambitions of commerce and finance to a nicety. Europe had, of a sudden, left the human world behind. It had become *'developed'* (to use a later phraseology). It now embodied a self-proclaimed, nay flaunted!, catechism of *'progress.'* It also embraced, and enshrined, a corybantic *materialism*—to the point of supplanting all other pre-existing norms.

Materialism was Science. Materialism was Philosophy. Materialism was, even more, the general rubric of *All* societal drives and motivations, insinuating itself into both means and ends. It was armed both with the glib canons of 'universal rights,' and the even more palpable cannons of *munitioned might*. There was no further recourse to confiscate in the name of King, Country, or Christ. It would now expropriate in the grand name of *Civilization*. It was, in other words, ready to pillage, plunder, and rule, the world. And it did this, and still does it!, on a scale unimaginable.

❉

How is it all to be transcended? Let us return to a *realist* human anthropology, the only *Science* we need, in understanding ourselves. Contrary to Modernist dissimulations (which have gulled us all), *morality and civilization* (understood in the sense of *a pacification of the conditions of human existence, both natural and social*) are not 'choices' exercised by sovereign individuals, standing on the bold high ground of the Modernist escarpment.

It is a perennial anthropic necessity, imposed by indefeasible aspects of our very species-being. The need to raise the human infant safely through its early, vulnerable years, demands it: and *women*, given their early and intimate connection with this process, cross-culturally, become the first *guarantors* of minimal societal peace. *The mother-child relation is the constituent building block of anthropic society, its very first social, and moral, relation.*

All other societal norms flow from this genetic, nucleic matrix, depending on the *prevalent* conjunctural balance of *gender-struggles. Men and women, universally, are equipped by nature with differing instincts: and so are, each, quite distinct sub-species of the human family.* In this struggle, *Women* seek, eternally, to 'build,' and preserve the *artifacts of civility* which *Men*—whose feckless depredations, in the arenas of violence and domination require such measures—accommodate, according to their lights: now more, now less, ever fluctuating, in nip and tuck fashion.

In effect, women are, inescapably, the trustees, the custodians, of both civilization and morality.

We are, as a species, *in essence,* not 'light-seeking,' but, rather, far simpler 'heat-seeking' animals: and no, 'freedom' is *not* an intrinsic anthropic value of any evolutionary consequence. Modernism invented the doctrine to 'free itself' from all communitarian bonds such that it could go about its inexorable *avarice* in unbounded fashion. As tribal entities we do not, instinctually, seek *'freedom,'* by any stretch, but rather *the hospitality, security, and warmth of the societal sanctum,* wherein all our *anthropic needs* (survival/propagation) are met *affectively* and abundantly.

So, the grand litany of the hollow freedoms of Modernist fantasy, when/where swallowed whole, has ensnared the European to the point of being hopelessly lost in *Two* very vital senses: *not knowing him/her-self, 'internally,' in this abnormal, individuated form; nor having a cradling societal sanctuary in which (s)he can find any extended rest. These are the Primal Alienations of EM, for which there is No Salve: not yoga, not 'socialism,' nor 'humanism,' nor 'personal growth'—those being merely the desperate, even pathetic, 'pillar to post' avenues of a foredoomed path of Escape.*

This accounts for the turbulent *vagabondage of spirit* that informs the confirmed EuroModernist, defying the very notion of *contentment* itself as dire anathema (yes, we *must* 'climb every mountain,' as the refrain goes). Tragedy is that, plunged in ceaseless war with their own spirit, Europe exported this maleficent, misanthropic model to all peoples, over time, by dint of force, fraud, and attrition.

Given the foregoing, it may be readily understood that, for having made human existence, natural and societal, even more precarious than ever, Europe's fateful trajectory has been only to streak straight from barbarism to decadence—wholly innocent of the critical desiderata of civilization. As such, it is trivially true that the earliest of human tribal societies attained, almost effortlessly by comparison, a far higher degree of civilization than any Modernist European entity. Realism demands that we know 'ourselves' as *tribal animals: hominids*, gifted with ascertainable traits that make the world what it is, for better or worse.

In stark terms, anthropic society is, at base, an instinctual society *wherein 'nature' and 'culture' coincide—with No 'opposition' between them.* Modernism, *au contraire, 'invents'* a novel societal order, *culturally* speaking, willy-nilly, with its philosophers spouting quixotic visions, ungraced by any anthropic insights, and with its prophets, similarly, proclaiming insensible, ignorant chimeras: but the limits of such unfounded intellections are all too quickly, and often very tragically, reached.

Indeed, the dominant *Anglo-Am* societies, today, have only revived, and restored, for all the vain proclamatory zeal of Smith, Locke, and Paine, the grisly mores of the Modernist *jungle*, as the operative norms of public policy and every-day life. *Life as a Lottery is the great, Modernist, Anglo-Norma contribution to history (Smith was wrong: not a 'nation of shopkeepers'—and trade is of much utility—as much as one of Inveterate Gamblers).*

Indeed, the follies don't stop even there: for now, their follow-through, imminent, feint is to ungently move us all to an approaching *Transhuman* future built on biogenetic robotics: thereby bringing the hoary Project of Evolution to a dismal, abrupt, depraved, and extropian *terminus*. EuroModern *anthropology* fails to comprehend any/all of this for being really a potent *misanthropology*, fatally disabled by its *Two* overriding *system-imperatives*:

a) the demands of Empire (*i.e.*, of maintaining a 'necessary' distance between Europeans and *Others*, and between fact and fantasy: in its favor*)*, and

b) a Judeo-Christian ideology that fails to equate 'humans' with 'animals' (of course, in the usual *modus* of apparently chronic 'double-standards,' European ideologues happily consigned women and aboriginal peoples to '*nature*'—think of the appellation '*natuurvolk,' e.g.,*—whilst reserving, for themselves, the high trope of 'culture,' free of animalistic attributes).

At any rate, given our 'essence,' *our deepest anthropic drives derive from an affective attachment to 'family,' 'clan,' and 'tribe,'* far from Modernism's tendentious imputations of our being just so many isolated, individualistically moved, 'rationally' (whence, *materially*!, in its confounding logic) calculating automatons.

Stated simply, emotive affections rule the human animal, en générale: it is this innate proclivity that is turned upside-down in EM conditioning that seeks to subdue/subvert it *via* the cold blooded, instrumental, calculus of canny calculation of material advantage (as pointed out, Anglo-Am societies have 'internalized' this *geist*—or is it an *anti-geist?*—early on, and far more completely, than any other societal grouping on the face of this planet, to momentous effect).

So long as the 'material economy of interests' delivers expected 'goods' the latter fantasy can be indulged (i.e., we can't be persuaded to be pigs if the trough is empty!), albeit at cost of the far more meaningful 'moral economy of affections' that it perforce supplants: but the moment it cannot, which is where the EuroModern Economy is at today, the haze wears thin—and people return to the soon remembered bosom of their birthright very swiftly.

As such, all prolonged 'depressions' and 'crises' *spontaneously* revive calls for 'socialist,' communitarian, and kindred, modes of economy and society. Of course this '*reactive*' force is strongest where EM has least penetrated popular consciousness: *this might explain why socialism, contrary to Marxian expectation, took root in the East rather than the 'advanced' (i.e., the more deteriorated) West.* This process is already commenced, globally, and will gather steam proportionate to the ongoing subsidence of the Modern system.

Looked at more analytically, it is the entire world-view of a mistaken, and antiquated, materialism that is being—and needs be—jettisoned. In Science, this has already been accomplished, with Physics serving as the lead discipline *(via* Quantum ideas) placing *human subjectivity* (in the *collective* sense of a communal 'consciousness') at the very center of the world of the 'things' being examined. The old 'determinisms' have given way to a more probabilistic, and less mechanistic, ways of understanding the universe, both social and natural.

EM Philosophy had adjusted itself, also, to the change, since Einstein, if in typically unhinged ways, with self-styled '*Post-Modernism,*' at its apex, making a philosophical mockery of the real *science* underlying such changes in its vacuous '*anything goes*' postures and dispositions. *The great Einstein, himself, was wrong:* 'god' not only plays 'dice,' but, apparently, all manner of incomprehensible games that keep us guessing—with the ratio of the known to the unknown being an ever-diminishing one.

The idle bluster of Stephen Hawking, made in his heyday in the closing decades of the twentieth century, that a putative 'Grand Unifying Theory' was just a hop and a skip away, not only calls to mind another vacuous swank of one of his forebears (Lord Kelvin, *circa* 1900: 'There is nothing new to be discovered in physics now, All that remains is more and more precise measurement.'), but also illustrates the quintessentially triumphalist arrogance that has always marked EuroModernist *scientism*—and its Anglo-American *avatar,* in particular.

Abandoning a discredited materialism is not to embrace organized religion(s) (old or new), or any of its own brand of suppositional, and delusive, idealisms that deny extant realities in favor of a *Utopia* in the *Afterlife*: it is rather to understand that the real, anthropic world does not support such *a priori* noetic postures, though it can still yield us, within strict *species-limits*, an arguably provident life on the good earth.

Being ineluctably human, this sloughing off of the Modernist yoke is far from being difficult: it is easy, for being *instinctive*—and will presage a gradual return to our *species-being, mortally* traduced centuries ago. However, old habits do die hard: and so Europeans will find it possibly harder to give up customary modes of thought than non-Europeans who never really assimilated the perversions of their ideology 'in their bones.' Indeed, we may have to abandon many EuroModernist, divisive, binaries of like-nature: '*Left vs Right*,' for example, that have deceptively mesmerized generations raised in dour EM tutelage.

Left *vs* Right are the vapid options *within* the arid world of EM; what is needed is a flat rejection of the *world entire according to EM: tout ensemble* and *tout a fait. Think again of the universal archetype of the human family: it is neither democratic nor egalitarian, nor 'free' (nor left-wing or right-wing), but it affords all humans what they crave most—sanctuary, conviviality, and societal affections.*

Our anthropic future need not rest, anymore, on the grim prospect of a permanently *divided-Self*—living precariously in an insuperably banal dog-eat-dog world (despite, in all irony and paradox, the hypertrophic paraphernalia of 'equality,' 'liberty' and 'rights,' *etc.)* where the race, in a rigged game, is ever to the oligarchic captains of the commanding heights of wealth and power.

Centers do not hold, and it is likewise with *epicenters*. Modernist entities have been held up only by sheer *force,* be it economic, political, or ideological: now that the force is found flagging, the exalted towers are, slowly, starting to lean. At base, to continue the metaphor, we remain, intractably, *instinctual.*

When 'superstructures' crumble, the foundation becomes freed of its burdens. So it is that, universally, centrifugal forces are compelling the human world, in these times, to adapt to an incipient *Great Inversion:* a return to our original, anthropic attributes. In this rebounding is restitution: nature and culture may yet again, coalesce, and be *One.* The enduring anthropic pastime of irrepressible cultural innovation/differentiation can then resume: to adorn the planet with continuing variety, diversity and heterogeneity—reflecting, once again, the unquenchable genius of our species.

And EuroModernism, together with its stultifying asphyxiations, and the fateful sub-continent that bore it, may all retire back, in time, into more proper, and just, historical, and geographic, proportions.

Whence Evolution, perhaps, can yet again recommence its (rudely interrupted) immemorial, timeless, sway.

29

A Farewell

It is time to prepare to bid farewell to the long reigning supremacy of *Euro*Modernism. This may appear absurd, given its willful hegemony across the universe today. But it is time, nonetheless. The global struggles of our times, howsoever disguised by our own misconceived vocabularies/viewpoints, are, in essence, a clash between Modernist and non-modernist ways of life, ideas, and practices: indeed, the oft-reviled Sam Huntington was not far wrong in his depiction of this as a 'clash of civilizations.' He was off-base, however, in equating EuroModernism with a form of *civilization*—instead, of being its very *antithesis*.

So, more aptly, is it a struggle between barbarism and civility, between material-ism and morality, between the calculus of accumulation and the mores of empathy (or, perhaps more succinctly, in my own usage: between mammals and reptiles).

It is (Euro)Modernism that first erected an unbreachable wall—between our anthropic natures and our societal being. The Modernist Revolutions, ideational and material, from the late sixteenth century on, which now stereotypically define the 'west'—in their own eyes—saw to that. Briefly, it did so by the adoption of a vision of society as a '*contract*' (*i.e.*, a '*balance of interests*'), rather than the ancient compact of a '*balance of affections.*' Secondly, it, perforce, '*individuated*' humans, *i.e., cleft them from their societal bonds*, those tensile hoops of affective steel!, so they could, then, in all sordid, self-destructive, alienation, see 'society' as but a *means* to deliver personal, individual *ends.*

The West did not invent *individuals*—they are *universal* to all anthropic societies—but rather 'individualism': of an *asocial* nature. In a stroke, the *moral* basis for societal conduct was expunged—paving the way for a still devolving *'amoral'* being, increasingly obsessed with advancing a purely private interest, knowingly, *against* the pre-conditions of societal, and ecological, well-being.

Gemeinschaft village communities, under the impetus of greed and trade, were breaking up, and being swallowed by the new *Gessellschaft* formations, belonging to the *genre* of *empires*—ending in the now familiar modernist *'nation-state'* (that emerged in the thirteenth century, maturing later, finally, with the Treaty of Westphalia).

Modernism is the most far-reaching Empire ever constructed by the (evil) genius of Men (gender intended), providing, for four centuries now, the stark mismeasure of human inclinations, aptitudes, and dispensations. In that same vapid devolution, speaking in metaphor, mammals began to morph into reptiles, conviviality yielding to calculation. These two mutations were situated within a new outlook that adopted an aggressive *materialism* both as a general philosophy, and as a measure and standard, of both personal and societal welfare.

The sciences of the time, *positivist* in the main, handily assisted this makeover, objectifying *'nature'* (which in Euro-Christian usage did *Not* include the so-called 'god's children,' i.e., Europeans—*whilst subsuming Women, and 'Other' cultures within it!*), and creating a cheerless universe of *things: both social and natural.* Its impact on the so-called *social* sciences—which were no more than blunt devices of *social control* designed to contain the revolutionary stirrings of the times (Comte's vast repertoire of works are a good example)—was immediate: with someone like Durkheim, *e.g.,* asking us to *'consider social facts as things.'*

As Sartre commented, this could only be possible *where 'things' had already become the dominant social facts.* The *Age of Quantity* was beginning its long, triumphant, destructive, march. Any and all forms of *idealism* (especially *moral* idealism) were consigned to the pound of a now devalued *religion,* whose tenets ran seriously afoul of the drives of the commercial classes. Protestantism eventually overthrew the increasingly anachronistic strictures of the Church of Rome, and forged an individuated, and *'reformed'* Christianity, that, possibly not by coincidence!, better fitted the needs, nay the demands!, of commerce and industry. Simultaneously, morality was banished, and assimilated to the boondocks of religion, with *utilitarian* and pragmatist social policies being their new-fangled, stolid, surrogates (*via* the likes of Bentham, *et al.*). Dickens's Mr. Gradgrind quite epitomizes that banal outlook. *Social Engineering, on behalf of the dominant, acquisitive classes*, the Great (if as yet unfinished) Modernist Project, had begun.

My very first scholarly work describes how so-called *'laissez-faire'* (Kanth, 1986) simply disallowed only *anti-establishment* interventions, *not* pro-system subventions. The new 'Social Science' was undermined inevitably by its 'law-and-order' biases, much as philosophy was hopelessly overdetermined by church *vs* secularism issues: each, thereby, inhabiting a self-imposed prison which offered little scope for either objectivity or insight.

On the other hand, Modernist *philosophy*, to take up the other major link in the ideological chain, was always a morass of *partial* speculations. Indeed, *European* philosophy, *where uninspired by Greek ideas*, simply could not exist as a viable entity. At any rate, in the seventeenth century, the former project took unsteady hold, with Descartes sounding the pioneering bugle. If compared to the originality of the Greeks, or India, it was, and still is, wholly unremarkable—indeed, to this day.

The reason is simple.

The Greeks were not self-limited by the parameters of Judeo-Christian norms: nor should their contributions be assimilated to *'European'* philosophy gratuitously, as the North Atlantics have done—they were part of a great *Pan-Mediterranean civilization* whose ideas were part of a vast, melting pot, affected, in particular, by the seminal influences of Asia and Africa. To give but a trivial, if telling, example, *Aesop's Fables*—attributed to Greece, much like the 'Theorem of Pythagoras'—have their origins in antic Indian *Panchatantra* tales, themselves deriving from a dateless antiquity.

Descartes, Kant, even Nietzsche (and Schopenhauer), quite consciously, were all dealing, for better or for worse, with various tenets of Christian *theosophy*. The German philosophers, in particular, were also specially tutored in newly translated *Sanskrit* texts. Descartes was explicitly religious: Kant, somewhat more implicitly (it is said that Kant found it only societally *utilitarian* to believe in god *as a means to succor morality, not because it was 'true'*: at any rate, he helped *divorce faith from reason*, permanently, in EuroModernism, to the lasting satisfaction of the emergent overseers of both church and state), with 'freedom' (read *Christian* 'free will') being a notion that still had to be retained, as a necessary *a priori*. In fact, *sans* Christian 'free will,' Kant's project vanishes almost entirely: a clue, possibly, to its putative 'greatness.' As was, apparently remarked about Andre Gretry's harmonies, *'between his high notes and his low, you could drive a chariot'*: a critique that, usefully, applies to *all* of Post-Renaissance, *non*-Greek, European philosophy.

Even the 'rejectionist' Marx was, no less, moved undeniably by the gospel(s) of Christian humanism (the adjective being as important as the noun, whence his ready contempt, *vide* his writings on India, for the beliefs of *Other* cultures: a stance that is extant to this day amongst his epigones). In fact, as often as not, Marxism itself is a species, only, of a *loyal* 'opposition' to Modernist agendas. To state the point brusquely, Christian myths are, *en générale*, believed, privately, even by the intelligentsia, as loosely *historical*—with all *Others* being treated, privately again, as *suppositional.*

Anglo-Am *media* (is there another kind?), a cut below academic scholarship, *e.g.*, to this day carry narratives of *Jesus, e.g.,* without qualification, as a 'historical' figure: whereas any references to *Krishna*, e.g., are explicitly couched in condescending terms suggestive of myth, lore, and legend. In effect, the EuroModernist 'progressivist' could have his/her religious/cultural cake and eat it too: whereas all *Others* had to surrender, and sacrifice, their traditional belief systems to climb up to the Modernist altar. European 'secularism' is, thereby, not very much more than, nor ever very far from, Protestant *theosophy.*

In other words, even 'progressivist' Modernist agendas—such as 'communism'—were but extensions of essentially, deeply inscribed, pan-Christian ideals. Indeed, take away the King James Bible and there are but few themes/tropes remaining in the Anglo-Am literature/lexicon of the higher imagination (Shakespeare's writings might follow as a distal second, in impact, but are, also, similarly, drenched in biblical imagery). So, this was not philosophy that was wholly 'open-ended,' like that of the Greeks, or the Indians: it was, of necessity, *constrained*, to its serious detriment. Its greatest, if late, exemplar is, of course, *existentialism:* a striking example of Christian passions battling Modernist debasements, howsoever fruitlessly. As such, its fruits were/are quite bare. Virtually all of it is a *cri de cœur,* a grieving, for the moral/affective ties lost, or scuttled, by the societal artifacts of Modernist 'progress.'

Indeed, speaking only of philosophy, if the entire tradition from Descartes to Quine and Putnam, in our own time, were to vanish, not much would be lost that could not easily, and far more suitably, be *re-acquired,* say, by a quick delve into the antic *Vedic* treasure trove (much of it still in need of translation). This should not be surprising since Christianity itself is no more, philosophically, than a humble variant of Buddhism—as the latter was but a deviant (*naastika*) strain of mainstream (*aastika*)Vedic thought. *This should surprise no one*, since Buddhist influence flowed far, in both east and west, from India: until the later rise of Islam checked its advance, terminally, westwards.

It is only with Wittgenstein, and much later, with Chomsky, that European philosophy takes up original subject-matter that was not inherently part of, or influenced by, the old, hackneyed, struggle between church and state, or religion *vs* secularism (as, say, moved Kierkegaard, and Nietzsche) *via* the novel study of *language*: but, in so doing, Chomsky only revives pioneering Indian ideas of thousands of years ago (originating with Panini, to name but one).

Of course, Linguistics is not, *prima facie*, part of philosophy at all, but is rather a sub-set of a *possible science*: of *Anthropology*. *In fact, there is only One social science that is feasible, and includes all else: a realist Anthropology of our species,* yet, it has never been achieved, within EuroModernism, owing to, (a) its imperial origins, and, (b) its contamination, *ab initio,* with Christian, and Modernist, ideals (such as 'equality' to name but one: I have tried to sketch the initial prodromes of such an anthropology in my *Lectures* previously referred to).

European anthropology is better termed a '*misanthropology*': to which the only fitting correction is what I have termed '*reverse* anthropology'—a field that has only just begun to be assayed. Wittgenstein's initial notion that words are pictures of reality and, later, that meanings are socially constructed, would not have fazed Indian linguists of antiquity in the slightest.

Indeed, the West oft claims too much for its philosophers; Kant's 'categorical imperative' has been compared, for instance, with the biblical 'Golden Rule,' as amongst the noblest canons of human invention. Firstly, it's a *moral* canon, and not a necessary derivative of his *philosophy*: secondly, in all irony, it offers the engaging *mantra,* no less, to a society, an emergent *civil society,* which, *ex definitione,* is driven precisely by the *severely anti-social frame of a 'universal egoism': where each uses the other as a means to his/her own advancement.* Thirdly, its enduring novelty is a function, merely, of its *denial,* or *absence,* within *Modernist* society, and its 'universality' is quite untenable since it requires an atypical, abnormal, focus, like all Modernist Projects, *on the premise of a sovereign individual* in 'free' association—which is not sustainable (even unthinkable) for the vast majority of anthropic societies, past and present, untouched by Modernist corruption(s). *It is akin to applying gesellschaft criteria to gemeinschaft entities.* Finally, if you are seriously seeking moral canons of genuine 'universality,' Jainism and Buddhism is where you would, more profitably, commence the search.

The more contemporaneous John Rawls's acclaimed contribution is, similarly, also interlaced with strands of Modernist pedantry. *Justice* is *not* reducible to 'fairness'; fairness is simply, to use a vernacular idiom, the *prima facie* 'cover charge' to be paid to any petition for 'justice,' *ab initio.* '*Fairness,*' *or impartiality rather, is therefore more of a rule of legality, or procedure, not justice, in the first instance.* Like all Modernist systems, Rawlsian criteria are formalistic '*universals*' only, and evade substance (ideas such as '*equal rights,*' and '*egalitarian economic systems*' that lace his arguments, are abstract, Modernist notions that perhaps dodge, if not actually fudge, and divert attention away from, the more vital, *historical* issue of '*initial conditions*': so 'distributive justice' even *à la* Rawlsian criteria cannot undo a *default* in an *initial* dispossession, say, *via* theft, fraud, or conquest—an issue that he was, of course, fully aware of).

Rawlsian ideas, are, thereby, a celebration (in the customary vein of triumphalism) only of the *possibility* of Modernism crafting 'the 'Good Society' as a project of *social engineering* (if permitted by the ruling interests!)—another 'ideal' that one must, perforce, set in stark contrast to prevalent, ontic *reality.* More fundamentally, any notion of 'justice' (and there are several: restitutive, retributive, *et al.*) is *relative always to prevailing norms,* so it is a societally specific notion: it cannot be elevated to a 'universal' discourse. Rawls does just that: and, as such, *Rawlsian criteria are specific only to Modernist ideology, and are not relevant to non-Modern formations,* which makes of it far short of universality.

Anthropic Society is not a voluntarist engineering project that one 'designs' like a gulag, or even a gated-community with member-prompted 'rules' (which is how both capitalist and socialist planners, *i.e.,* the two dominant strains of Euro-Modernism have viewed matters): *it is an organic entity that evolves, naturally and spontaneously, building consensus, over millennia.*

Of Late Modernist *will o' the wisp* billows such as Structuralism, Deconstruction, Postmodernism, *et al.,* the less said, perhaps, the better: they never ascend to the scale of serious philosophical systems, and are no more than passing fads, the *'bas morceaux,'* of very minimal lasting value (despite assisting, inevitably, a host of *avant-garde* careers: for academe is also a rich backwater of minor spoils).

In the choice of depth, seriousness, and nature of subject-matter, Anglo-American philosophy of today scarcely touches the hems of the ancients. As in so many regards, Modernism as an intellectual force, remains, to employ terms I have applied, hitherto, to its *economics* only: *a self-referential language game.* Of course, it is, and can be, 'interesting'—as a T.S. Eliot character has it, in one of his plays, in context of someone finding another's poetry interesting: *but only if you are, a priori, interested in it.*

Modernism, in all its stances, to underline my meaning, is inescapably *misanthropic, tending to a dour anthropic entropy,* in its very constitution. It leaves us all, if swallowed whole, fit only for 'treasons, stratagems, and spoils': which, if thoughtfully considered, is no more than the grisly record of the European Drama—at least, since Columbus.

Let me relate but one minor moment in the latter's register of infamy, in a poignant tale. One of his victims, a native aboriginal about to be burnt alive was approached by the stand-by Catholic priest who asked if wished to be baptized (as prelude to the broil). He asked why—and was regaled with vistas of the joys of heaven. At this, he asked only if his tormentors were also headed there: and, receiving the obvious answer, said: *'No, I don't wish to meet your kind again, anywhere.'* I dare say he spoke a mouthful there—for millions more to follow.

❄

I have taken my stance, in many of these posts, on the premise of the possibility a real anthropology of our species, so my 'critique' is—leastways in that sense—non-arbitrary. What do I mean by it? *That we are 'programmed' as a species, much as our other animal cousinages are*, and the one obvious way *of just beginning to read* the *modus* of this conditioning is the obvious one of looking to *instincts*: which hold vital clues not merely to 'human behavior,' but more accurately, and importantly, to the *differential behaviors of men and women*– who, whilst sharing some instincts in common, also have *distinctly differing* instincts.

Modernist ideology tendentiously subsumes men and women under the solvent rubric of 'equality' (thereby joining women, to men, gratuitously, in the ghastly epics of male depredations). This is a vicious canard: men and women have played very different anthropic roles in human evolution.

I have argued that both *morality* and *civilization*, understood as *the pacification of the conditions of human existence,* derive from the structural roles/responsibilities of *women,* not unrelated to their instinctual endowments and biological capabilities. Patriarchal ideology—*men being the ruling sex universally*—could not admit disclosure of the fact that *male societal violence* stands in outright contrast to the female record in this area, cross-culturally: whence the feint of speaking, in terms of a *'human' propensity for aggression, etc.,* cannily evading appropriate gender responsibility.

I have already pointed out, in the earlier section, why EuroModernists chose *not* to take the requisite *empirical* route of real anthropological analysis. Instead, the 'rationalist' *modus* was adopted, by and large (a tendency that peaks with Levi-Strauss and French anthropology of that *genre*), in keeping, partly, with Modernist 'ideals' of progressive humanism. Christian myths of human genesis, in turn, also played a role in the *refusal to classify Europeans alongside animals as animals,* despite the genius of Darwin—although cheerfully applying such derogation to Women and non-Europeans.

Besides, the needs of *imperium* dictated that *Other Cultures* should be studied only to measure their 'distance' from the European master-model (Said's *Orientalism* was amongst the early works to define this tendency, though Fanon, and others, had gotten there long before academic scholarship), alongside the need to 'crack their codes' for colonial and military objectives. Also, Modernist 'requirements,' as in Economics, did away with the embarrassing aspects of human biology, such as 'needs'—in favor of duly manipulable, and indefinitely expandable, 'wants.'

So, all of the above made a hash of anthropology as a science: instead, it became like economics: yet another *unsound* pillar of Modernist, ideological propagation.

In sum, we know not who/what we are, as a species, let alone why we are here.

The First task, left to 'science' never really got off the mark, as just discussed; the Second, left to religion (and philosophy) meant that only generous fantasy prevailed. Yet, it behooves us to ask these questions, again, and start over: and in so doing, we shall be returned, perhaps, to the procreant musings of the ancients which offer a trove of insights that we can pursue further—subject to our own genius.

A realist anthropology, unlike the *mis*anthropology bequeathed us by Modernism, could offer invaluable insight and guidance as to the real parameters of the 'human dilemma.' Until then, regrettably, we will only be (mis)led by the canny subterfuges that undergird the sordid plans of the Modernist Project.

❉

How can one be reasonably sure that this 'saga of our times' is all set to expire? Well, again, the facts lie stark, nay blatant, before us. I call the phase after the Reagan-Thatcher *coup,* the era of *Late Modernism,* where it begins, finally, to *self-cannibalize: and that is likely the certain Prelude to Unravelment.* Marx once wrote that the Middle Ages could not *live* on religion (even if it swore by it): and neither can Late Modernism live on Finance and Munitions (these latter are bad enough simply in their own terms, but, in combination, they are a fiendish mix). *Finance cannot feed, Munitions cannot minister.* Empires, like ambition, need to be forged of sterner stuff. *Au contraire*, we have all seen its delegitimization proceed precipitately, as the many, increasingly, see through the spin.

Our doughty Anglo-Am governors apparently forgot the old dictum of Napoleon: that you can do anything with bayonets, save sit on them. *One cannot simply bomb one's way to enduring legitimacy, in this age and time.* And global *hegemony* is not built by explosives, though the latter was undeniably the *simpliste* European basis for *domination*—which is a far lesser-order phenomenon. Consequently, *sans* the necessary fig leaf, the world can see, all too clearly today, only their ineffable brutishness.

When/Where a basic licitness is lost, little endures. The tribes that looted much of the world pell-mell (American drives derive, innately, from their *English* roots: accordingly, that generative island-cluster I christen *the Brutish Isles* for their regressive impact on the globe), in a historically unrivalled orgy of extirpation *cum* extraction, are now in sullen state of an unaccustomed abatement—with confusion rife in their ranks and banners.

One might think of it, perhaps, as a species of suprahistorical *Karma?* Of course, EuroModernism will not simply cease to be: it will only begin to (con) cede hegemony. To be even more specific: its dominant, if aberrant, *Anglo-Am,* form will now draw down, forever (unlike, say, its Icelandic cousinages, which, reined by abiding, antic, communal-tribal norms, will yet hold their own).

Whence I conclude this piece—with a mini semi-dirge, as a sort of a prevenient requiem.

A Farewell

We will Heed no more the Call of the Wild
to fulsome seductions in Whimsy's wan pall
few Artless amongst us yet Lost in the Woods,
in goblin ensnarings, rapt by Sirens in Thrall—

We stride swiftly by Quicksands, past Pythons of Blight,
abeying the Tempters in Revels of Night:
The Long Dance quite ended, the Tables full Bare,
The Candles still flicker, but the Music is spare—

Carriage wheels clatter, gates creak to let go,
Wry catcalls ricocheting, Wraiths take to the Tow:
lolled in their penumbra, we grew sere in its glow,
but the Dread Lot is past, new Salves are aflow:

Time pratfalls in Trespass, life still is Unclear,
But the Vigil is demitting, neap Redemptions appear:
We fain sense the sunrise, we feel it loom nigh:
Burnishing the damson of a still smould'ring sky:

The Masque is untwining, the Ghouls are in flight,
Vampire and Werewolf, all glid into Night:
We who Adored them now resolve to Revile—
For We shall Yield no more to the Call of the Wild

30

Rethinking 'Democracy'

There are a good many sacred cows in the Modernist world. One of them is 'democracy.' It's rather a fine myth, as myths go. As ever, even the brightest of us fall for its disarming allure. The only myth greater than it is possibly the notion that it is (yet another!) European gift to the world.

Europe, as it happens, links itself, quite gratuitously, to the achievements of Ancient Greece. Then it suggests that the Greeks invented it, and thereby, by extension, it 'opts-in' as one of its Co-Legators. But facts, being stubborn things, deny such a facile attribution. As I have argued before, Greek Civilization was a part of a great *Pan-Mediterranean* Civilization that included several others, itself, fertilized by a host of ideas emanating from Egypt, India, and China.

North Europe, the least cultivated region of the sub-continent, first received exposure to Mediterranean Civilization, *indirectly*, in 'twice-removed' fashion, *via Roman* conquests. Then, of course, the *Crusades* had the former stalwarts brought, finally, back into *direct* contact with the region. *In consequence, the so-called 'Renaissance' was the Great School where North Europe learnt of exotica like high culture.*

A bit later, the generalization of European Conquests, globally, netted them the bounteous troves of the wisdom, science, and technology of the East which helped bring about their own, vaunted, 'Enlightenment.' At any rate, the Greeks no more 'invented' democracy than they discovered the theorem attributed to

Pythagoras. That much is simply part of the smug folklore that was constructed to project the later European Empire as great, wise, and beneficent. Democratic institutions existed in both ancient Civilizations, like India, and tribal formations, long before Greece.

At any rate, *EuroModernism* did not, by any stretch, enter the world bearing the olive branches of 'freedom' and 'democracy': but rather, swept in by sword, cannon, and civil war. *If one reduces 'democracy' to a mere voting rule, then it was, within Northern Europe, localized entirely within the ruling class, as say, within the landed elites—not exactly the most progressivist of the extant societal orders—of Pre-Reform England.*

Later, it was actually fought for by forces set against them, as with the *commercial* 'middle classes' who ably exploited the *working-class* Chartist Movement to secure their own 'voting rights' in 1832. And it was only in 1867, after long, long, struggles, that Workers, in England, earned that nominal privilege. Of course, it took Women until the twentieth century to wrest that same 'right.' As for racial and ethnic minorities, a comment or two, below, will clarify matters.

If we date the onset of the Modernist Impulse as somewhere in the late sixteenth century, even *limited democracy* took two centuries to be accepted, largely by dint of the struggles of an 'internal opposition.' Of course, History is written by conquerors: and it is *written such that we assume that Modernism simply dawned one fine day, smiling benignly, and brimming over with a cornucopia of such gifts, scattering them to all and sundry—like manna from heaven.*

On the other side of the Atlantic, 1776 gave White Gentry Patriarchs that same privilege, but keeping it safely away from all else (minorities, women, and the *sans-cullotte). Never mind the Franchise, the property-less couldn't even count on the services of a fire brigade in the land of the free.* Women resisted, and gained the franchise in the twentieth century: and, with Afro-Americans, it took the second half of the twentieth century, almost two and a half centuries after all those fanciful 'Universal Declarations,' to be recognized as even having the franchise; though, to this day, with public discussion in the US on whether 'Black Lives Matter,' there is a certain undeniable fragility to it.

The domestic struggles for the franchise were aided also by fortuitous international factors. Women got the right to vote in the US, in context of the Russian Revolution, and WW1, which shook the confidence of *all* ruling orders. Afro-Ams were assisted by the heat of the Cold War, where the US was forced to compete with the USSR, in appearing to be benign and "human-rights oriented' in the eyes of the world. And so it goes.

One must pause. *Recall, we are talking about a mere Voting Rule only, no more, no less, In Modernist democracies, the 'people' elect delegates to an Assembly only*: they elect, in effect, the would-be *governors* (in most cases, these 'representatives' are then swiftly bought out by 'special interests'). *Voting places people in office: it does not, necessarily, put them in power.* Stated another way, the *governing* class—a functionary *political* class—need not be the *ruling* class: in fact, the greater the distance between the two, the more effective is the propaganda about democracy. So, we need, first, to understand the nature of *power.*

Power can derive from a monopoly of *force,* but that can, *en générale,* only be temporary. As Napoleon had it, one can do anything with bayonets—except sit on them *More securely, it stems from effective ownership or control over the means of social production and reproduction. So, effective power lies, for the most part, in the hands of an unelected class of landed, financial, and corporate wealth. They are the organ grinders*: the *governing* class is a *political* elite that is elected, but is just the front stage player-performer in the Game of Politics.

The ruling class is more continuously stable than any such governing class, which comes and goes as elections dictate. And no set of governors can, for long, defy *their* special interests. Now we begin to get closer to an understanding of Modernist 'democracy': it is no more than a *legitimating* device (now if that sounds 'Marxist,' in origins, *beware*: it is actually a rather prosaic Weberian argument). One might also recall Adam Smith's bland statement that 'governments' are constituted to *'defend the rich from the poor.'* Yes, Adam Smith: our ever-glorified 'Free Marketeer.' *So, 'democracy' provides the comforting illusion that the 'people' are in charge of their own socio-economic destinies*—regardless of how often that myth is punctured, again and again, by overt political realities. So we need to try and see through the charades, or become stupefied by them: as an acute thinker once wrote, 'if appearance and reality coincided, there'd be no need for science!'

The crash of 2008, and the gratuitous bail-out of the very folks that helped manufacture that crisis is just one more drab and dreary lesson that is likely to go ignored as to the reality of the power of the real rulers. It gives lapidary proof of Santayana's *dictum* that democracy is the *'paradise that unscrupulous financiers dream of.'*

Let me make this clear by pushing the argument forward. Had the 2008 crash posed an *irreversible* threat to the ruling class, even such 'democracy,' as exists, would have been suspended (even beyond the *de facto* suspensions one observes today): as it well might, in any such future crash. And, as it is, a *passive* 'democracy' was deployed to deck the perpetrators, wantonly, with oodles of our tax monies.

❄

Power, to be stable, needs *legitimacy*. And 'democracy' is a useful *tool of legitimation*: indeed, few of us stop to think beyond having voted. That mechanical act effectively terminates the exercise of the 'power of the people.' *After that,* the real powers that be take over: and run the show. *De facto* Dictatorship, *within 'formal' democracy*, one would think, never had it so good! We elect 'representatives': and these are then 'commandeered' by the power elites. Yep, and so we do, routinely, get the 'best government money can buy'! But this is not to entirely discount the concept.

From the point of view of the *sans-cullotte*, democracy offers the meager possibility that, perhaps one day, some charismatic demagogue, riding the crest of a strong,' populist movement,' *may* author policies that at least, indirectly, benefit them. Yes, trickle-down benefits are possible, and even be at times critically important, but to imagine that rulers simply hand over control, let alone ownership, to the 'mob' (as they see it) is laughable. If this sounds cynical, remind yourself that even elite US educational institutions—such as Princeton—have, recently, sponsored studies that establish the *fact* that we live under an *oligarchy*.

So you don't need a Piketty to announce, with the air of *nouvelle* 'discovery,' in the twenty-first century, that the rich are getting richer, so to speak, 'behind our backs.' They have done so, systematically, since the system began. *What else would you expect under Capital-ism?* It is not, even nominally!, labor-ism, middle-class-ism, minority-ism, or women-ism, surely!

In fact, even more sobrietously, there is an Iron Law of Oligarchy that obtains in all societies that are 'class-divided' between labor-owners and property-owners. Barring the rare instances of revolt, that is the *status quo* that prevails, *en générale*.

Now, Churchill offered a rather classic defense of 'democracy': *it is the worst way to run a government, said he, until you consider the alternative.* As with much that he said, off the cuff, he was dead wrong. Actually, democracy is, by far, the safer tool for Modernist societies than dictatorships, because the latter are rarely stable—given the ever-present danger of *revolt. In effect, 'democracy' is, so to speak, the perfect sop for the masses.*

Indeed, the truth is even more bitter. *There is a saying that whether the melon falls on the knife, or vice versa, it is the melon that gets chopped.* So, the everyday peace of Modernist democracies (which are law and order entities) may be far preferable to the iron fist of Modernist dictatorships: but in *either* case, in the final analysis, *it is, en générale, the same sheep that get sheared.*

So, this is the great tragedy of Modernist politics: *that generations of the property-less pin their faith, again and again, over time, to achieve societal justice at the polls—and go home unrequited* (even in everyday political rhetoric, note that they offer you 'peace and prosperity,' but not *equity and justice*). It's not unlike that Peanuts gag where Lucy holds the ball down, and invites Charlie Brown to come running and kick it, only to whisk it away at the last minute: *time after time*. Only, it's not funny. Ask yourself who is responsible for the sad denouement: Lucy, for tricking Charlie unabashedly, or Charlie—for believing Lucy over and over? So it is necessary to understand the *limited* value—if value, nonetheless—of Modernist, *top-down*, democracies, from the point of view of the under-classes. *Democracy from below*, is quite another matter, obviously (but where, one might ask, is that permissible?)

The far superior 'alternatives' remain *tribal, i.e., consensual* societies where 51% cannot trump 49%, as a matter of course. Indeed, instructively, many European *tribal* Democracies, like Denmark or Iceland, fare far better than, say, the UK or the US, for being far more genuinely considerate of the larger interest. *It follows from their homogeneous, tribal, constitution.*

The *fatal flaw lies in the make-up of (Euro)Modernist 'civil society'*: once you sanction *unbridled greed*, and set up an *adversarial* society where each sees the other as rival and competitor, and society itself as but a means to advancement of personal self-interest, you have created the pot-holed Hobbesian world where '*Hell is other people.*' So, not merely 'democracy,' *any means of governance* fails in such a disastrous minefield of malintentions. *Where empathy is dead, and amorality is alive, you get the familiar, anthropic prospect of a Modernist wasteland, debauched of all co-respecting content.*

Now, the *Convivial Society* is still possible, for having viably *pre-existed* our deformed Modernist 'states of being.' Its *eternal locus* is the template of the *anthropic family*, which is more or less intact, in truncated form, even under severe Modernist duress.

How we get back on that felicitous track is the Prime Question for our troubled times.

In effect, our *tribal essence* is ours to reclaim anytime we wish. *It is, no less than our anthropic birthright*, sadly expunged by four centuries of EuroModernist depredations. Perhaps we might start *rethinking all issues* considered settled for us, by *Europe* in 1776 and 1789, and soon: lest we continue the precipitous slide into what promises to be an indefeasibly radioactive future.

31

East and West

Aeons ago, when I commenced my academic avocation, as an Assistant Professor at the then newly opened, and highly innovative, Jawaharlal Nehru University, in India, at the ripe, green, age of 21, I had, *sub rosa,* but one real intellectual 'quest': to discover the *'essential'* (I use the word advisedly) difference between the classically stereotyped duals of 'east' and 'west' (for those innocent of such *genre* of old hat, I commend Kipling's ringing, heroic, ballad, '*The Ballad of East and West*' that immortalizes that 'divide'). Only very recently, about 2007, did I finally put it all together. Yes, it is true: I, now, have found—if to my own satisfaction!—The Unholy Grail. If there were false starts, and mis-steps, along the way I am unaware of them, since I feel I had my eye on the 'prize' from the start.

But, there was a certain streak of Brahmin perfectionism (much is made of the Protestant Ethic: but it pales, like a lover's face in moonlight, before its sovereign Brahmin predecessor) that wanted every Argument to be in place before I announced it to the world. This I did, on January 4, 2007, at my (previously mentioned) *Festschrift* at the Chicago Meetings of the American Economic Association.

My book *Against Eurocentrism* (Kanth, 2005), but, more so, my follow-up Book, *The Challenge of Eurocentrism* (Kanth, 2009) spells out the Theses in much detail. I had doled out bits and pieces of the *Argument*, at various invited gatherings, but given that most at such events were Economists, the ideas, likely, went over/past all but a handful. At more mixed public gatherings, there was enthusiasm, but I was not always sure of genuine comprehension.

My very early correspondent friends (and I have really been blessed with the best)—the late Robert Heilbroner and Paul Sweezy; Noam Chomsky, and Roger Owen—probably got what I was driving at: but maintained a certain (necessary?) discretion *vis-à-vis* my ideas. Immanuel Wallerstein also read bits of my work (commending it publicly, if cautiously). I had met the late Roy Bhaskar early on (in Oxford in 1987) and liked him and his work; but it was apparent (at least to *moi*) that my own ideas were heading in quite another direction (though his later work it is said, may run at least tangentially close).

However, the one I made acquaintance with, very late in his short life, the inimitable Paul Feyerabend, was hewed of another clay. If the above were all canonical saints, he towered over them like a god. In him, and his work (for the twain were the same), I found a near-*Total Resonance*. I still treasure his beautifully handwritten epistle, but a few months before his tragic passing, bemoaning the fact that only a few really understood where this chaotic Age of ours was headed.

I must not omit Vandana Shiva who helped, like Feyerabend, to foster a critical attitude toward *scientism*. Shiva and Maria Mies (like their own predecessor, De Beauvoir) also emboldened my latent *Feminism*—and, importantly, brought its intimate connection with *Nature* into play. I must mention Edward Said and Gayatri Spivak, also: though with them it was ever a feeling of travelling along parallel tracks, if not within the same Arena. David Bohm and Krishnamurti also helped in strengthening my convictions, though I found the former by far the more insightful one, with his brilliantly discursive style of open discussion.

Just when I thought all the ducks were, at last, in a neat row—no, not to be shot at, but to be admired as a formation—I ran into the lone work of Amit Goswami (now quite a cult hero) that patched the very last pieces on to the evolving tapestry. He is, I think, amongst the most gifted of contemporary physicists (and, also, happily, likes my work).

Other than Heilbroner and Sweezy (though they were anything but conventional economists), I have not mentioned 'economists' in this story, owing to the simple fact that economics is a barren, sterile, and axiomatic, discourse that needs be wholly overhauled, if one is to further an understanding of the human condition.

If Economics is to be vindicated as a discipline that yields any usable fruit, I can only think of Ravi Batra's brilliant '*The Myth Of Free Trade*' work, which patiently, and with painstaking gathering of data, indefeasibly disables the very Greatest Myth of Classical Economics. The only other Project I am aware of, of finally, after two long centuries of vacuous fantasizing, attempting to place the subject on some minimal kind of an *empirical* foundation (if only in text-book form) is the work being pioneered, under the stewardship of Neva Goodwin at the GDAE (Tufts).

Now, I have saved mention of Classic, Canonical, scholars, who did not jump on the Modernist bandwagon, to the last. I will single out but a few: F. Nietzsche, S. Kierkegaarde and C. Jung on the Continent; and J. Ruskin, W. Carlyle, W. Wordworth, R. Southey, and O. Goldsmith in England, were grappling with issues whose unravelment helps unmask many, if not all, of the High Pretenses of Modernism.

On the India side to this, I must mention the bejeweled tradition of *Vedic* Ideas (which so influenced Spinoza, Nietzsche, Schopenhaeur, Emerson, Jung, *et al.*), as distilled by Adi Shankara, and including its Greatest Critic: Siddhartha, the Buddha. Many were the laden nights that I listened, in awe (in translated audio text)—at their prismatic insights into the Human Dilemma. Closer to our times, Vivekananda and Gandhi, who straddled the awkward gap between Tradition and Modernity—if, in different ways—helped me think through many issues that are part of the narrative of a distinguished, but rather convoluted, Vedic lineage.

Now let me state a very important axiomatic of *Eurocentrism* (and many named above are wholly within a Eurocentric paradigm, though they are all, *à la* Shakespeare, honorable men and women): *it simply will not allow perspectives outside of its Universe. In effect, and in all irony, the 'Other' is compelled to borrow, even its very Critique of Eurocentrism, from European thought, if it is to get a hearing*!! Only the 'loyal opposition' is granted play: if one dares to 'break' with European ideas altogether, one is dismissed as, the ultimate insult!, a *'Nativist.'* Well, I have 'broken with the Enlightenment': and I am wholly at ease with name-calling (*believe me, and I know: it doesn't stop with name-calling…*), of any kind.

❊

The 'East-West' dichotomy is, in this context, a rather bland misnomer. The 'difference,' today, really, is between Tradition (in this case *Late Tradition*) and *Late (Euro)Modernity*. Europe suffered its Modernist Revolutions, long prior to the antic Civilisations of Asia, who, with the possible exception of Japan, received 'Modernity' only *via* the rigors of Colonial Conquest. The latter: India, China (and its early periphery of Japan, Korea and Vietnam), Persia, the Mediterranean, and much of West Asia (in the Tigris-Euphrates area)—I omit Egypt from the Mediterranean clutch since its civilization did not endure into Modern times—were, unmistakably, highly *evolved* societies in relation to Northern Europe.

Northern Europe, largely unaccomplished in the material and civil arts (save Warfare) conquered the Mediterranean first (the 'Crusades'), and assimilated its original cultures into itself, even claiming putative descent from it (the so-called 'Renaissance'). Next, it subdued the native peoples of North and South America. Then, it turned to Asia, Australia, and Africa: and ransacked as much of those spaces as it could. Its own brand of Modernism was then imposed, as if its various extractions were not enough: on culture after culture.

Regrettably, there is a Gresham's Law of Civilizations: the less evolved tend to overrun the more evolved—the 'Barbarians at the Gate,' of the Other, were Europeans.

How were they able to do so, even granting 'advantages' of cannon and chicanery (of course one can hardly belittle these devices: EuroModern despotism was built upon outrageous fraud—*indeed, EuroModernists, are arguably, the Greatest Deceivers of All Time*—of which the latter-day WMD ploy is only a trivially abject example. Of course, their hegemony was always buttressed by the—now openly confessed- doctrine of outright, and permanent, Military Supremacy)? Civilization, or the lack of it, provides the clue. Why is it that India and China lay next to each other, more or less peaceably, for centuries—whereas Europeans past (and present) could not go through even a century without fierce warfare?

The ravening European hungered, and thirsted, far more than his 'Eastern' cousins: was ready to leave 'home' and spend lifetimes—nay, generations—in distal, inhospitable foreign shores, seeking the most humdrum manna, the drabbest mess of pottage, of the mundane earth: because His own *Locus,* His Native Lands, were so very devoid of such fare. So, the very mastery of the civilized arts, in India and China, limited their appetites for, and any tendency to, sustained, long term 'adventurism.' I am reminded, to digress but a little, of the Last Mogul, the indolent Bahadur Shah, who continued to scribe his beloved love poems, despite being made aware that the Brits were on the march to lay siege to his demesne in Delhi. Silly, isn't it? Or, is it?

Similarly, the many Indian tribal chiefs that stoutly resisted the British, when not militarily vanquished, threw in the towel all too prematurely, anxious to return to convivial enjoyments: only the hapless, stolid, steadfast, British trooper, joyless, visionless, far from home and hearth, with only duty and booty (*i.e.,* cupidity merged with stupidity) in mind—in other words, already a zombie—stood everready in the mid-day sun, to die, in any dirty ditch, for the Crown, as required by Orders from above, and so, eventually, prevailed.

European barbarism, relatively speaking, provoked their own fitful Exodus: Asiatic civilization, au contraire, restrained such impulses, for the most part. But this, though true, is question-begging. Did the 'wanderlust' of the European really arise solely from the putative 'paucity' of their resources? Not entirely; for then, *mutatis mutandis,* one might think, all Aboriginals would have, similarly, rushed out to conquer us all.

So, it was a species of critical *metaphysical change(s)* that produced this miasma of 'discontent' (that has not left them yet!). Modernism (as I define it) is the encompassing term I designate that covers that fateful orientation and outlook. I have defined the concomitants of this process elsewhere (in Works cited in the References below) so I won't repeat it here.

Suffice it to say, that this was the First Break of Humankind from its own long-standing 'species-being.' All the 'normal' polarities of anthropic society were soon overturned, or reversed. Individuated, and anti-social, Greed, perforce, led the way into an everlasting, seething Ocean of Discontent (like Midas, they didn't anticipate the inevitable). There was so much to be pirated and purloined, they discovered—during their contact with the more opulent world during the Crusades—if only they didn't have their own selves as obstacles! Thus did the *nouvelle* European 'states' (a state being simply a permanent camp of armed men who claim monopoly over a stretch of land, and its unfortunate populace): Spain, Portugal, Netherlands, France, and England, amongst others, battle each other for supremacy.

The Wolves were extirpating each other—for the right to be sole Ruler of the Lambs that lay Without.

Many 'sciences,' and 'technologies,' were fine-tuned by this deathly serious competition. Ideologies that held them back, like the Traditionalist notions of the Catholic Church—the Laws against Usury, or the notion of *justum pretium*—were gruffly set aside (*i.e.,* the 'Reformation'). Societal obligations that limited the rights of these new 'merchant-prince-pirate-plunderers' were swiftly snuffed out (the Enclosure Movement, the Poor Laws, the various Statutes that manacled laborers). Of course, every such capitulation to the calculus of greed was preceded by a noble, if dissembling, declaration (Malthus, *e.g.,* argued against welfare subsidies saying they were too 'patronising,' and 'paternalist,' an affront to the dignity of the laborer!) of *high principle.*

Thus were Asia and Africa conquered, if one is to believe this bilge, as a form of 'upliftment' for their own benefit: such was the touted 'civilization-mongering' norm within the casuistry of the ideology of the 'White Man's Burden.' Similarly, Chinese coastal cities were shelled into submission only so they could be welcomed into the civilizing world of *'free trade'*—in opium, no less. Today, the rickety old 'Human Rights' claptrap is deployed in much the same way, and spurred on by the same nefarious intent. The domestic societal cost, within

Europe, was horrific, the flip side of the casual genocide inflicted on much of the Non-European world.

Family ties, tribal ties, community ties, were all rudely sundered (to the everlasting distress of the subaltern orders). Desolation, alienation, and *anomie*, rose as defining attributes of the 'West' (and remain so to this day). Oliver Goldsmith's wrenchingly plaintive '*The Deserted Village*' poem touches upon it all, in inimitable cadences. The European, severed from the healing hospitalities of anthropic life—family, community, tribe—became, in large numbers, and for the most part, a rather wretched creature: cheerless, restless, and rootless. Minus the pumps of sugar, caffeine, and alcohol—or worse—he remains that still, mired in various modalities of existential *angst*.

Now Greed, and its Object—an equally asocial, profit-led-*Productivism-cum-Consumerism*—took over Life itself: not as means to an end, but as Ends in themselves. The filigreed, multi-faceted, richness of societal life was thus reduced to the dull abasement of producing and consuming, at cost to all, of the simple felicities of *Being*, and *Living*—in a degrading Libel on the Human Race! 'Ill fares the land, to hastening ills a prey, where wealth accumulates and men decay': so intoned the moving dirge of Goldsmith dedicated to that process.

Drugs, drug-wars, senseless mass-shootings, species destruction, ecological degradation, nuclear contagion, toxification of nature's troves, pesticide contamination, food crop spoliation—the monotonic cadences run on. Yes. For they all add up to that humming, hi-octane, world of ever-augmenting GDP the North Atlantics are so inveterately proud of.

❃

This unwholesome *European Way* was adopted wholesale by its rebel progeny: North America—which was to lead the world to a new, even higher (or is it lower?) climacteric in these regards. *I have said that Modernism, as I define it, was history's First Break with the norms of Anthropic Society.* But North America concluded a *Second Break*, which was even more final—in its Breach of Human Civilities.

Up until recent times, and for millennia, we '*homo sapiens*' have known but *two* dominant societal norms: *Morality and Immorality*. Anthropic societies are, *primarily—like the human family—Moral Entities.* But America led us into *Late Modernism, the Second Break,* by initiating, virtually singly, a new nadir of devolution: the oxymoronic, *Amoral Society*.

EuroModernism triumphed by deracinating Communal obligations, and a host of interdependencies, that marked the 'social compact' of pre-Modern Europe, across the board. Late Modernism, in motion since about the period of Reagan-Thatcher, for its part, turns and twists the knife, this time, upon its own corpus: cannibalizing itself by undermining its own ontic bases (economic and societal infrastructures)—and, as such, is little other than an inglorious suicide mission.

Now, the Moral and the Immoral presume each other, limit each other. But the 'Amoral' is a brand new vista of utter *normlessness*. The *only limit* to any societal disorder within the *Amoral Regime*—cupidity, violence, chicanery—is the Law alone (rather than moral regard or ethical norms). Small wonder that 94% of the world's lawsuits are filed in America. And the peace is kept, and broken, by naked armed force: more guns, and more gun deaths, than any society on earth. And more people, *percent*, incarcerated (a fact lately turned even more hypertrophic—to feed the profits of a privatized prison-commercial complex). Is this, at all, an Anthropic, *i.e.*, a *human*, society, held in check, as it is, only by mutual terror?

Traditional Societies are based, like the anthropic family, on a '*Balance of Affections*' (take any Native American tribe, *e.g.*). Euro-Modernist 'societies,' in Emergent Modernism, were/are held together by a '*Balance of Interests*' (the so-called 'Civil Society' of 'universal egoism,' where each sees the other as a means only to some private advantage, and where, famously, 'Hell is Other People'). But Late Modernist 'societies' are 'held,' if at all!, only by mutual intimidation, or a '*Balance of Terror.*' The emergent, permanent, *Security State* (droning, surveillance, profiling, *etc.*) being exported globally today, is chillingly emblematic of that new, apocalyptic *genre*.

❊

So now we know why Europe 'pulled ahead' (though the merit to such 'gain' is, clearly, to be questioned). It stood ready to do *any*thing for material gain (Slavery, Fracking, *et al.*). It was ready, also, to inflict *any* quantum of violence to achieve its *Ends* of mastery (Hiroshima, Nagasaki, *etc.*).

I will give but one antic, counter-example, to illustrate by contrast. Anyone familiar with ancient Vedic Classics, in everything from Science to Metaphysics, cannot help being struck by the fact that the *Knowledge Quantum* existed thousands of years ago, in the Indus Valley region, to lead an inexorable drive to amassing vast material wealth. But they did *not* take that route: it was a sort of societal, metaphysical, 'choice.' They were 'rich enough' (and a lot richer, by far, than pre-Modern Europe): and that was enough. That mode of Materialism, that was to overwhelm Europe, was *Not* found to be in favor.

Sanatana Dharma (or Vedic theosophy) assigns the commercial sphere exclusively to one Caste, so as—perhaps—to limit, and localize, its corrosive impact. China, on the *autre* hand, pursued *technology* far more vigorously than India (whence their ancient 'lead' in technologies over other societies)—Confucianism was far more pragmatic than Brahmin Idealism—but they, too, did not encourage, rampant, runaway, wealth-seeking. Yet, today, the entire gamut of North Atlantic societies (yes: the precocious American Child has assiduously 'fathered' the European Man) are ready to colonize the Moon, and Mars, if need be, to fill the deepening voids of its own tragic emptiness.

I have used metaphors to capture this vital 'difference.' *Since the sixteenth century, Modernist Europe gave up its natural 'Mammalian' heritage, to adopt increasingly 'Reptilian' traits.* So, the current, global, 'war' is between the Mammals and the Reptiles (no offense to either species): between the grimly cold calculators of material advantage, and the more warm-blooded, emotive, custodians of their, much simpler, domestic weal.

Take the BRICS, *e.g.,* and compare them to the G7. How do they differ? Very, very, importantly. *The BRICS are uninterested in Hegemony (or 'full spectrum dominance.'). They are not ready to risk genocide, or mass annihilation of our species, to achieve their socio-economic ends.* But can we not object, *e.g.,* and say that, surely, India, China, Russia *et al.*, are all now *en route* to the same Valhalla of reckless Marketization, and Globalization, as in the West?

Fair question, but one that begs the prior query: for who were the Comity of Nations that conspired, for decades, to force them, kicking and screaming, into that unfamiliar compass, using every means, fair and foul? Yet, despite all that, they are still *not* akin to the West—as yet!—on the *Two Vital Parameters* noted above. They are still 'Satisficers' in the Profiteering Game, not insensate Maximisers. And they still cling to the quaint old nostrums of Morality and Immorality. In other words they are still, despite their enforced marketization, *anthropic* societies.

Civilization forbids. Russia recently passed a Law that prohibits swear-words in the public media. You can guess where the loud howls of protest came from: yes, it was from the G-7. *After all Milan Kundera fled ('defected') to the West, and was duly received as a Culture Hero, to gain the inalienable right—yes—to pen porn.* It's the one, obviously vital!, higher-order, 'freedom' that even western security states do not care to tamper with.

✳

It is time now to sum up, in *précis* form, the difference, between 'east' and 'west,' or rather between the Late Modernists and the *Late Traditionalist-turned-Ambivalent Modernists.* The European, bereft of even the bare material artifacts of comfort and convenience (*i.e.,* 'civilization'), beginning in the sixteenth century, swept across the globe like a holocaust, plundering, pillaging, and expropriating. This catapulted that *Sub*-Continent (*no, Europe is Not a continent*—that being a usage inspired only by their smug '*apartheid*'—but a rather small part of the landmass of *Eurasia*), materially, above a world much of which, like India and China, was far and away ahead of them in virtually all regards.

In this process, the European shed vital anthropic traits, one by one, dissipating the precious, rarefied qualities of societal life, in favor of cumulatively possessive quantitative cravings. Family and Community—and its binding forces, such as kinship and kindred—fell prey early on: so *He* (*I use the Masculine Voice, since Women remain the 'Other,' in All such matters of Empire and Power*) increasingly subsisted in a sordid moral vacuum, isolated, forlorn, and 'alienated.' When aware of such deprivations at all, he sought to, desperately, recreate these Lost Affinities, in hapless 'modernist' fashion, *via* wan Utopian Cravings—such as 'Communism'—as mark the *cri de cœur* works from More to Marx, including the short-lived vintage of the 'Noble Savage' idiom.

Speaking metaphorically, having '*left home*'—*i.e.,* the matrix of kin and kindred, the only sanctuary of bliss that anthropic life affords us all, high or low—he looked everywhere (and still does), in all the wrong places, and in vain, for the 'paradise lost.' Nietzche, Kierkegaard, Goethe, and German Romanticism, like Russian Romanticism, (Pushkin, Tolstoy, *et al.*), both nations being late comers to Marketization, bemoaned the Great Bereavement, as philosophers can and do, in powerful works that are still resonant. Carlyle and Ruskin, Blake, and Southey, did much the same in England, if in the form of 'voices in the wilderness.'

But, for the most part—and this is important—*He* embraced his own wretched *anomie,* wore it proudly like an ornament, and a badge of a higher attainment, and projected his 'loss' and 'discontent' *externally* in malevolence, misanthropy, and misogyny: content only when razing culture and civilization wherever he encountered it—'leveling' the world, in grim satisfaction, in his own, unhappy, morose, image (*and serving as a living testament, en passant, to the Marxian idea that the 'bourgeois' have no values—save that of deriding all values*).

At any rate, the Non-European world was uprooted: and turned into that pathetic morass of wretchedness that were then contemptuously titled the '*third world,*' by the very grandees that willfully and ruthlessly manufactured, by brute force, that staple brand of societal tragedy. Europe created, *via* classical Colonialism, not 'poverty'—which is a relative term—but acute, and real, *deprivation,* globally: its own enrichment being directly proportionate to the havoc wreaked on the 'Other.' The wretchedness that still litters much of Africa, at its base, is of

European origin, much as the demoralization of 'Native Americans,' a continent away: they forcibly broke the natural rhythms of tribal life and tribal ecology, to feed their extortions.

Slavery, genocide, and civilizational destruction: these are the momenta of Modern Europe's Great Ascent. India, arguably the wealthiest civilization on the globe in the sixteenth century, using Europe's own misguided yardsticks (though far richer than even that within its own civilizational scales), was calmly and rationally looted and shattered, reduced to being, within two centuries of British—or shall I say '*Brutish*'?—barbarism, for a while, the world's most successful beggar (and one might, equivalently, guess who the *world's most successful thief* is—or was).

Sixty years after a nominal independence, today, it is finding its own footholds again as a solid, senior, member of the BRICS configuration, albeit still working within the given Rules of the Game of its former Oppressors. So what, or where, is the *Critical Divide? It lies in the Blanket Philosophy of Materialism that Europe adopted, covering ALL social spaces: science, philosophy, religion, morality, and culture. (Euro)Modernism is built upon Materialism: it deploys a materialist science to advance an economy and society driven/riven by materialist values, using illimitable material force, as needed, to further its insatiable materialist ambitions.*

Sadly, EuroModernism is Wrong on All epistemic scores: categorically misleading in its Science (latter-day Physics defies much of Classical Physics), False in its Metaphysics (Newtonian Materialism is unsustainable by today's scientific discoveries, its 'Determinist' world now replaced by a 'Probabilistic' world), and ever so hopelessly barren, and denuded of amity, convenance, and grace, in its Amorality. And all of Traditional—tribal—society stands, as it has always stood, in Grand Negation of virtually every canon of that tawdry Enterprise.

In consequence, the Late Traditionalists (largely *Non*-Europeans), deep within their psyches, remain closer to their anthropic *geist:* and thereby are, relatively speaking, more stable, more centered, more concrete, less abstract, less alienated, less anomic, more affective, more emotive, more contextual, more *whole*—than their average EuroModernist counterparts.

These key differences of 'temperament'—*not all of which necessarily produce virtuous outcomes*—are *not* inconsequential, but have a decisive impact on epistemic orientations and ontic practices. Stated starkly: the world is safely left in the hands of a Masai—not so in the hands of a NATO General, a Corporate CEO, or a D.C. Beltway Politician. The disembodied, cool, calculating 'rationality' of the EuroModernist has, and has had, its uses in various contexts: but, in Late Modernism, its utility is wholly eclipsed by its strident penchant for stark robotization of human traits, turning flesh-and-blood humans into mechanized automatons, 'living by the book,' knowing little other than 'the book,' and bereft of any and all creative imaginations that transcend the 'for-profit-market-nexus.'

At any rate, returning to metaphysics, *Human Subjectivity*, far from being an odd, even anomalous, reflex of barren matter, as in Classical Physics, stands instead, now, owing to Quantum science, at the very Epicenter of our otherwise inscrutable cosmic reality. As Goswami (Amit Goswami) puts it, we live, ineluctably, in a '*Self-Aware*' Universe: to which I add—and a '*Self-Fulfilling*' one, as well. It may be recalled that European Social Science, at its early inception, was wholly dominated by '*Physics-envy,*' (*i.e.,* of the Classical Newtonian paradigm) and needs, now, to be suitably expurgated.

And the non-European World, though increasingly cast (not by any accident, but by the fact that the world is dominated by the West) in that same recreant, EuroModernist, image, is still not entirely 'emancipated' from its own 'traditionalist' value structures: and this applies, even now, in the twenty-first century, to virtually all of Africa, Asia, and South America. Thus are the Mammals yet set apart from the Reptiles.

And thus is Late Modernist Barbarism, entirely European in provenance, yet checked by the admittedly fading premises of a Traditionalist civilizational genius still residing in the *Other*: that, for all its own undeniable, internal, petty, brutalities, cruelties, and infelicities, which I do not mitigate, has never threatened with extinction, willfully nor inadvertently—indeed, not even in its wildest dreams—the essential, and enduring, hospitalities (such as they are) of our transient, planetary home, their ambitions and joys, even predations, being, ever, wholly local, in origin and impact.

All other despotisms—and Masculinity ensures, universally, a none-too-benign outcome whenever, and wherever, it runs amok—left both Society and Nature Untouched: it was the North Atlantic's 'Manifest Destiny' to disrupt (let us hope not irreversibly) the normal functioning of both—and in record time.

Those who wish to, and stand ever ready to, press that nuclear button, past and present, are firmly, and irrefragably, of the amoral, Late Modernist, ilk. The sad truth is that anthropic existence is, even at best, tenuous and transitory, leaving very little to be cheerily glorified: and yet, a small part of the human populace has put even that minimal boon, of the baseline survival of *all* species, at risk—*via* its demonic zeal for unceasing surplus extraction from both society and nature.

It is EuroModernist values, or, perhaps, its striking *dearth of anthropic values!*, that benumbs us today—like a miasma hanging over all—with a universally felt apocalyptic fear: of encroaching, impending, Doom. Tragedy is that there is no *external* force powerful enough to halt its runaway chariot: yet, ironically, its tumultuous reign may yet expire, and in the none too distal future, owing to the giddy overreach of its own titanic, if truantly ill-conceived, eco-political ambitions.

It is, in other words, as already hinted, providentially, *Self-subverting.*
Sic transit infamia mundi.

32

And There Was Blight

Summary Notes on the European Saga

Anthropology was simply the Study of Non-Europeans by Europeans, as prelude to Conquest. Later, Europe taught carefully inducted Non-Europeans to 'study themselves,' deploying European lenses. But the time may be ripe now for some due Correction, which I term 'reverse anthropology.' Its import will be understood in the reading of this very short 'Cross-over' Note, intended for the lay and scholarly reader, but not for the faint-hearted in either camp, on an important subject.

A necessary caveat: this Note takes aim at the dispositions of the past-present governing elites of Europe-America; the governed, though occasionally beneficiaries of their policies, cannot be seen as responsible for them (nor are East Europeans included since, for the most part, they, like Chayanovian peasants 'exploited themselves,' rather than cruised the globe seeking manna.). Also, I present suggestive ideas only, and will not defend them as infallible. I do think that they are, right or wrong, serious Arguments—to be taken seriously, by the serious. Of course, I exaggerate the 'reverse' anthropology feint: for the civilized may not stoop, and Truth is reparation enough.

❄

It is possibly the single most astonishing fact of its kind, in social history, past or present, of the human species. Even more breathtaking is the allied fact of its *near-absence*, as an important issue, within social discourse, of the more official kind. I will explain what I am referring to, shortly. But, let me commence this gradual unravelment, firstly, on a personal note. Science prefers us not to be *ad hominem*, and yet, as a hominid, this may be not an impossible so much as an unreasonable requirement.

I happen to think one can be *factual,* and still remain *'personal'* in one's 'scientific' pronouncements. As the late C. Wright Mills once wrote, with much dignity: *'I have tried to be objective, I do not claim to be detached.'* At any rate, I am somewhat 'personally engaged' with the subject-matter of this Note, as will become apparent: and I can only hope that such an 'involvement' does not prejudice the content of the latter—in terms of its truth-value.

On a trip to New Orleans, years ago, *en route* to yet another disheartening Economics Conference (which I attend not for its economics but for its incidental felicity of gathering people in one place that I might wish to meet), I encountered a Haitian taxi-driver who spoke of matters that are, *en générale*, not associated with cab-drivers, leastways in the US. Looking into the reflector mirror, he asked me where I was from. I said India, and he kept quiet for a minute. Then he said, with a thin half-smile, 'then we are brothers.'

Where are you from? I asked, interested in identifying the basis of the kinship being alluded to. Haiti, he said. I settled back in the seat, my mind running over the many crises of that unfortunate nation. India, and Haiti. I pondered the common ground between these far-flung societies. He cut short my thinking. *The European messed us both,* he said, *forever.* I felt then, as I do now, that he had offered an avenue of thought that could occupy a dozen Conferences—somewhat more appealing, perhaps, than the Conference I was going to that prized itself on its superior knowledge of R-Squares and Beta-Coefficients.

❋

I have mused on his comments since then, off and on. *The tragedy of Haiti is emblematic of the Tragedy of Innumerable Non-European Spaces trampled on, with impunity, by (past and present) European presences.* And yet the matter is not always understood as one pertaining to the specifics of a *human 'tribe' within an essentially tribal history of humankind.*

Social Science reifies, and abstracts: Colonialism and Imperialism, *e.g.,* or, Commercial Capital and Financial Capital; Or, Capitalism and Feudalism. I myself, in not dissimilar vein, have written of Modernism, Tradition, *etc.* That is to say, analytical concepts often, howsoever unintentionally, abstract away the palpable human-societal entities underlying the notions.

Human agency cannot always be thus absolved. So, blaming 'Capitalism' for this or that societal evil, as is often the case, *omits direct reference to the actual groups/individuals that have to, in the end, 'choose' one action over another.* When a worker gets laid off in a cyclical downturn, it is not *'capitalism'* that let him/her go: it is a specific capitalist employer, with a name, that did so. *The 'morality of choice' is an inexpugnable issue.* I could say 'Colonialism pillaged India': or I could equally validly say that very canny, identifiable bands of *'white,' English, Governors* personally, and willfully, saw to the organized theft of resources And at times, reality is better unmasked when it is located simply, stripped of the cover of such abstracting nouns.

What if we understood Western history, First Millennium onward, instead, as a *free-for-all,* given a Latin Rome in decline, between various *European Tribes* (later to graduate to so-called 'nationhood'): Angles, Saxons, Celts, Gauls, Normans, Franks, in one cut—Slavs, Bulgars, Huns, Avars and Alans, in another, to but name some important ones? And, if we also omitted a few other Eco-Political *'isms,'* then we could say, matter-of-factly, that the *Angle-Saxon Tribe* wantonly invaded North America, vanquishing pre-existing Native American tribal societies in their wake [of course, the term 'Anglo-Saxon' deserves some explication. Angles and Saxons were Germanic tribes who invaded England fifth century C.E. onwards, only to be subdued in turn by the Norman Conquests of the eleventh century. So, a more accurate appellation might be *'Anglo-Norman':* but in this *Note,* I am following a more customary usage]. Or, that the Spanish Tribe looted the Incas, and the Belgian Tribe ransacked African Tribes in the Congo, and so on (it's quite a long list, so I will pause there, for now).

I said *'Western History'*—as if it were all now safely removed to that omnibus, catchall, dumping site of the *past,* of the *bad old days* when, presumably, *'humankind,' as a whole, were All mean, cruel, and ignoble. After all, there is no dearth of war, murder, mayhem, plunder and pillage amongst the tribes of the Non-Europeans,* if one but glances, even casually, at their own uncharming histories. *Of course, we remind ourselves that History is, in such choice regards, entirely His Story.*

And we could also, naively, *imagine* that all that is over and done with now, given the presence, today, of International Law, the UN, Amnesty International, and, why not?: GPS.

Imagine!

※

But, I wish to pursue the ideas of my Haitian Taxi-Driver. His last comment before he dropped me off was, *'we would all be better off if Europe had never existed.'* Now, there's an interesting, even original, thought. And I would like to pursue it, simply, as a grand *thought-experiment.*

Let's glance first, superficially of course, at the *negatives* of such an *absence*. Just possibly: no underground, no railways, no airplanes, no cell phones, no automobiles, no flushing toilets, no microwaves, no electric lighting, no laptops—and, alas, no *crème brûlée*. On the *autre* hand, some equally clear *benefits*: no nuclear devices, no dropping of Nuclear Devices, no Cuban Missile Crisis style nuclear brinkmanship, no World Wars I and II, no Cold War, no Star Wars, no Modern-day Colonial Empires/Imperialism/Slavery, no Globalization, no Terminator Seeds, no GMO's, no TRIPS, no BGH, no MNC's, No World Bank, IMF and WTO, and no CIA, NSA, nor the Seventh Fleet.

So, the moral can hardly be escaped: the boons of Modernism may be swell—but are simply not cost-effective. Here, one must pause: given what we know of the European and non-European World, it is also evident that *we can be far more certain of the second set of absences than the first*; for, surely, Japan, India, and China, left alone, would have gotten to the basics of *latter-day* science and technology (they had their own sciences from Antiquity) on their very own. And Russia?: a conundrum: for are they European, or Asian? In fact, one can press this divide even further.

Why is Europe a 'Continent,' at all, for starters (because Europeans claimed it is so…)? Who, so anxious, or insecure, one might ask, as to 'separate' themselves from the 'Other,' by drawing an imaginary line within a continuous landmass? Surely, it was, thereby, the very First 'Gated Community'—holding off the Undesirables. The Berlin Wall (a tremendous Cold War boon to the West: *where is the universal outcry at the barbed wire 'Wall,' built by the hand of the free, to keep out the 'huddled masses' of Mexicans?*) may have fallen, but not so the less visible, but perhaps more permanent, if only imagined, Walls of a pre-conceived *Apartheid*.

Now Europe and Non-Europe are easily demarcated, but Russia presents a challenge. It covers both Continents in terms of land-mass and ethnicity. Suffice it to say that Western Europe treated it, until the Russian Revolution, as its economic colony; and most Anglo-American governors, to this day, have viewed it—*after the Revolution*—much like China, as a sort of a natural rival, if not an archenemy. This much can also be said: that in its adherence to international law, and its willingness to live within its borders, Post-Revolutionary Russia has always been far more *'Asian,'* unlike its European /Anglo-American counterparts, in tone and temper, than 'European.'

Even during this *Soviet* Era, its internal Asian Principalities largely gained at the expense (much like Cuba was a drain) of the Central Government and Western Russia, in the distribution of resources; so there can be no question of an *internal* Russian *'empire'* (nor an external one) *of an economic kind* (as apart from a *'political'* one), after the Socialist Revolution, despite staple, Western, Cold-War propaganda. So how does it all hang, on balance?

We shall return to this a bit later.

❄

To press on. Let's take a look at Europe, in the early centuries of the Current Era. There is the Latin Empire of Rome to the West. Celtic peoples, in Central and Western Europe. The Germanic tribes, Saxons, Jutes, Nordics, Vikings, Normans, Danes, and other Germanic tribes, Goths, Ostrogoths, Vandals, Angles, Saxons, Lombards, Frisi and Franks, toward the North. In Central and Eastern Europe, the other, equally fierce, nomadic tribes: Huns, Avars, Slavs, Bulgars, and Alans.

The Evolution of Modern Europe is the story of the Fall of Rome, the dispersion of the Celts, the maraudings of Germanic tribes, and similar depredations of the Eastern nomads, punctuated by Islamic forays after the seventh century—all to be followed by the all-eclipsing, apocalyptic finale of *European Expansion into every corner of the globe. Southern* Europe was a distinct part of a *Mediterranean Civilization,* itself a fusion of Greek, Roman, Egyptian, and Asian (India, China) influences *The pedigree of ideas runs, in terms of sheer antiquity, India and China to Egypt to Greece to Rome, and then centuries later, with Islamic additives, to Northern Europe—which, then, assimilates it all, to itself, as the 'Renaissance.'*

What can we say about *North* Europe, inclusive of England? Not a lot. Cold and, for the most part, inhospitable, and lacking a ready bounty of natural resources. And an aggressive *wanderlust,* perhaps in consequence?, captured well in *Beowulf*—and practiced, true to text, by the Vikings, Normans, Danes, and the other Germanic tribes. Piracy, pillage, and plunder was the effective language and currency of these Norsemen, who colonized England, Iceland, Greenland, and much of Northern Europe, even parts of North America (I was told, blandly, in Denmark, by learned scholars no less, that the Vikings were, 'first and foremost'—*nation-builders*).

North Europe became firmly linked to the South, during the Crusades, which provided the necessary *knowledge-links, via* the mercantile Latin City-States, for further expansionism. Once the lure of the Colonies turned into yet another choice avenue for competitive zealotry, they went looking for spoils, fighting each other like hyenas, in intermittent skirmishes, over the 'kill' of the hapless societies overrun by sheer military prowess and chicanery.

Whilst Britain was the ultimate, and supreme victor, in this tribal internecine struggle, there was, nonetheless, as much *colonial* space to be had, and *shared,* as force and guile permitted. *After all, the Non-European world was bigger, and richer, than the European one.* If Britain was the lion, which claimed the lion's share of the Non-European world, the hyenas and jackals of the Lesser Tribes had enough to feast on, and not merely left-overs. Thus did England, Holland, Germany, Portugal, France, Denmark, Belgium, and Spain, amongst others, ransack the globe creating the basic '*Division of Spoils*' that has marked the world indelibly ever since. Asia, Australia, the Americas, and Africa, all fell easy prey to their inveterate zeal.

The *Lands, Labor, and Resources,* pillaged from the four Continents made the European (including his now hypertrophic American protégé) the *Master of the World* He is today (gender emphasis intended). The truth is simple and stark: *minus* its original Non-European Colonial Empires, later to be vastly enhanced by further exploitative commercial, trading, industrial, and financial links, Europe, including its North American progeny, would be no more than a fair-size pygmy, culturally, economically, and politically, amongst the Comity of Continents—as it indeed was, prior to their intensely motivated 'explorations.'

No '*Renaissance*' (*i.e.*, *Northern Europe's* acquisition and revival of Mediterranean artifacts including Roman jurisprudence, Greek philosophy and culture, and an Islamic amalgam of ideas, amongst others); no '*Industrial Revolution,*' whose capital, labor, many techniques, and raw inputs came from the non-European Colonies (and its own eastern European ones); and no '*Enlightenment*' (spurred by its thoughtful mining of Arab, Persian, and Oriental, treasure trove of philosophical and scientific knowledge).

Now, I have spoken of the *Northern* European tribes *collectively,* given their joint status as the super-exploiters of the globe, but far and away is it *the Anglo-Saxon Tribe that must be singled out, from its Northern European Cousins, for having triumphed like no other tribe in history.* It occupied, by dint of enterprise and conquest, all of North America and Australia—and ruled over much of Asia, Latin America, and Africa as its own, private, Colonial Empire.

The later rise of its fateful American off-spring has given it, today, the *Greatest Empire in History*, albeit an Empire under definite challenge. *That we all speak English today, the world over, is but a small acknowledgment of its total hegemony.* Of course, this burgeoning empire was to be challenged by the (European) *Late Comers* to the Great Game of global exploitation, namely Germany, and Italy, and the one *Non-European* Power, Japan, *almost successfully*—were it not for the decisive military sacrifices of a Russia (*i.e.*, the *ex-Soviet Union*), decisively broken with its own imperial past *via* its own epochal Socialist Revolution.

China and Russia were the natural *'Other'* in relation to the European onslaught, and today are finally in position to resist Anglo-American hegemony, perhaps alongside their partners in the BRICS, decisively.

❄

To understand the extent of this cataclysmic *Fall from Glory,* necessarily accompanying the loss of Empire (that is, to understand the real penury of a *Capitalism without Empire*), one has only to examine the plight of Britain right after WWII: a crumbled, bankrupt, rag-poor nation kept afloat, like an abject welfare recipient, by its US cousineage, and its own continued stranglehold on Global Finance *via* the yet flourishing City of London. *So what was mighty Britain w/out her vaunted Empire? Minus* Empire, one might say the Great British Isles were stripped down to the rather unprepossessing *brutish* isles they always were, before their coffers were engorged by unholy Colonial loot.

Today, it is still the *City of London* that keeps Britain afloat, with its ever burgeoning financial scams, and the superordinating power of *finance* (*i.e.,* banking) capital at its disposal, richly enabling its hoary bilking of the world to continue with renewed vigor. Of course, its nuclear capability, and its deft piggy-backing on the broad US back earns it, even now, a quite disproportionate rent of respect in world affairs. It can only be much the same with the US, if, *par exemple,* the *Almighty Dollar* (which gives it a blank check on global resources) were to suddenly fall, if not unexpectedly, in this great *Age of Disorder.*

❄

I started this *Note* by alluding to an undefined 'astonishing' fact. Now, to lumber up to that. Imagine a circle of Late Modern philosophers solemnly pronouncing the *Equality of Men* (*sic*) whilst being served their afternoon teas, or mint juleps, by bonded *slaves.* Take pause, to digest this: *Slaves,* as late as in the *mid-nineteenth century,* generations after the American and, later, French 'Declaration of the Rights of Man, *etc.*' How's that for the high alembic of *'Euro-Modernist'* ideals? Or, observe when, or how late, the same set of worthies 'granted' *women* the most elementary right of suffrage; and how many decades later, one might ask, and after what sacrifices, did those 'freed' slaves gain *effective* rights on that very same score. Next, imagine a nation that prides herself a model *'Democracy,'* whilst retaining a *Hereditary Peerage* (92, of that feckless ilk, still sit in their Upper House), with full Parliamentary membership: and an entire coterie of parasitic *'royals,'* living off the commonwealth, one of whom is also the titular Head of State, not to mention the absurd pantomime of sundry 'lords' and 'ladies' strutting about, revisiting the abhorrences, proudly, of feudal rank and birth—in *the twenty-first century.* Useful to note, how many of the 'Germanic' states still follow this usage, albeit in far more modest and attenuated form.

Where, in contrast, are the Emperors of China, India, Japan, and Russia, today?

Or, imagine a tribe that drove the original, native peoples of North America—some 2000 or so tribes—to near-extinction, through a carefully planned *ecocide-cum-genocide*, whilst speaking glibly, and in exalted tones, of *liberty* and *self-determination* (and whilst loudly and piously condemning Cousin Hitler for his, not dissimilar, brand of depredations). Or, a tribe that left its brightest Empire in the East wantonly, and murderously, split viciously on religious grounds, a far cry from the way they found it when they first set foot there. Or, a tribe that denied *itself* the basic right of *Habeas Corpus*, aside from some of its other allied prerogatives, most recently, whilst claiming to be, no less, the 'Leader' of the '*Free World.*'

Or a tribe that has, since WWII, committed casual, but continuous *mass murder of Non-Europeans*, in Asia, East and West, *civilians in the main*, under the guise of making the world 'safe for democracy.' Indeed, this latter fact is so scandalous as to deserve strong enunciation: the bald truth is that, *White Men, of the various Eurotribes, have murdered Brown, Black, Red, and Other peoples indiscriminately, for centuries, under one guise, one pretext, or other, with wholesale impunity.*

This combined racist /imperial terror today brings all the *Euro-Tribes* together (shall we call them, to coin an acronym, NATO?) as they lay waste West Asia, and parts now of Africa, to secure resources vital to their wants. *Afghanistan is a living (or do I mean dying?) reminder of their conjoint tyranny in the twenty-first century, much as South Africa was the 'poster child' (!) of Classical European racism, circa late twentieth century.*

Now, let me offer a telling contrast: the *Manu Smriti* is an ancient Sanskrit document (of antiquity unknown) that lays down a *Code* (sort of a 'Declaration' in its own right) for *Vedic* society. But, it's brusquely iniquitous treatment of various subjects, especially women and the 'lower' castes, is all too painfully distressing (to the contemporary reader). *Yet is it, for all that, less disingenuous than the American and French Declarations, for I would wager that Vedic society, more or less, practiced the iniquity it preached.* This is far from trivial: even if it were true that ancient India and China had all manner of barbarisms (*viewed from a later/different lens*), they would still be far less *disingenuous*, on the whole, than the European—for the latter proposed lofty idylls ever so readily betrayed—especially in relation to women, native peoples, disadvantaged groups, and so on.

Another way of saying this is that *Modernism does not live up to its own ideals (and not judged within any 'outside' frame)*, whence the idea of a fairly consistent *Anglo-Saxon Proprietary Default in Public Policy*—then through now. *It raises, unavoidably, the issue of the good faith undergirding such lavish offerings.* In hindsight, it is not unreasonable to see such hyperbolic ideals as ruses, or *political formulas*, to buy off, co-opt, and defer, resistance on the part of the victims of their imposed policies. I have often thought that since *theory and practice*—especially in these times of the outright theft of the national exchequer by ruling elites—of 'democracy,' 'accountability' and the 'rule of law,' are so far apart from each other, that one simple way of 'closing the gap' might be to pass a *Hypocrisy Amendment* to the Constitution (and it's easy to pass any reactionary legislation today with near-100% support) that says, in just one line: *'All of the Foregoing may be taken to be pure Eyewash, with no bearing on the Rights and Entitlements extant of peoples in the real world.'*

Now that would restore a 'unity,' of sorts—and also render redundant the burden of this labored critique. At any rate, this *Vanguard European Tribe* invaded Imperial India, and turned that ill-fated sub-continent, the envy of the world for millennia, for its arts and crafts, industry, science, mathematics, and philosophy, within two centuries of planned fleecing, into a broken, *'third-world'* nation, with vast rural masses rendered redundant by imposed modernist land tenure–cum–confiscationary–tax systems, and left to rot in squalor as so much human offal (having bribed/cajoled the native rulers into co-operation).

Yet India has, nonetheless, gallantly, within but a few decades of a very *partial freedom* from their yoke, once again risen as a modest player in world affairs (Pakistan is still not recovered from the scars of its long spells of martial rule, duly assisted as it was in this deviation by the West in their decades long Cold War against the Soviets). It is this same tribe that set up an entire Southern Continent as a penal colony, driving its original inhabitants off their ancestral lands, and destroying their eons old culture and civilization.

To this day, where it goes, thither goes a very *late modernist* form of death, destruction and/or dissolution of one form or other—of culture, ecology, economy, or society. Of course, on the ashes of such havoc, it clones itself—like a virus—resuscitating the prostrate entity in its own image. *If it had its Will (as it pretty nearly did historically) every nation on earth would look like, and live like, it—sharing its own materialist monoculture—and, of course, be beholden to it.*

I am reminded of the famous English Colonial poem, by Henry Newbolt, entitled *'He Fell Among Thieves'* (yes, it may well take a Greater Thief to recognize the Lesser): Newbolt wouldn't have known it, but there is a certain poetic justice to a Global Thug (hung on his own petard) succumbing to a Local one. *No, it is not these facts that are astonishing: what is astonishing is the fact that Non-Europeans, to this day, have existed in a near-passive stupor, as but on-lookers—as this process goes on, even now, under the far newer 'entitlement' of Globalization.*

One way of dramatizing their infamous, yet undeniable, success is to recall the fact that, at any given time of their occupation of the India sub-continent, there were never more, perhaps, than a *hundred thousand* Brits actually available for empire-building (of course that includes the obligatory Celtic regiments that fought, loyally, for them). And yet, they had subdued a region where *millions* lived, with multiple opulent and entirely war-worthy kingdoms, who were never-theless all subjugated, or forced into unequal treaties. How is this to be explained?

⚛

The Anglo-Saxons distinguished themselves early on, beginning with the Cru-sades, as *formidable Warriors*. Yet their outstanding trait was not merely the *ability* to make war, but, more importantly, perhaps, the *willingness* to go to war. Both Russia and the US had the *ability* to make nuclear war, *e.g.*, during the so-called Cuban Missile Crisis: *but only the US was actually ready to push the button. A reck-less aggressiveness would therefore qualify as one of their prime characteristics.*

Now, the *Arts of War* also include *adroit chicanery* (parsed, more politely, as 'strategy') as well. The title of '*Perfidious Albion*' was likely a grim recognition, by their foes, of their mastery of deceit and guile in public affairs (the making and breaking of Treaties, and Covenants, willy-nilly). This, too, remains their very current idiom. The US, insouciantly, violates as many International Agreements as it makes—never letting mere rules stand between it and its interests. Britain, in its heyday, was no less devious and dissimulating.

Unbelievable valor/indomitable courage, obsessive, disciplined prosecution of a predetermined plan: these are, one would have to believe, Anglo-Saxon traits to a very high degree. The emergent *military technology* was but an (necessary) *adjunct* to those traits: and this is important to fathom. Usually, European conquests are explained away by Modernist historians as simply reflecting the objective tri-umph of their *technological* superiority. Not entirely true—because *it is in fact their primal aggressiveness that produced such technologies in the first place:* to make the point, the US is the largest military force in the world today simply because *it dearly wished/wishes to be so.*

Had Russia or China ever sought such a unilateral hegemony, they could easily be there themselves. *So, in effect, the Anglo-Americans gained military pre-eminence since they sought it so very relentlessly.*

This is instructive.

But the record of European (mis)adventurism in the non-European World is not explained simply by that remarkable passion for overwhelmingly indiscriminate, and gratuitous, violence. Giving this passion, the further fire of rabid motivation was the later additive of the *Litany of Greed Unbounded,* that the Angle-Saxon made his very own staple. Colonization was not driven by a vainglorious desire for world domination, but rather fuelled by that deep, brooding satyr-like hunger for riches. This Mercantile gambler's craving *to get something for nothing,* wherever, whenever possible is yet inscribed deep within their psyches. *One might usefully say that, in some sense the Anglo-Saxon governor, at heart, has never stopped being a pirate. Now, to put it all together: an irascible, restless, fearless, valorous aggressiveness, combined, later in their evolution, with an inexorable Midas-Mania, is what marked out the Anglo-Saxon for that special destiny amongst the European tribes.*

None of the other Euro-tribes, in effect, could muster up quite that high degree of intensity in either trait, despite their sharing those qualities, if in lesser measure.

And so, They Lead: where all Others merely follow.

And this helps clear up the matter of their taking of the Indian sub-continent, despite weakness of numbers. India had its own tribes, *e.g.,* Rajputs, Sikhs, Marathas, *etc.,* even braver, perhaps, than the English: but they utterly lacked the canny calculations of 'rational' political economy to prevail *in the long haul. They might win the occasional battle, but not the War.* Successful war is not merely valor and equipment, but canny economies and planning as well. *Indian tribal Rulers offered fierce resistance, but sans any extended staying power of Will, being ever anxious to return, as quickly as possible, to 'normalcy'—and the accustomed joys of excess living.* The idea of *permanent sacrifice,* across decades, maybe even generations, was a notion quite foreign to their extravagant tempers.

One more Anglo-Saxon trait must be mentioned, though perhaps more applicable to *civilian* life: their pedestrian, prosaic passion for *Order,* and *Legality.* I have had many Colonial relics of the Old Raj still express regret at the British departure from India, on these grounds. The Brits delivered not *justice* in India (and couldn't, obviously, as Conquerors), but did offer more than a semblance of Order, and Legality. Of course, 'order and legality' may appear hidebound, even grotesque, when they are but the willful instruments for the delivery of *injustice,* as they were under British rule; yet, nonetheless they made for a certain *explicitness of rules* that is grist to the mill of the rational mind that values, prudently, *predictability* over other felicities.

This ran, however directly contrary to the spirit of 'creative anarchy' that informs the genius of the Indian psyche (which is why legality and order, of the formal kind, are still, even today, a touch-and-go affair in everyday life in India: where an *inclination to riot* is palpably ever-present) but was warmly welcomed by the *professional* classes (who were, of course, largely trained by them). *The Anglo-Saxon does not live by rules*: but rather *governs/misgoverns via* the *instrument* of rules and regulations that can be ignored, applied, deferred, misapplied—*as statecraft demands. There is, in effect, a real passion for (due) process that trumps any inclination toward substantive justice.* At any rate, the English prevailed, in the Sub-Continent, by the sheer pig-headed doggedness of ingrained *discipline,* and *sang-froid. Stated simply, mere Satisficers can never hope, perhaps, to overcome the sustained zealotry of inveterate Maximisers.*

This is a vital point. Culture is a series of *'choices'* that order possible societal values in a unique way. The materialism/aggression of the Anglo-Saxon is as much part of his cultural endowment, as being other-worldly/sybaritic, in the main, is part of, say, the ancient Brahmin-Hindu tradition. To put it another way: anyone who has read Vedic science and mathematics is instantly made aware that ancient India could have gone straight into the sort of 'technological revolution' that Europe embraced—long before Europe.

But it didn't. The *'choice'* was made not to expand material indices. The choice was also made not to convert science into 'pay-off' technologies, on any appreciable, far-reaching, scale. But, *au contraire,* Science, in the European tradition, was ever quickly 'cashed in'—a trait that still epitomizes the European Way. Science was a willing handmaid of the *desire* to amass wealth and conquer, in Europe. It is super-abundantly clear that this is *not* how knowledge functioned in India or China. The 'enlightenment' of the noble Siddhartha is cut of a very different cloth than the 'enlightenment' of the European.

A la Adam Smith, the newly 'self-aware' (*i.e.,* 'enlightened') Anglo-Saxon looked deep inside his troubled soul, and found the proverbial parody of the 'Scotsman' lurking within, brimming over with those ever-agile propensities to 'truck and barter.' Not so, apparently, *his* (gender intended) Asian counterpart. Be that as it may, to this day, neither India nor China have been remarkably *'expansionist'* in the way Europe/America still is. Yet, the paradox must also be noted: India and China, in medieval times, still accounted for some 50% of World GDP, despite this dearth of a 'zeal' for accumulation.

Apparently, they could easily outproduce the Europe of its time, without any serious recourse to geographical expansion, capital accumulation, or a thirst for far-off resources. *One might say that, unlike Europe: what they didn't have, they didn't crave.* So, despite having the means to go 'expropriating,' they showed scant interest in doing so, in any systematic sense. The Emperor Asoka sent missionaries to the East, not invading navies seeking plunder (of course Indian traders also went where they could, but w/out the intent, or the impact, say, of the East India Company), or overthrow of regimes. Some Southern Indian rulers did send navies eastwards but with no calamitous urge for serious accumulation. So, much of South East Asia was '*Indianized*,' but mainly culturally only.

The Chinese, similarly, also sent navies across the seas, under the so-called 'Eunuch Admiral,' but to little, lasting material effect. Imperial Russia expanded around its physical borders Southward and Eastward, sixteenth century on, annexing Siberia, and then occupying Alaska (and parts of Northern California) two centuries later—but after its sale, remained more or less within its own bounds. Imperial Japan commenced its own colonizations late nineteenth century onward, setting up puppet-states where possible: and some of it, perhaps, was a 'defensive' colonization, in the main, *vis-à-vis* gathering European encroachments in Asia; and, again, as an Axis Power, at war with the Allies, in the mid-nineteenth century.

Yet, for all that, there is very little in the experience of the above societies that can seriously compare, in size, scale, and scope, not to mention impact, to Europe's expansion around the globe. Now it could be argued, and is sometimes argued, that Europe was genuinely *resource-poor*, unlike Asia, so had '*no choice*' but to go foraging. Again this is question-begging: Australian Aboriginals, similarly, did not have any spectacular abundance of material 'resources'—yet did not set off to colonize the Americas, or foreign lands, in consequence.

It is putting the cart before the horse to say that 'Capitalism' drove Europeans in such a direction, since it begs the question as to what 'drove' Europeans to embrace capitalism to begin with. The answer can only lie in a culture, an ethos, that supported it philosophically. There is no 'materialist causation' (which is the staple of liberal and Marxian historiography) that does not presuppose materialism itself as a philosophy.

Capitalism did not descend, unbeknownst, like a meteor from the sky on Europe: it was eagerly embraced by its feudal rulers (and then foisted upon others). That *fatal embrace* did not take place in India, or China (or Russia), in comparable historical time, and on a comparable scale. And the rationale would have to do with basic *civilizational* and *cultural* values. The '*dispassionate passion for rational calculation*,' and its sustained application in the pursuit of unlimited accumulation, never took firm, or extended, root in their soil (today's China, under massive investment from Europe, Japan, and America, may well stand at a *critical threshold*, where it could well cross over, irreversibly, into the Anglo-American mold: but it is still too early to call).

It is this highly portentous *'difference'* that Gandhi had in mind when he made that oft-quoted quip about 'western civilization' being a good idea.

It still is.

❊

Of course, the European can lay sound claim to virtually all the sciences and technologies of *Late* Modernism. Partly, this is because once Europe 'seized power,' globally, it either cannibalized, or constricted, further evolution of such activities amongst its subject-peoples. Native handicrafts and manufactories, much as knowledge-systems, were ruthlessly suppressed, by the British in India, and their counterparts elsewhere, wherever/whenever they threatened the interest of the Conquerors.

But it must also be recalled that we often equate Euro-Modernism with Modernism itself—which is a serious mistake. I have defined Euro-Modernism, in another Work (Kanth, 2005), as consisting of some Four Attributes: a less than critical 'faith' in Science, a Self-congratulatory notion of 'Progress' (measured, for the most part, in material terms), an over-riding philosophy of Materialism, and a willingness to, as even J.S. Mill averred, 'force people to be free' ('freedom' understood in their own terms). These are also the correlates of *Eurocentrism*, as I view it.

A Society can *Modernize*, as per its own mores and values, rather than have to import it all, perforce, from another, hostile, entity: which is how most non-Europeans were inducted into a *Euro*-Modernism. Without European Conquests, the world would have, in time, 'modernized' (not unlike Japan, the one major Asian society that remained unconquered by Europeans until the mid-twentieth century, when it was finally, with inhuman cruelty, atom-bombed into abject submission to the European Way), but it need not have taken a *Eurocentric* cast.

In other words, European knowledge was *culture-specific,* and 'functional,' only within a set *cultural* paradigm. For instance, modern European medicine is *not* superior to either Indian or Chinese ancient healing traditions. But European medicine had a skew that fit the society they were busy inventing.

Partly, they created novel public spaces/modes of living—like early nineteenth century London—that generated certain specific pathologies, such as cancers, and infectious illnesses: and so they had to pioneer treatment of such reactive/resultant ills. Not dissimilarly, Freud's psychoanalysis may have been of some solace to the neurotics subsisting within the decadence of Habsburg Vienna, but hardly of meaning to say, the Masai of East Africa. Partly, they developed not cures but *palliatives,* or symptom-suppressing medications, of which the American drugstore is the emblematic apotheosis.

And partly, they absorbed the medicine and pharmacology of *Non-Europeans without due acknowledgment,* such as Native American herbal discoveries (the 2000, or so, Native American tribes compiled a cornucopia of herbal remedies, many of which, like *arnica,* were to be adopted by mainstream medicine w/out acknowledgment). And it wasn't just in healing: Ben Franklin got his notion of the '*separation of powers*' from the great Iroquois Confederation.

But, *en générale,* India led Europe in the *Sciences* if we trace the time-frame from remote Antiquity to the 1500s. Trivially speaking, *e.g.,* the *Pythagorean theorem* (or the value of *Pi)* was calculated in India long prior to Greece—and yet bears a Greek name of original discovery. Calculus was developed in India centuries before Newton and Leibniz, yet Europeans prefer to date it from the latter. And so on. And China led Europe in *technology,* similarly (in paper, printing, gunpowder, the compass, cannon, rocketry, paper money, *et al.*). But, after European mastery of the world, and its mining of their discoveries, the native traditions of India and China, not to mention West Asian (Arab, Persian, Turkish, *etc.,* in Chemistry, Biology, Mathematics, Engineering, Architecture, Optics, *et al.*) ones, were either forgotten or shelved.

If one takes up Philosophy, the record is even more compelling: the German Enlightenment was based, heavily, on the discovery of *Sanskrit* Texts that stirred the imaginations of Nietzsche, Schopenhauer, Jung, Freud, and Goethe (and Spinoza, but in another tradition). I rather favor the idea that it was their *Non-European* Colonies, and dependencies, that stimulated the Enlightenment even more than the revival of Greek and Roman ideas during the Renaissance. *But, as we all know, history is written, and recorded, by Conquerors—to the lasting detriment of the conquered.*

✳

It may not even be possible to take the full measure of the staggering Angle-Saxon achievement (and also—it must be noted—the prosaic, unheroic, even careless, *modesty* with which they abide it all). Their irrepressible materialism built a material society whose 'laws' have now come down simply to but three injunctions: '*Consume, Obey, and Be Silent.*' And that self-same Materialism has also virtually *Unbuilt* that same society, today to the point of widespread nihilism, anomie, dysfunction, and dissolution.

From More to Marx, European *Utopianism, the anthropic reaction to the fatal embrace of materialism,* has been a pathetic *cri de cœur* seeking salvation from the very ills that come, paradoxically, with the Modernist package that they would yet support, in the misguided name of *'progress': i.e.,* 'freedom,' 'individualism,' 'equality' *et al.* (which come parsed in societal reality, unfortunately, as the atrophy of affective ties, the breakup of familial relations, angst, and existential despair).

Life as a Treadmill is the only real original invention of the Late European Angle-Saxon Avatar. Hitherto it was reserved, by rulers, for the many, or the few, whose miserable destiny it was to be drudges. But Late Modernism made it the *Blight of All,* rich or poor, high or low. To be striving endlessly, competing endlessly, seeking, wanting, and craving endlessly, and without respite, in isolated, sordid hells of an individuated Self that can know neither peace nor contentment—that is the burden of its dehumanizing catechisms.

Their Constitution sums it up aptly when it speaks of the 'pursuit' of happiness. Indeed. It is only the vain, alienating, solitary, asocial, *pursuit*—that is mandatory. It is the *process of* getting there, and the more *roundabout* the better (curiously, their Capitalism is also based on that very same notion: the more layers of intermediation to a specific production, the more costs to be added on,—including profit as a 'cost'—the more 'valuable' it is). For, once 'attained,' it is never attained (for ceasing to hold interest). *A contentment that 'comes easy' would be pagan, heathen, and insulting to their catholic taste: heaven is dearer the more distal it is—the more pitfalls twixt it and the soul.*

What a curious amalgam: of *Beowulf, Luther, Calvin,* and *Smith.* And, even more sobering thought: if they could do what they did despite the accouterments of '*Christianity*'—*the meek and humble ideology of slave revolt:* what more could they not have done had they *not* been thus 'hampered'? It boggles the mind.

But, a little more more prosaically, to list the *Tableau* of their Accomplishment(s), nevertheless. They, physically, occupy *Two* entire Continents outright (let us also take some liberties with this 'Continent' terminology), or a vast portion of the Earth's habitable land-mass. Their Language is the universal language of business, diplomacy, science and aviation. Their Institutions (World Bank, the UN, WTO and the IMF *et al.*) dominate the Globe, laying down rules that may not be breached. Their Financials control, in the main, whatever can be bought, leased, or optioned, on the planet. Their currency is the World's Reserve Currency. Their Legions are posted around the planet in Full-Encirclement. Their Media own, operate, and/or dominate all, or most, international media. Their Entertainments, Film, TV, *etc.,* reverberate, and resonate around the world, even in imitation. Their Consumer Technologies are All-pervasive, globally, Laptops,

IPods, *et al.* Their entangling web of new-fangled Universities sprawl across the world tutoring all in the *Tao* of the Great Anglo-American Way. Their Fast-foods, and drinks, near—iconic.

And so on.

Walmartization of retail, McDonaldization of food, Monsantoing of agriculture, J.P.Morganing of Finance, Microsofting of computer technologies: Who can be, who has been, so Unimaginably Powerful? *And who, thereby, so strong, as to be able to cope with all of that brazen might?*

❋

And the *Costs* of this Great Hegemony?

In particular, if we now bring in their honorable country-cousins from Europe. Who there to reckon it? Who there to bear witness? In how many millions shall we number the victims (maimed, torched, killed, enslaved, pauperized, displaced, driven, deprived, enserfed, humiliated, robbed, incarcerated…)? Native Americans, Vietnamese Peasants, Men, Women and Children in West Asia today, Africans, Incas, Latin American and Central American Peoples, Indian peasants and ryots, the people of Hiroshima and Nagasaki, Gypsies and Jews, East European Peasants, Chinese Opium addicts of yesteryear, Australian Aboriginals, Other Species, and …?

What Tribunal could scale all that? What Nuremberg could, willingly, sit over it in dispassionate judgement? How many years would it take to simply catalog the crimes, let alone adjudicate issues? And what, and how long, would be the *Charge-Sheet?* Mass murder, genocide, ecocide, pillage, bombing, invasion, piracy, plunder, looting, extortion, theft, fraud, swindling, and..? *No, the Charge Sheet today Exceeds All those issues combined. It is the European Way (supernal Greed wedded to execrable Violence) that has brought the societal world to breakdown, the cultural world to abasement, the economic world to collapse, and the natural world to near-extinction.* In short, in these times, the Planet *reels* from the impact of European practices.

And it's no affirmative defense to say that the *Non-Europeans, today, play the very same game,* for that only points to the stratagems of *Those that compelled them to join in on pain of destruction* (ask yourself, *e.g.,* the *Efficient Cause* as to why the Soviet Union resigned itself to an abdication of its own Agenda, or why China was able to enter, and then sustain, its present trajectory). I have, elsewhere called the struggles of our time as that between outright *barbarism* and the glimmer of a possibility of *civilization*: or a clash between '*mammals*' and '*reptiles,*' *the warm-blooded and the cold-blooded.*

Why? Because material dialectics, based on mechanical *determinisms* (borrowed from Classical Physics) has viewed anthropic social relations as contractual, rationalist, competitive, optional, and based on a mutuality of sporadic eco-political interests: rather than affective, necessary, organic and entwined by irreplaceable bio-social needs.

The one viewpoint is *'masculinist'* in inspiration, and leads indefeasibly to *Euro-Modernisms*, to the sort of 'civil society' of 'universal egoism,' where the social is merely a means to secure private, individual ends (and, of course, 'hell, is other people,' similarly motivated), and an asocial individualism keeps us all as the isolated, icy 'equals' of a cold, calculating social nexus with the great 'liberty' to live and die alone within a solitary suspension of social life. This is the vaunted 'freedom' of European fantasy that cripples them even as they ponder, near-eternally, how to get out of their own self-imposed, existential misery.

The Other view, *feminine* in the main, leads us to our inescapable, instinctual, tribal, communitarian heritage as hominids, warmth-seeking, not light-seeking, mammals, who huddle for comfort within the refuge of kinship, and affective relations, where society is not a voluntary contract but our simultaneously natural/social precondition, and the convivial domain of our most expressive engagements.

Most significantly, this Second Perspective is not at all 'Utopian'; since formations embodying it have already been achieved, in anthropic history, by tribal societies— across space, time, and culture.

The *First* view has now come to threaten the very existence of society, and aspects of the natural environment vital to the survival of the various species on this Planet: and the *Second* allows All the possibility of co-existing, peaceably, in a benign reciprocity—*whence the inherent Barbarism of the one view, and the hope-giving Civility, and Benefice, of the second. It is no less, perhaps, than a 'choice' between Life and Death, Collectively, for our Species.*

However, the Great Wheel turns, inexorably—and I can say, with only deep-seated intuition at this time, that Europe has had its long day under the sun, and it is likely that there shall be *near-balance* again amongst the Comity of Peoples: for the notion of *'checks and balances'* also applies to *inter-tribal* relations.

So, all bemused, I can only return to the Haitian cab-driver, that unhappy philosopher of the road, plying his lonely trade in New Orleans (where Hurricane Katrina exposed the predictable abandonment, by their governors, of its largely dark-skinned inhabitants in their time of dire need).

Yes, it is an interesting question he had posed: *where would we all be, without Europe?* In remote Antiquity, possibly?—where India, China, Persia, and what I term '*Mediterranean Civilization*' once held grand, autonomous, sway (of course, I may have to rest content, bereft of *crème brûleée*: some treats, it seems, may just cost too much).

Or in its Creative Recreation, all over again, with the benefit of hindsight, in a Poly-Centric World of Evolving Anthropic and Non-Anthropic, Possibilities.

Just imagine.

33

By Ideals Alone?

It is easy to believe that because certain subjects have been gifted names, they are real. That form of *nominalism* is natural, if misleading, especially in context of the varied conversations within Modernism. Philosophy has always been at the obscure end of the speculative train of modernist thought. If we look at tribal formations, they have magic/religion at one remove, and technologies at the other: that is, where they are at all differentiated. More likely, the two areas are merged in one interlocked system.

With Antiquity, East or West, it is quite another matter: being far from their tribal roots, and closer to being incipient Empires, they could 'afford' the luxury of *speculation*—a sure sign of schism, doubt, and discord: be it Greek, or Indian. In some senses, it is a parasitic pre-occupation, of a rather idle coterie (possibly then, as now).

Religion and Magic are 'problem-solving,' like technology: and tribal formations had need for them. But one cannot, *en générale*, find a tribal *philosopher*. At least, in part, this is also because they had no use for sophism: this latter is a later state in anthropic *devolution*. Being authentic, and consensual, the need for guile, in such societies, was not primary. In fact, one way to define EuroModernism would be *via* its primary moving forces: calculation and guile, or calculation in service of guile (and, to be sure, *vice versa*). Double-entry bookkeeping, and compounding of interest are merely the arcana of that grim credo. It is this that gave European rulers the decisive edge over Non-Europeans, less than technology, or even cannon: chicanery was—and is still—their *forte*.

England mastered the Indian sub-continent more by its adroit skullduggery, than valor (though that quality was far from absent). So, we can easily understand the role of the philosopher: be it in Antiquity, or today. As with Kautilya, or Machiavelli—to take an example from Antiquity and the near-Modern era—it had to do with craftiness, applied to politics. With Modernism, its need becomes paramount. A system that needs a philosophical mirror to view itself is either narcissistic, or aiming at spoils, of one kind or other: or both. As such, European Commercial Society (*i.e.,* Modernism) is simply overrun with them, at its early, formative stages. Partly, it would deploy its sophisms against the received lore of religion, in effect 'trumping' the latter, as needed. The *Philosophes* of the French Enlightenment played a very useful role here, not always successful solely owing to better arguments. Apparently, the intelligentsia, then as now, were bowled over by the power of rhetoric alone.

But after that function was discharged, it turned duly narcissistic, even self-destructive (as in certain variants of 'deconstruction' today) given the confounding stresses of the alienating 'civil society' it had helped usher in with so much fanfare. Of course, the oppressed orders, within and without Europe: women, serfs, slaves, peasants, and tribals, could only marvel at the hypocrisy, then as now, when they came close to self-awareness at all. Besides, the real Masters of the New Order had already started to replace philosophy with 'social science,' so as to consolidate their gains, near-permanently.

In the latter cadre, 'economics' was to take over the trusted, even vital, function of apologetics. Indeed, quite explicitly, 'moral philosophy' (Adam Smith) was to be, very hastily, replaced by 'economics' (Marshall). Today, the economist is the one dragged out of bed, at odd hours, to defend the system, in public media, not the philosopher: when need arises to 'explain' the *status quo.* Yes, best to leave it to a Paul Krugman to 'explain' the ploys of empire: a Rawls would be far too equivocal.

But, today, this *modus* is fast becoming history. We have now entered a phase where even economics—the prime tool of Modernist hegemony—is becoming obsolete. After all, the 'economy' has become *finance*, only (yes, the Modernist Emperor has finally revealed his charming undergarments: to the dismay of the naïve, who were so taken, for so long, with the outer accouterments). And finance rules by practical *fiats,* in its own domain, not *theory* (as a Rothschild is supposed to have said it, more or less: 'give me just the power over money, and they can make all the laws they want'). It is self-justifying, simply, by cumulating wealth and power: each battening on the other. Wall Street cares not for the hoary, old fashioned, *Tools of Hegemony.* The gloves, and the fig leaves, are off. So, it is all really rather pathetic.

The traditional salves of order: religion, philosophy, and social science (economics)—more or less in that historical sequence—are all become utterly marginal to public life. It is, henceforth, to be a wholly privatized, *Trans-Human* world, with but two sacred parameters left standing—*money and technology.* Only two orders, thereby, are to retain privilege: the Profiteers, and the Technocracy. And they work together, to mutual glory, within a common Post-Human ethos. At least, that's the plan, for now. As for philosophy, it will just 'wither away,' taking economics with it for company. Not an enviable lot (for philosophy, that is).

European Commercial Society was once described, aptly, as an amalgam of British Economics, French Politics, and German Philosophy. Well, now that politics is being replaced by a *Managerial* Order, all three planks of Modernism are being summarily set aside.

So, welcome to the future. That is, welcome to *Late Modernism* (my term). At least, we all know its static 'Laws of Motion' by now: *Consume, Obey, Be Silent.* That is the crass Endgame of all those fanciful 'Declarations' of 'Rights' by which, *Ye Olde* Europe had nearly all of us thinking it had pole-vaulted over the 'wretched of the earth': *by ideals alone.*

About four hundred years ago, European ruling interests scoured the globe, seeking spoils, by hook and by crook. At about the same time, they also began developing fanciful ideologies of 'freedom' and 'equality'—used as cannonades against the *ancien régime*—that were to become the sacral mantras of Modernism. A simple analogy might help: it is a tragic witticism heard in Africa that when the European came, *he* had the Bible, and *they* had the land: within no time, this ontology was reversed. It is something similar with the secular replacement for colorful biblical images.

Only a few then (and even now) noted the grand disjuncture between the high theory and the depraved *praxis.* That itself is a primer on how *hegemony* is achieved, and maintained. Millions, entire societies, perished at their hands then, as they still do today, even as they still wrap themselves with the sham frippery of 'human rights.' Of course, they may be the only ones left now still believing it.

34

A Summing Up

Commencing early in 2014, I have been detailing the modalities of the current global crisis: from causes to consequences—and even salves—in my various writings: *they represent, perhaps, the first comprehensive, Non-Eurocentric/Non-EuroModernist accounting, and outline sketch, of global societal phenomena in their evolution under the heel of European Hegemony*. Here, I present, in truncated form, ever in acute brevity!, their essential import. So, some repetition is not only to be expected, but required. A necessary *caveat*, or two: adding to the Poet's admonition, a little knowledge is not merely a dangerous thing, but also, in some regards, merely embroiders extant *ignorance*. That is to say, my rendition hangs together—*i.e.*, stands or falls—*only as a whole*. So, a little patience will 'pay.'

It is also, unmistakably, and antipodally, antithetical to received information on the subject(s), stemming from vainglorious Modernist accounts, within which we have all been tutored, for generations—be they liberal, conservative, or otherwise. *As such, it were helpful if judgment on parts were suspended, until the entirety of the presentment is both read, and understood.*

Now, I am not seeking accord: far less, acquiescence (from anyone). Quite the contrary: it has been said that '*history is a fable, agreed upon*'—far more utilitarian, perhaps, if it were viewed, instead, as *a parable, disagreed upon.*

Finally, I scribe, not fuelled by customary drives of 'ambition, or bread,' but moved by pain—from the piercing pangs of keen 'awareness' of our rather desperate constitution on planet earth, especially in these latter days of mayhem and turmoil.

To explain. *Exploitation* and *oppression* are very different things. The former is oft not known: nor even 'felt,' when known. But oppression is, always, *both known and felt. Modernism oppresses, like no other, even if it exploits no more than any other form of Patriarchy—which is the inexpugnable bane of our species.* I write to dismiss, and so help diminish, the oppressive weight of its shibboleths, which are a further, gratuitous, tax upon an already foredoomed species—within an inexorably dying universe. Unlike many fellow critics, I would settle, readily, for but a *'cruelty-free'* social universe, though that simple pleading may go wildly beyond what any and all utopias can even promise—let alone deliver. Indeed, as I will suggest, *all* (Modernist) Utopias are sadly, if necessarily, *'anthropology-free'* (to their eternal detriment).

And our anthropology 'locates' us, in our *'being,'* much as the planet does so, spatially. So, I am sort of saying: *know your anthropology, and go and sin no more.*

❄

The world is upside-down today owing to the cumulating consequences of the Modernist Revolutions that rent the societal fabric of Europe, sixteenth century on. As such, unequivocally, European governors bear full responsibility for the inglorious disarray of our times. It is almost truistic to note that we have all been brought, today, to the very brink of the extinction of both the planet's material hospitalities *and* human society's own, antic, civic decencies. And the 'agency' that ensured this obnoxious outcome was the wholesale embrace of *materialism* as the ruling *'geist'* in all matters: in the sciences, arts, and societal modes of living. As I have previously written, materialism is *sham science, shoddy philosophy, and shabby ethics.*

The endemic crisis in sustainability and human well-being is, thereby, the infelicitous 'gift' of *EuroModernism*, a gift that was, perforce, pushed down the throats of all *Other* societies by the simple fact of European domination of *All* societal spaces, globally: economic, political, cultural, *etc. Modernism is an ideational construct built upon: (a) a self-serving view of progress, (b) a materialist scaling of the latter's desiderata, (c) a chronic attachment to 'scientism,' and (d) a readiness to use (illimitable) force to achieve putatively 'progressivist' ends.* As such, it covers both (European) capitalism and socialism (the difference lies in the fact that the former relies on an '*individualist*' ontology, and the latter on a '*collectivist*' one).

Whilst 'Europe' is its inescapably generic, matrix *source,* it is also clear that it is the *Anglo-American* formations that have 'powered' the appalling declension in world affairs (in consequence of Modernist theory and practices) with all their might—a process not at all abated even today (not all societies, nominally 'European,' had either the head or the heart for this sustained crusade).

The Celts, as just one example, were subdued early on, and brought into the fold by force, but remain, to this day, with some reservations, 'a breed apart.' Ditto, with many regions of *Eastern* Europe never wholly won over by the Modernist Revolutions.

✳

For those who might object that some major '*Non-European*' societies were also '*materialist*' in philosophy, as, say, China (which is why Buddhism—itself imbued with a pragmatic materialism that challenged Vedic idealism—did as well as it did there, unlike, say, in India) the answer is that *no society other than the European ever acceded to an 'individuated self-interest' modus; for it is this latter predilection that virtually guarantees the repudiation of ANY notion of a public, or general, interest, that can—be it abstractly or concretely,—be expected to supersede the sovereignty of individual (self) interest.*

Once that genie is out of the lamp, there is no turning back. Stated differently, China was indeed *materialist,* but retained serious *societal responsibility and accountability* as governing norms of public policy (and that to this day, despite being inundated by Western *accouterments).* So, it is the invidious *combination of materialism with an asocial individuation* that explains the distinctive structure and trajectory of European formations, after the sixteenth century. It also explains their palpably common Modernist 'signature' conditions of *angst,* despair, loneliness, and restlessness.

Which is why the 'lights can never go out, the music must always play,' wherever EuroModernism strikes unwholesome, noxious, root. A soul, ill at ease, can seek only, for ever more!, crass, and unrequiting, satisfactions.

✳

Of course, this 'fateful embrace' went directly against the very grain of our *anthropic being.* And it is this materialism that has always stood, defiantly, as the impenetrable obstacle to the prospect of a European *Civilization (understood as a pacification of the conditions—natural/societal—of human existence).* Once society was seen as a '*social contract of interests,*' rather than a *compact of affections* and, further, *only a means to individual ends*—the fall from grace was both certain, and precipitate. Every vanity, especially *greed*, was given full, nay utmost, rein: and the societal tie, in dire, straight-line acceleration, wilted and withered.

In the singing words of Goldsmith, '*Ill fares the land, to hastening ills a prey, where wealth accumulates, and men decay.*' Indeed. And the fetid decay is spread all around us, like a virus. Morality, *which is but the collective cement of a human community*, now dies a morbid death, gradually asphyxiated by the extinction of culture, civility, and goodwill. In its place arise the dry desiccations of Modernist 'rules, laws, and constitutions': in short, '*legality*' takes the place of moral norms, and, of course, gives us the cheerless, fateful, '*Amoral*' society, whose paramount example is latter-day America, the derelict wasteland, *where the only, last, threadbare, restraint on anti-social behaviors left, if at all, is Fear*—of the Law.

The radical transition should be noted: Modernism destroys the convivial, *affective*, basis of morality, and replaces it with a tawdry, *fear-based* system of punitive legalisms. It explains why police shoot to kill in America even for minor, inconsequential, civil offenses—and not even a few demur (indeed, they kill even when *no infractions* are at issue). It is as one alien does—to another (for they are all, 'alienated'). Not so in Denmark, or Iceland, which, despite their Modernist garb, yet retain the tribal, communal, tie. In effect, in Anglo-Norman societies, *Gemeinschaft* is replaced with *Gesellschaft;* civilization, with the laws of the jungle; mammalian traits, with reptilian ones; the paradigm of *femininity* (caring, consideration), with the paradigm of *masculinity* (aggression, greed). Yet '*(Wo)Man*' *does not, cannot, live by dread alone*—without embracing dire *anomie,* and its indefeasible consequent: gathering *insanity,* as enshrouds the budding psychopath and the sociopath.

❋

I write often of *morality*—a topic conspicuous by its striking *absence* from the daily vocabulary of EuroModernism. No wonder: having destroyed its *affective* basis *viz., family and community,* it can scarce comprehend its relevance, let alone its meaning. In fact, for most purposes it is, in layperson's terms today, equated with *ethics,* and hence left up to *individual* taste, and choice. This is little short of an unspeakable travesty.

Morality is the interlarding fabric of anthropic society, and stems from its very primal building block—the mother-infant relation: the inexpugnably vital basis of anthropic evolution. As such, it originates, primarily, with *women.* The vulnerable human infant requires time to mature to adulthood: whence the entire safety-security set of relations/conditions that constitute the cultural 'cordon sanitaire' of 'pre-requisites' (of what we might understand as 'civilization') assuring that this may be accomplished, regularly, time and again—*i.e.*, the *pacification* of the extant conditions (natural, social) of human existence.

Given that the greatest threat to this nurturing process is always the on-and-off nature of male depredations, it is women, again, who are the primary *trustees* of civilization (whence, also, of *civility*). *So, both morality and civilization are serious, structural, societal 'needs,' not arbitrary, personal, 'choices,' mediated, in the first instance, by women.*

The fact that EuroModerist society finds both to be no more than dispensable artifacts only illustrates the real basis of its continuing, steady-state, observable, *dissolution*—as an *anthropic* society. I have also argued that men and women are, *two distinct sub-species*, divided by *differentiated instincts*, something known to all but the Modernists who sweep radical distinctions under the *dissembling* rug of a presumed, ideological, '*equality*' of the two: *au contraire, women are 'arguably' superior to men, using the realist, and non-arbitrary, standard of bearing propensities that ensure the possibility of the survival of the species.*

Stated succinctly, women (universally, and across millennia) quietly, build the templates of reciprocal convivialities, even as men, somewhat less modestly, raze them. As an important aside, the relationship of *Men* to power and domination is, at root, *instinctive:* it is the genius of matrilineal tribal formations to, more or less, enchain this 'drive' within the bonds/bounds of the affective ties of kinship: thereby placing it, howsoever ephemerally, 'under restraint.'

Where such restraint is absent, or weak, empires result, of one kind or other, within the firm grip of a burgeoning 'iron law' of *oligarchy.* It is this latter propensity that obdurately undermines and vitiates all Modernist projects that aim to thwart power and curb domination, even when nobly inspired. At any rate, 'Equality' is but one, powerful, if largely exploded, myth: there are many other notions that are shot through with a slew of epistemic and ontic disclaimers, non-starters, and sheer bad faith. *Which brings me, now, to my Major Thesis: that All varieties of Modernist philosophy, and social 'science,' fail, utterly, for Not being located in real(ist), human, anthropology.*

Regrettably, Modernist anthropology was hopelessly vitiated, *ab initio*, by its *a priori*, all but unconscious, 'assumptions,' drawn, loosely, from a secular version of Christian theology, which ascribes a *teleology* (of '*progress*') to the human species, alone amongst all others.

Now, am I suggesting, perchance, that 'anthropology is destiny?'. Not necessarily, though even a casual perusal of history will confirm the trivial truth of my propositions about men and women. Instead, let me say that we must, in all caution, resist the temptation to be delusional, in the grandiose, Modernist, manner *of pontifical, even 'universal' declarations that suggest that we can be 'anything we choose,' as a species. In fact the only 'universals' are our instinctive, anthropic drives, though mediated by culture. And culture is 'difference,' writ large.* Modernism, *au contraire*, standardizes and homogenizes any and all cultural/institutional 'differences,' so as to better co-opt, control, and dominate the world.

The entire set of Modernist declamations, upon which its applecart rides, most insecurely, is specious *cant*: alternately, false, misleading, tendentious, empty, shallow, anti-social, and misanthropic. Take, *e.g.,* the vaunted, abstract, 'freedom' that is the *primus deus* of Modernist ideology: indeed, it is but little hyperbole to claim that all variants of its spectrum swear by it. Careful scrutiny will, however, reveal more holes than may be found in the common run of Swiss cheese.

For starters: freedom from what, for what? Next, what the (actual, potential) limits of this 'freedom'? Then, perhaps the key *lacuna*: it is ever an *individuated* concept of freedom, which underlines its asocial, and even anti-social, credentials. Now, to its realist, ontic, correlates. For the luckless consumer, it's the meaning-laden 'choice' between Coke and Pepsi. For the citizen, the solemn election between Two Parties divided only by One, common, idolatry (Republican, Democrat). Any other freedoms?

Yes, largely to live and die alone—in 'solitary,' as in prison parlance!—formally 'equal' to millions of others similarly marooned, drowned, and foundered: in an irredemptive swamp of loneliness, disaffection, and despair. *So much 'Free Will,' one might say, so little Self-Contentment.* Ah, but it does have a 'real' side to it, wherein the real clue to its ideology comes revealed: the *Corporate Governors are 'free' to do what they wish, as they wish, when they wish: upon whom they wish.* And now, thanks to an insensible Supreme Court, they too are *'individuated'* by *fiat*: yes, they are 'individuals,' nay, 'persons' with 'rights' (if not responsibilities). For them, rises the Statue of Liberty, but with no parallel statue, not even a tiny hand-puppet!, of Responsibility, or Accountability, to offset it.

Let the meaning be clear: 'freedom' is a Modernist, corporatist slogan that arose in European history, when upstart commercial classes wished to rid themselves of the nuisance-laden restrictions of the *Ancien Régime*, Canon Law, Laws against usury, and such, that frustrated their insidious advance to absolute power. It served to dupe and mobilize the masses, who fought and died for it, only to be tragically robbed again of the societal *protections* that once immunized them, howsoever minimally, against want and privation.

More profoundly, individuated modernist 'freedom' goes against our given *anthropic grain:* the modicum of contentment that is possible for us is found only in close-knit, emotive, tribal *reciprocities* that are emphatically *not* based on any such abstract 'freedoms.' *The human family illustrates my meaning, irrefutably: it is not equal, not democratic, not free—yet gives to all, high and low, east and west, Modernist and Non-Modernist, that miniscule dole of warmth without which life would be unbearable, unthinkable, and unlivable.*

Not for nothing did Alexander Selkirk name his very own private island the 'Island of Despair.' Once again, we need to know our own anthropology to resist the *genre* of false, and dangerously misleading, temptations. Real 'Freedom' may well be, as has been held, if within limits, the *recognition of (anthropic) necessity.*

❋

Instincts impose many *caveats* upon 'human' (*i.e.,* male/female) behavior that would be, and have proved, quite foolhardy to ignore. One telling, and related, example of radical misreading of human behaviors, is how the *pseudo-science* of *Modernist* economics is all agog, bursting at the seams with '*wants,*' but (tendentiously) forgets '*needs*' altogether, to its utter, disadvantage (yes, and workers, *e.g.,* are but '*hands*' only, 'freed' of the inconvenient, fulsome, burdens of bellies and mouths). And Economics draws from *Modernism,* the *motherlode* whence it springs—which conceives us all as mechanical, rationalist, *automatons,* not organic, biological, beings, having epistemically 'freed' us, *from our very placement in Nature itself* (whilst yet leaving, leastways in its early idylls, *women and 'primitives'* to stew in that latter, primal, slime: yes, both the 'Shrew' and the 'Aboriginal' required much 'taming,' and 'uplifting,' to meet Modernist standards—Shakespeare, attending to the first, and Kipling, to the latter, at least allegorically).

The madness runs several shades deeper: one Nobel Laureate, in Economics, whom I will not name out of embarrassment for *his* sake, in full flush of Modernist triumphalism, argued that '*we can do without nature*' (what a pellucid manifest of *Self-alienation*!, quite aside from the fact that, regrettably, *the truth is, exactly, vice-versa*). We are, in all its drab pathos, but *animals* (if shaped in 'god's image,' this god could only be a great, even glossy, *Ape*) who, lofted by sheer imagination, and equal measure of egotism, soar higher than nature allows: but, just as gravity brings us 'down to earth,' if we are not properly equipped, so do our instinctual natures drag our (utopian) projects down, when we strike out for the empyrean—unequipped with due understanding of our obvious flesh-and-blood limitations.

Regrettably, All Modernist paths are the same: they lead nowhere.

Flights of fancy, be they of 'Left' or 'Right,' are destined only to crash-land—worse, in a place not of their choosing. Durkheim understood the 'socialism' of his time, shrewdly, as a tragic *cri de cœur*—at a paradise lost irretrievably: and Marx's 'communism' of the future was but a Modernist make-over of so-called 'primitive communism,' *which is no more than the tribal reality I have been drawing attention to in these essays.* So, our ineluctably tribal essence asserts itself, even in Modernist pipedreams.

✳

How is all this to be reversed? I have argued that there is no earthly, temporal, force that is, today, stronger than *EuroModernism.* Thereby, it is perhaps quite fitting that it will, in all probability, and all by itself, undermine itself. Its parasitism has now turned into an even more deadly *'self-cannibalism'* (I call this the phase of *Late Modernism*). For four hundred years, Modernist Europe (*via* its savvy governors) swindled the *Other (both external and internal to it), t*o attain its vast bounty of resources. We all know—or should know—the means deployed: slavery, genocide, expropriation, occupation, war, conquest, pre-emptive trade & commerce, colonization, and empire. In effect, workers, peasants, farmers, women, serfs, slaves, chattel, the indigent, and the impuissant, the world over (again, both internal and external to Europe) *labored*—so European elites (and their usually dependent cronies/allies elsewhere) could live in the glitz and glitter that attends them still.

And today's 'globalization' has replicated that so very remarkable process of a wholesale transfer of resources/values—even more smoothly. Then, in the closing decades of the twentieth century, with apparently little left to dominate (other than the Moon and Mars)*,* and brimming over with bravado at its 'victory' over the oppositional, if hapless, 'socialist' comity of nations—it *turned on itself.* With Productions virtually ceded to the 'New Emergent Periphery,' and its own traditional working-class(es) similarly abandoned, the *Anglo-Ams* (in an earlier Chapter, I have detailed the historical uniqueness of the Anglo-Norman as a force in world history) are now spearheaded by the perhaps the purest form of egregious parasitism conceivable within the modernist economic paradigm: *finance.* Banking capital now superordinates, and controls, all other capitals, owing to a gargantuan size and scale made possible, ironically, by its very *fictitious* nature. *The unproductive rule the productive, the drones command the bees.* It has given but behind-the scenes, credit-wielding, speculative, cyberfunctionaries, life-and-death power over agriculture, industry, *etc.*, and, as such, over *real* livelihoods, and economies, globally.

Small wonder, possibly, that many of their technocratic philosophies, in shallow echoes, see little difference between the real and the *virtual, in grim forewarning of an encroaching Transhuman future.* It is, emblematically, the very height of (Euro)Modernist tragic absurdity that scraps of paper (oft-times, even *less*: but mere digital entries!), no more than IOUs, can yet purchase outright, vast, incalculable, swaths of *real* resources, both societal and natural—with malefic intent, and deadly effect.

Thus, the '*Great Reversal*' of this self-immolating agenda is written into the script, from the start: already, derivative gambles exceed the value of world GDP by a colossal factor—*i.e.,* a sudden, and cataclysmic collapse of finance is only a little short of inevitable. And with it, howsoever buffered by public budgets, will go much of the flimflam and fluff of Western Economies—and the hegemony of the North Atlantic Powers. Of course the *Costs* of its fall, economic, political, *etc.,* similar to its initial, cataclysmic, rise, will be borne by those (*Other* cultures, *Other* species, and the teeming strata of the underprivileged, under-represented, and the resource-starved) who can least afford it.

When a Gulliver falls, a lot of Lilliputs can only find themselves placed in radical jeopardy.

✳

The world will not, of course, be taken by surprise. Our intrepid governors know full well what they are, and have been, doing. It has, rightly, been termed '*failure, by design.*' And many, if not all, amongst the *Other*: Russia, China, India, *e.g.,* are also catching on, howsoever slowly. Indeed, the BRICS have already taken the first, hesitant, baby-steps to climb out of the deepening morass. And many, many, others, will follow their example, perhaps even take lead. So, yes, this 2.0 version of the Titanic will—finally!—be abandoned: if, unhappily, as with the original, perhaps too late for the many.

The real economy will revive, all over the globe, and an antic sanity will, yet again, get restored. That much is also written, nay *coded*, into our *species-being*. And it can only be beneficent—to all. Once again, it will be a *poly-centric* world, free of hegemons: a motley crew of nations/societies, living/experimenting—according to their *own* cultural lights. We can only hope that the incumbent pioneers can generate the needed 'escape velocity' to leave Modernist ideologies behind, permanently. And they will need to dig deep within: to recover buried realms of past heritage, whence they can yet again derive norms, values, even small felicities!, of real anthropic import and meaning lost, for so long, in the turgid *melee* of modern-day consumerism. It will, doubtless, also, take some time to retire all the false, meretricious gods to their sordid lairs in misanthropy. This is quite comparable to the state of the world *prior* to the onset of the great saga of European Adventurism, so it is neither fantasy nor utopia.

Of course, the enforced letdown from their dizzy heights will be hard to swallow for the Older Hegemons. But they, too, will need to adapt—and learn to live more peaceably with a world that they have thus far, and for so very long, owned and operated, willy-nilly, as their very own fief. Better humble pie, one might say, than no pie at all? So, as the good bard has it: the best, just possibly, is yet to be! Although, given what we know of the crumbling present, even a return, simply, to the *status quo ante* might serve just as well.

Part VI

Futures

35

The Future?

For over a year, I have disinterred, possibly *ad nauseam,* the various logics of Modernism, both overt and covert. Stated simply, there is little that is redemptive about it. *Au contraire,* it represents the most sweeping about-face of baseline anthropic values in the history of humankind. The consequences of that fateful eventuality are all about us: to witness—and despair. The fact that it fell to Europe to lead us all, ready or not, on that choice path to perdition may or may not be fortuitous.

Here, I won't go into that set of issues. Instead, I will spell out, briefly as ever, what is to come. First, who we are. Whether we evolved or devolved, we are *hominids* with some unique instinctual traits. Our closest kin, bonobos and chimps, differ radically amongst themselves. The former are female-driven and relatively pacific: the latter are male-driven and aggressive. We fall in between, albeit closer to the chimps: with virulent patriarchy slightly more nuanced in tribes within matrilineal contexts. It would appear, importantly, that male aggression can be tempered, if not tamed, within the affective ties of kinship, *i.e.,* within a *moral economy*—usually worked by either women, or the 'feminine principle,' as I have termed it.

The *material economy* is largely, perhaps even wholly, a male enterprise, dominated, and driven by men, or what I term the 'masculine principle.' Milder tribal forms devolve into empires when the latter force, no longer bounded by affective restraints, runs amok. Simple gender constraints, it would appear, break, yet again, into class divisions with the discoveries of settled agriculture.

Knowledge of these simple facts might have pre-empted much of the vast trove of vacant philosophizing as to 'human nature' and 'human perfectibility,' as characterized the so-called 'Enlightenment'—when Europe, shrugging off biblical restraints, nevertheless retained basic biblical notions, if now transmuted into secular form(s).

Modern *Utopianism*, right or left, however, founders, ever, on the immutable shoals of our received anthropic *instincts*. Curiously, both Soviet communism and the non-descript hippie commune break up on that same set of traits. Stated semi-seriously, bonobos cannot be chimps, nor *vice versa*. More specifically, men and women are gifted with differing instinctual traits (denied fervently by many brands of Modernist thought) that have huge consequences for society. It is nonsensical to believe, as with centuries of Modernist sloganeering, that we can simply 'declare' ourselves into a benign state of being. That modus of grandstanding—*liberty, equality, etc.*— was either tendentious and hypocritical, and/or wholly a creature of fantasy. *Contre* Rousseau, we are not 'born free'—except, perhaps, in a derelict Modernist ghetto beyond the pale of society—and even less, to design ourselves as we please. Everywhere, *Men* tend, in the domain of power, to *oligarchy,* and near-despotism, whenever/wherever opportunity affords regardless of the political set-up.

So, notions such as 'democracy,' *etc.,* are simply the savvy rhetorical flourishes by which we are gulled into believing in patent counter-factuals. It is in this arena that EuroModernism has us all, even the quick-witted, swept clean away. We remain ever a *totemic* species, so modernist 'leaders' can and do beguile us, especially given our loosely tied 'contractual' societies, with self-interest as the sole binding force, and lead us willy-nilly (that is what Weber understood as *'charisma'*) into this or that exit into (usually) a deeper damnation. This impetus, by its nature, is a force for both good and bad: *i.e., charisma* can break the bounds of the Modernist Empire of today, much as it can lead us into a Jones-style mass-extinction.

Modernism, *an alien form*, was imposed by brute force on communities linked by antic hospitalities, universally, East or West. It dissolved our tribal nexus, and cut us adrift into so many free floating islands of *anomie* and *angst*, if we were at the bottom: and into towers of profiteering, profligacy, and power, if at the top. *But it allowed no one, high or low, the grace of contentment: so it is with EuroModernism that the Age of Discontent begins.* Restlessness is its intrinsic norm. But we are ineluctably *tribal* in our very natures, and so this unnatural restlessness can only lead to collective suicide, if unchecked.

Much of Neo-Lib or Neo-Con radicalism, as with the incredible huckstering mania of Wall-Street (to which they bear an umbilical connection), is a sort of a runaway death-wish unchained: with each faction charging ahead—to see who can go over the cliff first. For such is the madness that takes over when we, *qua* Modernists, deny ourselves our *species-being* of communal existence. It might simply be a species of karmic justice if all of their ilk were to rush over that precipice, if we could but stand aside and watch: but that, alas, is not to be. They appear determined, instead, to drive us all into a Finance-Capital Jonesville, of catastrophe and cataclysm. It is this ferocious doggedness that sets up the reality scenario that I have termed, only partly satirically, as the extant struggle between mammals and reptiles: that is to say, the warm-blooded and the cold-blooded. Who shall win?

Keeping an eye to the current setting of the Doomsday Clock, it might appear that the Modernist reptiles shall overrun us all. And, for years, I had feared that that fate was to be borne through, inexorably. However, the latter-day insights of Quantum Physics, much as the ancient intuitions of Vedic wisdom (with which they seem, at times, to be in synch), now has me give pause. We live in a *self-aware* universe: that much is not mumbo-jumbo, but physics. But I go a step further than Amit Goswami (whose eloquent phrase that is). I feel—regret I can't 'prove' it—it's a *'self-fulfilling'* universe, as well. In effect, a universe that, apparently, wishes to behold itself albeit, for now, *via* human eyes. So, if we were to be extinct now, so would the Universe, with us. What an egregious waste of super-colossal effort/energies 'invested,' over billions of years!

So, surely, it cannot be: we are to stay, perforce!, and survive. Right now, developing facts appear tending that way: it is Modernists—EuroModerns in particular who lead that choice band—who are in panic, in flight, in disarray, in indecision, globally. So, our 'choice' is simple: any way we can, we need to try and get out of the way of their careening Juggernaut, and build ourselves simpler, humbler shelters of conviviality, community, and co-operation.

Yes, we need to revive moral economies (I said revive, not *invent*: so 'utopia' is, simply, *rediscovery*), such as the human family (which is defiantly, nay instructively!, *Non-Modernist*: it is *not* built on equality, freedom, or democracy; yet gives us all, pathetic hominids that we are, what we crave most, as a species: warmth, shelter, caring, and kindness).

For you see, there is but one real human need (left or right, east or west): to huddle. If so, the 'future' is no more than a return to our antique past. Ironic, is it not?: that those who sought to leap over us all, *via* cannon and chicanery, into a neon future of consumerist gluttony, based on the drudgery of the multitude, may now have to walk the plank, in ignominy, back to the ingenuous burrows—where we all started *together,* a long, long, time ago.

36

The Final Hour

The Doomsday Clock, for all species that inhabit this earth, was set into motion only with the arrival of the European as a force in World History. The planet had mustered an ill manner of maladroit *equipoise*, despite the tyrants, East and West, that come and go with such monotonous, and ill-fated, regularity in the iniquitous annals of the universal Archetype of *Patriarchy*. However, all of them, even taken together, could not have hoped, in their wildest orgies of despoliation, to even dream of approximating the realities of the all-Extirpating scourge that Europe, in its Modernist *Avatar*, in its unseemly haste to streak straight from barbarism to decadence, unleashed upon this world.

The *modus* of 'Modernism' it invented and embraced—and which rules us all today, East or West—robbed the species of little choice other than to go further and further along that path of collective self-immolation. *To iterate the obvious, when I make reference to the 'European,' I am always denoting their governing orders—not the hoi polloi, who, like all subalterns, scramble but for the crumbs, material and ideological, that fall off the regal table.*

The extraordinary thing is that, to this day, these worthies remain all but unaware of their incredibly apocalyptic, historical 'mission.' This might appear surprising—until one fathoms the underlying mystery. Unlike, say, their Eastern counterparts the genius of the European has always lain in precision-mapping of all things: *especially in their micro-domains.*

Here, I must interject a *caveat:* this prepossession, whilst a generic trait, is far more pronounced amongst the *Anglo-American genre* than, say, in their German or Latin cousinages. So, the *'Big Picture'* is not, in the first instance, their real concern: Anglo-Norman empiricist, pragmatism has a taste, nay a fascination, for mundane *'facts,'* rather than grand *theory:* so they dig deep, and like moles, stay stupefyingly immersed, up to their gills, in the dirt of the datum. This has many obvious benefits, which we associate now, in sum, with the Hesperian 'Way of Life' that dominates the globe today. But it comes at quite a prohibitive cost. *Put metaphorically, they crave Knowledge, as it gives them Power: but not the Wisdom that might confer Felicity.*

In antipodal contrast, is the Vedic tradition of Ancient India, which imbues all knowledge, *ab initio and post-factum,* with the pervasive spirit of a perennial *wisdom.* You both begin and end with the *'big picture'* in the *latter:* not so, in the *former.* The latter project, in other words, is, ever, a *moral* undertaking: the former, only a *material,* instrumental one.

Thereby, the former are unable, in effect, to arrive at an intrinsic, 'implicate,' comprehension of the Whole.

Indeed, *morality* (being always *societal*) is constituted at the level of the whole, not its parts: so our Micro-modelling geniuses cannot put it all together, *speaking metaphorically,* any more than they could patch-up Humpty Dumpty, *post factum,* at time deferred. Stated differently, the Cartesian 'mechanical' metaphor of society simply fails with organic entities. The (Modernist) Enlightenment researcher, in his/her 'value-free' *cum* materialist garb, was appropriately 'color-blind,' with respect to perceiving the *moral cement* binding societal entities. This might help explain why Adam Smith, *e.g.,* is lauded very widely for his *Wealth of Nations* tome, but few even recall his *Moral Sentiments* work. To underline the critical import of this 'difference': the nuclear bomb cannot be built, or even thought of, in the one world: but it comes about all too easily in the other.

❆

EuroModernism effectively begins with the adoption of *materialism* as its guiding metaphysics: wherein its supernal success—and abject failure. Since this stance is openly flaunted as a *virtue,* not least by 'progressive' trends within it (*e.g.,* some variants of Marxism), I will not expend any time in establishing the fact. More interesting, perhaps, might be to indicate *why* this happened. The 'Reformation' paved the way for *Modernist Greed:* this could only be done by wholly demolishing the Late Christian ideology of the *ancien régime.* So classical Christianity (Canon Law, *e.g.*), of a monist-idealist bent, was swiftly subverted, and stood on its head, with a banal, materialist calculus replacing it.

But it is, perhaps, even more profound than that. When *gemeinschaft* was dismantled, with it fell the *moral* economy upon which it rested: the new '*social contract*' notions of society (*i.e.*, the *gesellschaft* form) could only conceive of society as a '*balance of interests,*' rather than a '*balance of affections*' (*i.e.*, care, consideration, *etc.*)—it is in this pivotal moment that the '*material*' economy replaced the more ancient, and *anthropic,* mode of social *being.* Given that Europe became *Modernist,* in this sense, far ahead of others, it embarked upon the *road to ruin* well before the rest.

Morality is not an arbitrary episteme, a 'choice' as Modernism views it: it emanates, in fact, from our anthropic being, as an ontic necessity. Its eternal provenance is the need for secure child-rearing (at once, both a natural and social necessity) in the warring warren of what I have elsewhere termed the 'paradigm of masculinity.'

Given that women are the first providers of infant needs, universally, it falls to them to be the *prime custodians of morality (i.e.,* the guarantors of the security of the newborn). *Indeed, the first moral (at once natural and social) relationship is the mother-and-child one. So, the 'material economy' inhabits the arena of masculine drives (greed, power), whereas the 'moral economy' thrives in the hinterland of feminine hospitalities (nurturance, care-giving).* The broad distinction between the 'public' and 'private' domains corresponds to this divide. *So, Morality is the gift of Women, much as Politics is the bane of Men.*

I have previously defined civilization as the (continuing) process of pacification of human existence: and, so, again it is women who are its eternal guarantors. Prior to the advent, and domination, of EuroModernism, even the *material* economy was, if only partially, offset by the persistent demands of the moral one. But with its outright triumph, it erodes, in straight line depreciation, to the point where, now, in the US, it has virtually negated any signs of the *moral* economy—outside of the vanishing residual of the nuclear family. As I have already mentioned, the US is, in most regards, now an *amoral, Post-Human* Society: which is the 'face of the future' of all Modernist formations of today.

Now, as for *materialism* itself, in this age of Quantum Physics, there is no necessity for proffer of argument (I have detailed its *lacunae* in previous posts): *it is, very simply stated, bad physics, faulty philosophy, and shabby morality.* Poignantly, in the words of Arthur Schopenhauer:' materialism is the philosophy of the subject who forgets to take account of himself.' And, as I have written in previous posts, it is in the *degree and intensity* of this paradigm of materialism that Europe, since the inception of Modernism, differs, portentously and prophetically, from *All* species of the *Other.*

❋

The nascent EuroModern economy leeched off all domains that it could annex women's labor at home; serf, slave, and wage-labor, abroad. It is this *primal annexationism,* beginning in the sixteenth century that explains its hypertrophic growth to *giantism* in the twentieth century. The gap between Europe and *Non*-European societies was not the painfully negative one it was to become—at the *start* of this process. One has only to gauge the pathetic riches of, say, England, in the sixteenth century, in relation to that of the Indian sub-continent, to understand this in all its dark poignancy. *It was Expropriation of all Other worlds that 'created' the 'First World,'* in its mature form in the twentieth century, despite the tendentious posture of benign concern for the former affected today by the North Atlantic powers (even whilst bombing, occupying, and looting them, willy-nilly!).

And what a saturnalia of accumulation that was! That lurid history covers the holocaust of genocide, colonial looting, slavery, and confiscation, where Europe ran riot throughout the world in an orgy of pillage, piracy, and plunder never before seen on the globe. Messrs. Attila and Genghis appear but mere village pick-pockets, and small-time hoods, in comparison. That same process gave the European that very current *elan* of being the Law-giving, ultimate 'Masters of the Universe' imprint that is such a hallmark of that ilk—as they still go about dismantling regimes, destroying nations, and debilitating cultures, globally.

❋

Strike One of EuroModernism was, as described in the foregoing section, the debauchery of *Other* domains of economy and society, both domestically and abroad (England, *e.g.,* colonized its hapless Celtic neighbors, even whilst subduing foreign lands). *Strike Two,* is the very *Late Modernist* one, inaugurated by the Reagan-Thatcher Anglo-Am set of Policy Initiatives that, essentially, in *self-cannibalizing* fashion, undermines, today, the very economic basis of Modernism—*via* its 'revised' manifest of illimitable (purely financial) greed *at any cost.*

Partly, this is to point to the quick transition from rampant *immorality* to the chilling *amorality* as was achieved, say, in the Post-WWII period. As anthropic beings, we are either moral or immoral: but *amorality* is a Euromutation of apocalyptic significance that surfaces first in the Anglo-Am formations. Not only is the *self-cannibalizing* extant within the social economy, in Late Modernism, it is paralleled also in the systematic 'deconstruction,' *i.e.*, annulment, of anthropic traits that the 'civilizing' process (where it exists) effects over time.

It means we are engineering, stolidly, a new generation of robotized, crypto-humanoids that will, fittingly, inhabit the urban wastelands that Late Modernism is 'creating,' with such breathtaking neglect, in its own decrepit backyards. But, mostly, I am referring to the entire set of *Neo-Liberal Strategies* that ended up empowering the most *parasitic* forms of capitals—such as *finance*—over the traditionally more societally useful, and productive, ones: to the point where the domestic economy is longer a primary base for sustainable *productions.*

The US, with its financially crippled middle-class, its demobilized, and demoralized, quasi-labor force of a part-time, itinerant, and non-benefited 'under-class,' and its fast-dwindling, traditional workforce, set against an all-powerful, all-appropriating, corporate, Financial Oligarchy is both a case in point, and a regressive 'model' for others. *Rentier* Capitalism, or the *regime of coupon clippers,* can only survive, bubble to bubble, tenuously, on financial scams and Ponzi schemes, crisis to crisis. *The system survives, precariously, today, on the continuous circulation and re-circulation of ever-escalating debt:* with industry shipped off abroad, and jobs with it, and with the consumer base thereby radically attenuated, Anglo-Am economies are held together, increasingly, only by this ever growing mass of *indebtedness*—public, private, and foreign.

As it is, we are now teetering on the brink of a collapse, or series of collapses, of the various mini asset-bubble economies. The Fed's propping of gold, control of interest rates, and pumping of liquidity into banks has mollified a stricken system thus far—if at grievous taxpayer expense. But the familiar salves of wars, sabre-rattling, and domestic repression cannot stave off the inevitable crash of Late Modernist economies (that are technically bankrupt already). So the Euro-Modernist world has, by now, and in these very times, reached the tail end of its overly long tether.

Indeed, few systems have tried harder to win this game of *self-subversion.*

❉

The choice before the world is, thereby, stark, and grim. If the Late Modernist rollercoaster is not halted, and *reversed,* in form and content, soon, we all go over the abyss into a zombie world already at the draft and design stage. Is there a fate worse than extinction? Yes, there is. The implacable misanthropes who pushed the nuclear button, back in the mid-twentieth century, can quite easily do so again. And that would, of course, end it all—for much that inhabits our little corner in space. *But if they didn't*—and actually succeeded in getting the world to bail them out with yet more blood and sacrifice, *then what lies ahead is little short of a dire dystopia that decisively punctuates, maybe even terminates, our long history of Anthropic Evolution.*

I am referring to the *nouvelle,* sci-fi, *TransHuman* world that latter-day Dr. Frankensteins and Dr. Strangeloves are busy concocting, in their hidden laboratories, albeit far from public scrutiny. Late Modernism achieved the *Post-Human* Society as its choice contribution to anthropic *devolution. Strike Three of Modernism will be the TransHuman Society that will halt about 200, 000 years of our anthropic existence.* This *emergent bio-techno-industrial complex* will, predictably, take-off, once every last vestige of real resources has been monopolized, and every nation reduced to vassalage to the North Atlantic Hegemons. *It will, very likely, transfer the Transgenic processes applied thus far to plants and animals to humans:* and *internalize,* quite literally, the new *genre* of bio-tech innovations— to clone a new class of androids and cyborgs, according to corporate taste and inclinations.

Projects of molecular nanotechnology all-purpose 'assemblers,' reanimation of cryogenically suspended patients, uploading of human consciousness to virtual reality: these are all, but a few of the ominous ideas that are being seriously examined and discussed, some even within the nether realms of Academe. *Much the same way that nuclear devices were first conceived of, then produced, and then deployed, so will the new human robotics, now being avidly researched, even at public expense,* be put to early, and diabolic, 'use.' *So, the bionic species is only, I suspect, but, a few decades away, if the current genre of Corporatism is allowed free rein.*

Once again, it will be our ever dependable *North Atlantic Anglo-Ams* that will pioneer and lead this fateful, even fearful, technology: so, with the characteristic twist of a Greek tragedy, they who spearheaded the Modernist cataclysm will now oversee perhaps, what may well be, the *Final Hour of the Species.* Of course, it will all be deftly marketed (as was the case with transgenic crops) as but the newest means to eliminate poverty, hunger, sickness—and the rest of the slew of cravenly dissembling shibboleths of public policy parlance. One can only hope there is, out there!, some merciful *'god-being'* to stop them, and in time—if we can't do it for ourselves.

Indeed, if IT doesn't exist, we may well have to invent it. For, they that set off the Doomsday Clock appear determined to make it, *asap,* entirely, and permanently, superfluous.

37

Everything, Reconsidered

I know: it sounds extreme. But that is exactly what my Critique of Modernism leads up to, ineluctably. Yes, it is not complicated. History (and sociology, and science, and… you get the picture) is written by *Conquerors.* EuroModernism, *via* its European grail-bearers, conquered the world, convincingly, eons ago. Then, they embedded that noxious philosophy of All Things, perforce, into virtually all peoples on this globe. Never mind that so much of it is rabidly anti-anthropic, it is also, frequently, wholly false in its specifications.

So, eighteenth century Anglo-Norman ideas and institutions have now become the parlance of the 'educated,' or the indoctrinated, the world over. It is a tight system, where if you buy one inch, you have to buy the whole caboodle. As a system, it is run through, quite hopelessly, with the twin evils of mechanism and materialism. The first is injurious to our anthropic natures, the second to our anthropic values (yes, and they both exist, demonstrably, despite Modernist efforts to relativize them).

For, contrary to its ringing, if febrile, declarations, we are, as a species, born neither free, nor equal to any other. The first attribute would thwart communal harmony, *i.e.,* it is *asocial;* the second offends the sheer diversity that cultures afford us, in the planetary panorama. I have never met my equal, but know many unequal to me: both up and down that scale. It'd be perfectly dreadful to live with, or in, universal *homogeneity*. Yet, that's where we are headed.

More seriously (!), equality has no ontic basis in the way Modernism is organized: hierarchical and oligarchical as it is. It is, in other words, yet another empty slogan, a travesty, to deceive the masses. Even the bland *One Person/One Vote* notion, which is as close as it comes to any notion of equality, is carefully undermined by ruse and stratagem (the bent of American Political Science in the Fifties/Sixties, to kneel and pray for a 'mass society' which would leave politics entirely to the elites, is but the tip of the ideological iceberg). Exactly like its Stalinist mirror-image, it said to its populace: 'you go and work: and leave governance to us, the bosses.'

The Anglo-Norman soul, being replete with the spirit of 'truck-and-barter,' *i.e., commerce,* loves flatness and uniformity, since it accords well with its long-standing ambition of 'full spectrum dominance'—for only a uniform world can be both conquered, and managed, at least cost. It also favors it because, of all peoples of this planet, it is one, *i.e.,* after it had fatefully donned its Modernist guise, wholly devoid of any unique culture. *In effect, it had no culture to lose.* Yes, I know: there's the Lincoln Center, and the Kennedy Center for the Performing Arts—whose extravagant 'exceptionalism' prove my point succinctly.

The continuous push to expand work, and increase production, leaves little time for leisure (outside of 'recuperation time'). Any real culture that yet endures in Modernist Europe, at large, is that which survives from its Pre-Modernist period (such as classical music, art, *etc.*). Eastern Europe is much closer to its cultural roots, though sadly under the heel and harrow of Neo-Liberal cretinism today: once shrugged off, like Russia, it can yet revive its roots.

The soul-numbing drabness of America is because it has no 'pre-Modernist' culture to draw from: it was born with Modernism instilled in its bones, so to speak. Like New York, it is little more than a large, lavish prison—enchaining the human spirit—lovingly erected, brick by brick, by its own inmates. And like its sprawl of prisons, yes—it does have color tv.

❄

I don't need to base my critique of Modernism on any manner of *arbitrary* values. I take my stand on our anthropic *species-being*, an ontic reality still standing, precariously, despite Modernist slash-and-burn atrocities. I am referring to the vestiges of tribal societies that Europeans, or their well-trained proxies, put into straight-line, accelerated retirement.

Yes, Sydney boasts unabashedly (Ozzie bigotry is highly educational, since it hearkens to a past that at least some Europeans would like to forget, much like erstwhile South Africa was a chillingly twentieth century Monument to, and reminder of, European Barbarism), a *Museum of Aboriginals*: whilst those wretched folk still walk the streets right outside—lost, and uprooted.

In America, they reserved spaces for their ilk—but only after they had done disporting in slaughtering as many as they could—on reservations, far from the madding crowd. Let me underline this: *no human tribes have ever, so consistently, over such a long period of time, in such large numbers, murdered their fellow-tribes, if of a different ethnicity, as Europeans have: and still do.*

Attila and Genghis (the usual Western favorites in such form of demonizing: recall, *en passant*, that Alexander, instead, is considered 'great') came and went, leaving not a ripple: but these worthies, like Tennyson's Brook go on forever. If that sounds hyperbolic, think: which Non-European governmental force is, today, in a European society, wholly uninvited, bombing the local populace as it pleases on one pretext or the other?

If such exists, it would only be but the exception that proves the rule. Yes, *they* embodied—*i.e.,* Bushmen, Aboriginals, *etc.*—*communal* anthropic values: all of which were shattered by the *Holocaust of Acquisitive Enlightenment* that we worship, mostly unaware, as Modernism.

Now it is EuroModernism I rail against: it is the dominant mode of 'Modernization,' which pre-empted all other modes, *via* outright conquest. The India sub-continent, like other regions of the world, was 'modernizing' (what an ugly word!) according to its own lights, and on its own timeline—*i.e., evolving*—before the *Brutish* Isles came tramping in, and turned that vast territory into a wholesale mining operation digging for whatever could be carried away. It is those deep values, of communal co-operation and conviviality that EuroModernism annihilated, in the name of a vacuous, puerile, asocial, antihuman, and utterly ruthless, notion of 'progress,' based on forcible extraction/expropriation.

Alas, that wretched idea still drives the Machine—or is it the Matrix?—today.

❊

To read their own accounts, that yet dominate even University education, they did it all *via* their own resources. *They invented everything, discovered everything, measured everything.* That's right: they had achieved it all—science, technology, civilization, philosophy, you name it: even whilst, let me note, daintily emptying their chamber pots out into the street in mid-nineteenth-century London (they could compare themselves, usefully, in this respect, to the disposal systems of ancient Harappa, millennia prior). Of course, this, like other such modes of self-aggrandizement, is an outrageous pack of lies. There is, fortunately, a burgeoning literature now that reveals the real origins of European science, technology, and philosophy: Northern Europe leeched off unacknowledged discoveries, in innumerable spheres, made by Mediterranean Civilization (Greece, Italy) to their South; the Arabs, India, China, *et al.,* as much as they made their own discoveries, to fuel its own Renaissance and Enlightenment.

In effect, both wealth and ideas, in different degrees, were procured/ purloined, where available, and then improved. Much of the German Enlightenment, for example, was the direct consequence of the study of *Vedic* works. I will be even more categorical: *all of European Philosophy, since the eighteenth century, could be seen as no more than a discussion and commentary, self-aware or not, on Jain, Buddhist, and Hindu texts of two Millennia, prior—certainly, it registered no critical advance over it.*

Never mind philosophy: those who still think Pythagoras was the originator of the theorem that bears his name need to think again: and no, Greek ideas cannot be blithely usurped as 'European'—they were part of a rich *Mediterranean* civilization that includes ancient, Nubian Egypt, itself in a fertile exchange and dialog, with the ideas of the East. Of course, as has been pointed out in a recent work, Europe first denounced non-European ideas as idiotic, next thoughtfully swiped them, then astutely sold it back to the world as its own findings.

The savage British despoliation of Indian industry, during their long orgy of looting in India, is a classic in this pattern. No, their history books would not suggest that, amongst other imaginative punitive measures, the hands of native, skilled artisans were cut off to stop competition with English products and processes, in particular in textiles: and this, in an epoch where J.S. Mill was extolling the virtues of human liberty, and Jane Austen was delighting English middle-classes with tales of sweet decorum.

Anyone in doubt of the efficacy of Indian technological skill, in other areas besides textiles, can view the solid iron pillar in Delhi, still standing, some 2,500 years later (that's a very conservative estimate), and still rust-free. And examples simply abound, of that nature. In fact, with the sunken city found recently in the Gulf of Cambay, the dating of India's civilizations is now pushed back to 15,000 BCE. And I rather doubt it will stop there.

And yet, the richest section of the Ancient and Medieval world was converted, courtesy of its European guests, thereby, in a few generations, into a 'third world' society, from which stigma it has barely emerged. Not merely its riches, even its accomplishments were to be pirated.

The '*Aryan Invasions*' travesty has Vedic civilization set up by conquering forces from, yes, you guessed it: Europe. And Sanskrit, once its being the parent of many European languages was understood, was deftly relegated to being no more than a late descendant of a pre-existing 'Indo-European' language.

Right: *Vedic Civilisation is a European gift to India!*

Even the dating of Indus Valley civilization was carefully structured: to be set up *after* the Greeks, so European *primacy*—priority—could be preserved. Africa was to be similarly besmirched: the European literati claimed, until quite recently, that the Pyramids were built by a European tribe that had wandered in (so Cleopatra could be played by Elizabeth Taylor?); even its languages derived from a mythical 'Hamitic' language, and so on.

I am still holding my breath to see when they will claim that an architect from Birmingham designed the Taj Mahal? V.S. Naipaul, no great friend of the colonized, called it a 'wounded' civilization: nay, it's a hung, drawn, and quartered, civilization. And is so still: despite recent material gains, still unworthy of its past. All this is a bit reminiscent of the vast 'foreign aid' drama of the Sixties, which ran thus: first, steal from the victims, then lend wee bits of it back, *at compound interest*—just to keep things interesting!—and call it '*aid*'; in return for which the ex-colonial world was expected to be grateful, and to open its doors freely to predatorial capital flows that would end up gobbling up its culture, resources, and sovereignty.

Is there, really, any other way of describing western 'aid' to Africa? What each ruling-elite European—not to mention his North Atlantic cousins—owes to the average denizen of Africa is, simply, whether in human or material terms, incalculable. Now, their patented formula for such accumulation was simple: amass maximal means of violence, and then extort, at gunpoint. It still remains their signature *forte*. In that sense, yes, they did achieve it all, by use of their own unique resources.

They certainly had a way.

❄

It might be objected that I am referring to, and harping unduly, on, *past* outrages.

Not true. What is this thing called Globalization, today, in its Neo-Liberal cast? What has it achieved, in the ex-colonial world? Who started it, and why? What new forms of slavery/serfdom has it not condoned? What instability and violence has it not unleashed? Look just to West Asia: the impact of today's imperium has quite exceeded the devastation of centuries of classic colonization. Half a million children dead, between sanctions and war, in Iraq, never mind anyone else. And yet is there no end, to this day: from the hunt for yellow gold in India yesteryear, to black gold in West Asia, in the present day.

Which entity, or entities, can be held responsible for the wholesale destabilization of the world?

Who feels secure, anywhere? What human, societal values, have not been scorched, globally, in the daily traumas of economic collapse, political instability, and random, unannounced violence? Within all this carnage, like the old song asks: *where do the children play?* What lengths have they not gone to, to secure the dour calculations of greed? When can, when will, it stop? Is Asia responsible for the mayhem? Africa? South America?

So, yes we know the answer: the very same forces that poisoned the air, water, and foodgrains, deforested the world, invested in transgenics, created terminator seeds, committed willful ecocide, murdered peoples by the thousands, and, *en passant*, equated 'pushpin with poetry,' yesteryear—are at it still today, with quadrupled energies. They, bless their savage hearts, now tutor the world, perforce!, to emulate, enlist, and join in the fun: or face unstinting persecution (and finding, no surprise!, many takers).

But how could it be otherwise? The ruling forces that could calmly drop nuclear devices on a prostrate, civilian population, numbering in the hundreds of thousands, are no part of civilization, or the comity of humankind: but are its very antithesis, its antipode. And I won't even mention those who gifted us two World Wars, and are now readying for a Third. Is it any wonder that even Nature seems to be in revolt?

Scientific materialism, a valued crown jewel of EuroModernism, is unraveling fast, in field after field, as Quantum ideas gain ground, by the day. New discoveries are putting the long-standing pride of European physics at risk: we discover there is more that is unknown (dark matter, dark energy) than known, despite its trumpery. This extends even to the great Darwin, who is under strong and serious challenge today: not from the idiot fringe, but from new discoveries that threaten to push human evolution to hundreds of thousands of years earlier than envisaged.

Some argue, like Michael Cremo (Archaeologist) that, perhaps, a theory of 'devolution' may be needed. And, Amit Goswami (Quantum Physicist) has suggested, *contra* received evolutionary ideas, that there is also accelerated evolution, *via 'quantum leaps,'* that may help cover gaps in the fossil record, and so on.

Possibly, no single theory might explain all the facts out there. Plural data might require plural hypothesizing.

In the so-called 'social sciences'—what a misnomer!—, the entire notion of 'contractual' society, and its pathetic economics of greed needs be jettisoned. Political forms, also, require rediscovery: plural, communal, local, consensual, self-rule ideas might help topple the top-down command systems that we have come to accept as inevitable. Curiously, many ideas of the ancients are venturing back to be validated: in food, in cultivation, in husbandry, in science, in medicine, in philosophy, in the fine arts of *conviviality*. We are on the verge, I am certain, of a Great *Involution*. In such creative periods, learning is unlearning, schooling is *deschooling*.

I am no great optimist, given the predacious drives of masculinity, of a tranquil order to come, but certain antic tribal forms (and such forms may not be impossible to revive) have shown us how those drives may be enchained, curtailed, if tied down by emotive, affective, bonds of kinship and community. This insight may allow for novel roles for women, in peacekeeping, for example, not yet envisaged.

Yes, there was a moral economy (constituted by women) before a material economy (dominated by men)—before Europe decisively thwarted the former: but it still exists, for being inexorably *natural*.

Indeed, there is, likely, a reservoir to the human potential undreamt of by the reductionist materialism of Modernist Europe that may still be gleaned by a patient rollback of received ignorance and prejudice.

The Physicist Goswami assures us, it is a *world of possibilities* in the universal consciousness that pervades all, and exists in a nether domain of *non-locality*. Unfortunately, under Modernist impetus we have been stricken with a regressive paradigm of constraints and artificial, contrived, 'scarcities' (which fuel the sordid banalities of Modernist economics) that chain us to the Wheel, day after day, in doleful drudgery.

Worse, it forces us to trade in the *communal love* (it is this love that Modernist economics economizes on, with severe stringency) that is our innate nature, for the discipline of the whip, 'managed' as we are by dread alone. What derogation, nay subversion, of our inherent birthright!

The Bushmen have more leisure than we do, and expend less time in foraging: and yet, we think we live in the best of all possible worlds, and think of them as 'savage.' What a tragic farce!

So, here is as much to be done, as undone. And the times appear propitious: I know few enlightened who wish to see the present logics of dire *exterminism* stretch into an eternity that they themselves forbid.

I am reminded of hoary Vedic ideas—that constitute a cosmic philosophy unmatched in its epistemic depth—that speak of the eternal human dilemma: *out of ignorance, we are prone to epistemic error, and thereby misconstrue the world*, grappling with windmills. It is the ignoble realm of *Avidya,* which ties us, unhappily, to *Mithya* and *Maya* (illusion and delusion). Yet is knowledge (*Gnana)* possible: it is, indeed, granted, us if we only open our minds to higher modes of consciousness—available to all.

That is a real *Moksha* (liberation), of sorts: in the present case, from the varied ills of EuroModernism.

38

The Cosmos

There is risk in using conventional definitions drawn from our received Modernist Legacy. Its division of labor between the branches of knowledge is not merely arbitrary, but capricious as well. So, anyone trying to say new things has to invent categories, alongside, so as not to be misconstrued. I see no particularly useful boundaries between the social and the human sciences, though one could, perhaps, heuristically, separate natural from social phenomena, for some purposes. Essentially, it would appear then that there are only *Two philosophies*—the 'science' appellation above is likely gratuitous—one natural, and one social.

The 'gulf' between them is not particularly wide, since we, as humans, are both natural and social beings simultaneously. Indeed, the social deviates from the natural, significantly, only because we, in nature, are self-conscious entities. So, I could also say that there is only *One philosophy*, *a philosophy of nature*, with a minor allowance made for the occasional arcana of us anthropic beings. Stated even more succinctly: there is but *Natural Philosophy* (comprising all the natural 'sciences')—and a *Realist Anthropology* (which subsumes all that is useful in the so-called 'social sciences').

The bias toward seeing a radical break between nature and culture, so dear to Enlightenment thought (take Levi-Strauss as a good exemplar) comes from its received heritage of Judeo-Christian ideas: in fact, Enlightenment philosophy is, in many senses, merely the secular extension of Protestant theology—here a 'perfectible' 'man' is situated at the center, and/or the apex, of the Universe, as the 'sovereign of the species' (even in Marx). The progressivist pose of Enlightenment thinking mirrors the 'Pilgrim's Progress,' in the arduous Journey to Christ, complete with purgatory and heaven (though, alas, one has experienced much of the former, and little of the latter in the four hundred years of EuroModernism).

The battle, marking the advent of the Modern era, in European history was between Two philosophies of the Cosmos: the one idealist, the other materialist. The former derived from the Bible, the latter from Modernist ideas that gathered force in the sixteenth century. To sum it: for One, in the beginning was the *Word*, for the Other, in the beginning was the *Deed*. Less enigmatically, to use Quantum Physicist Amit Goswami's usage, in the one there was '*downward causation*', from a Celestial Creator: in the other, '*upward causation*,' in a Darwinian progression from matter: atoms, molecules, cells—to beings like us.

The latter is the classical paradigm of 'scientific materialism,' which has dominated European science and philosophy. Its greatest triumphs would have to be the ideas of Newton, Darwin, and Einstein. Indeed, (so-called) social science took its obvious 'materialism' (Durkheim, Marx) from Newton, Bacon, *et al.* Yet, at the very zenith of the latter's success, cracks were to appear—lesions that would take the form of the Quantum Revolution in Physics. More of that, in a moment.

The classical paradigm faltered, a bit, on a Key issue: human *subjectivity*. It was with some unease that the idea had to be touted—to stay consistent—that consciousness is but an epiphenomenon of matter. Yet, Quantum discoveries were, quietly and cumulatively, working against such manner of reductionism. The so-called '*Observer effect*' brought the excluded 'human' back into the very equations, so to speak. Indeed, with Goswami, the argument gets nicely reversed. *Consciousness is the very ground of being*: so the material world is seen as located within consciousness. The wave-function 'collapses' into material reality—*i.e.,* the particle—upon observation, in the sub-atomic world. Goswami extends this idea to the Cosmos as a whole.

Now, there is no need for a 'quantum leap' (irony intended) from brain to consciousness: the brain, much as the material world it 'sees,' are only *possibilities* actualized when consciousness—independent of both—'chooses.' *This 'consciousness' is non-local, and exists outside of space-time.*

It is a very strong version of the so-called '*anthropic principle*' that posits that the cosmos is structured, rather precisely, to accommodate the (ultimately human) observer. It also carries the interesting implication of reconciling certain ancient (at times, even religious) ideas with science, *e.g.,* the Vedic idea of *Maya*, or the delusive aspect of reality. So, the issue is joined, albeit in extreme fashion. On the one hand: scientific materialism, where human subjectivity arises 'accidentally,' as an epi-phenomenon, in an 'upward causation' originating, so to speak, in 'mud.' Or, its polar opposite: where a *supramental* (Sri Aurobindo) consciousness is concretized, or made manifest, in material reality, in a 'downward causation,' originating in the ineffable.

There is another interesting twist: scientific materialism excludes teleology or purposiveness, but *monistic idealism* (this is Goswami's Quantum Theory of Consciousness) presumes it. There is purpose to evolution, where transcendent values—love, amity, *etc.*—come into their own, beginning with higher-order humans. Now, interestingly, on the larger notion of an anthropic universe the Goswami view is more consistent with Modern Quantum Science (*e.g.*, *non-local communication*, impossible in the classical paradigm, has been experimentally confirmed), than the classical, materialist paradigm. Now that does not make it right, any more than it makes the latter wrong: since paradigms are of human engineering, and reflect human errors (even at their most sophisticated). I call it, therefore, an impasse. I will now put in my own two cents (if safely, in bitcoins).

The scientific materialist paradigm would be vindicated if it could be shown, near-experimentally, that matter generates consciousness, even self-consciousness, *spontaneously* (without deploying the *post-factum* argument of the existence of humans, since that might well have happened owing to unknown, and unknowable factors, in our distant past). Put another way, that consciousness is an essential property of matter: at a certain conjuncture, that can be accurately defined (and demonstrated). Until this is accomplished, Goswami's ideas will hold the edge, if for second-order reasons: consistency, comprehensiveness, practical application, social benefits, and such.

I do have the intuition, though, that *ye olde* scientific materialism, the very bulwark of EuroModernism, may have to make way for something larger, more real, in the near future: it would still be preserved, in its basic essentials, though subsumed, or sublated, within a much larger framework (only partly, in the way that Newton yet survives in an Einsteinian world).

To deploy a line from the Swan of Avon: there may be more to heaven and earth than dreamt of in its mundane, even banal, philosophy.

39

The Day After

For most, regrettably, the collapse of the *ancien régime* of our times is still a probabilistic affair. Nor can one blame them, given astute government propaganda, a maladroit media, and a mostly soporific intelligentsia. Reminds me of the old joke about the late-night broadcast that said: 'World ends tonight at 9: details at 11.' But the sapient have to, necessarily, look beyond.

Pax Americana, inheritor of *Pax Brittanica*, has ended, although in both cases the *'pax'* part was a morbid joke. For at least 3 solid centuries the *Brutish Isles* (I am from India, and am more aware than most as to the choice gifts of John Bull to the welfare of India: *the abject destitution of India's millions at the time of 'independence' was a direct consequence of systematic British agrarian policy*, exacerbated by the apathy/incompetence of the carefully chosen Post-Colonial viceroys they left behind to govern in their stead), and their North American offspring, found a world lying prostrate at their feet. And they did with it as they pleased.

The resource transfer from the latter to the former, during this long period, exceeds any recorded pillage in history.

Gandhi once remarked to the custodians of 'independent' India (determined to emulate its departing masters) that it took 'puny' Britain 2/3rd of the world's available resources to 'industrialize': *how many globes will India need, he chided, if it embarked upon a similar path?* No one heeded him, of course, but the answer is now in: it will take 7 planets, it has been estimated, for the world to 'catch up' with North American modes of consumption (as it seems to be wishing to do).

Now the grand dragon is in a free fall, tail lashing at one and all. Not a pretty picture. *Hubris* is, in individuals as in nations, unedifying. But one that has to be endured, all the same. Yes, when giants fall they can crush a lot under them. The emergent global forces are largely centrifugal, but the Empire is now centripetally driven. After all it has to: consuming as it has, *without producing*, a full quarter of global resources for over a decade. Parasitism of that *genre* necessarily provokes a *slash-and-burn* approach to the global economy, which is in rich evidence.

The entire conceit of empire is to get something for nothing.

It is that '*empire premium*' that has seen a ridiculously overvalued pound maintain British *amour propre*, even as the pre-eminence of the dollar allowed the US to buy the world with paper. In each case, *financial monopoly*, itself the means to various other secondary monopolies, had both economies soar vastly higher than mere industry could contrive. Indeed, subtract this *financial power* and the two economies, to scale, do no better than Japan and Germany: and far worse than modern China (*indeed, it is fact worthy of note China is a World Power unlike any past or previous European power: it did NOT conquer, enslave, and commit mass murder to get to where it is. Nor did it deploy any form of a financial monopoly to reap where it had not sown. Of course, it did brutally suppress Tibet, but few critics would see any great economic fillip that this gained it for its economy*).

Of course, as the decades went by it took an exponential cost, in blood and gore, to maintain that antic monopoly. It is estimated that the US has spent over 7 trillion since post WWII, to maintain its hegemony over West Asian Oil. Now, the Fed has created 4.25 trillion dollars, *via* purchase of securities, to shore up the dollar (whilst keeping gold down: the threshold for the Dollar Index being around .80, and the maximum for the gold price being about $1450), and its related banking reserves—with no end in sight to the trillion-a-year expansion.

It's sort of a Ponzi scheme to end all Ponzi schemes. So the paper cost of maintaining a paper asset is now gone well past absurdity. Not to mention the *real cost*, in terms of an economy willfully torched and set to waste. *As every alert schoolgirl is aware QE was invented to keep the dollar alive, the banks afloat, the stock market viable, and real estate up.* Quite a menu. But production, consumption, and employment, in the real economy, all went out the window a long time ago. In short, the collapse of today rides on three bubbles: the real estate bubble, the stock market bubble and the dollar bubble, each linked to the other in a death embrace. This underlines the real story of the naked *parasitism* of the system.

Now the Classical economists were keen on the idea of distinguishing between *productive* and *unproductive* uses of labor (their latter-day successors deleted that notion entirely). As Smith had it: *There is one sort of labor, which adds to the value of the subject upon which it is bestowed; there is another, which has no such effect. The former, as it produces a value, may be called productive; the latter, unproductive labor. Thus the labor of a manufacturer adds, generally, to the value of the materials, which he works upon, that of his own maintenance, and of his master's profit. The labor of a menial servant, on the contrary, adds to the value of nothing.*

In other words, you hire a worker in a manufactory: s/he produces her own wage—and a net profit for you, which add to the real social dividend. You (society) gain by the hire. But, hire a maid and a butler and you (society) gain nothing. The labor in the first instance is productive, in the second unproductive: the first is an 'investment,' the second is 'consumption.' Hire many of the first kind, you grow rich: hire many of the second kind, you go broke.

Now look at the economy: when trillions are spent on paper derivatives, bonds, and real estate speculation, the monies add to consumption, in the main, not to any growth in the real dividend. That's why the economy is going broke. If finance is used to finance real investment the economy grows: when it is used only to buy more financial instruments the economy slacks (I am not an advocate for growth, like most economists: but it is clearly preferable, if *ceteris* is *paribus,* to opt for growth rather than gambling the entire national dividend away with impossibly leveraged paper assets).

Worse, when finance carries rich rewards, its skews all investments toward itself. If pure gambling is good business with guaranteed (*i.e.,* Govt-backed) profits, why would anyone consider the more humdrum agro/industrial class of 'real economy' investments that take years to yield returns?

So we have a near-pure *parasite economy*, on the general lines of Vegas. Now you understand why unemployment hovers around 13.5% (my own estimate taking a mean of Govt. estimates and alternative data). With inflation at about 4.5% (arrived at, similarly), *real GDP growth is virtually at zero* (despite official claims) where it has stood for some time now.

The *Official* Poverty rate is at 15% (47 million) and the Child Poverty Rate at about 21.8%: the worst figures since 2000. Being 'official' data one has to apply a needed upward corrective even to that. The *Gini Coefficient* (Inequality Index) at 44 (in household income) is the highest in 30 years. The US has the *lowest minimum wage* of any major European nation: at $7.25 an hour, it is an international disgrace (Australia at $15, France at $11, and Canada at $10.25—besides, all of these nations *also* provide health insurance for all).

Who says slavery has been outlawed? Slaves, and non-slaves, have all simply been turned over into serfs, if lucky enough to have a job. 50 million go hungry, and another 3.5 million, or so, are annually homeless. And budget deficits, that seem not to touch such data, are projected to go north of a Trillion annually, in years to come. The new jobs are virtually all at the non-benefited bottom end of the scale: parking lot attendants, burger flippers, waitressing, and such. So in what does the US, today, more than 'competitively,' out produce the world? Bombs, and armaments, *i.e.,* not even conventional means of 'consumption': one 'consumes' such articles only at peril.

From producing 'goods' they have embraced the recreant joy of producing 'bads.' Of course, outlandish profits have always been made in this 'gold-plated' —*i.e.,* Govt subsidized—sector ('defense' was 20% of the Federal budget in 2011, on par with Social Security: just compare for a moment, the two classes of beneficiaries!), much as in finance.

In sum: the real economy is all outsourced, the war economy is way up, and finance is run clear amok: all of which *'works'* (for folks at the top) so long as China (Japan, Russia, UK, *et al.*) buy our bonds, and hold our depreciating dollars: but these two latter conditions are now fast waning, to our peril. It is the Fed that is now buying most Treasuries (at well over 70% of net Treasury borrowings) thereby monetizing debt at a ruinous rate. Like the Red Queen, the Fed will have to run with this *ad infinitum:* until it all crashes. The dumping of even a trillion dollars by China would halt the game (or a move away from the dollar by the BRICS nations): it's a Razor's Edge scenario.

They can hardly be expected to stand by and watch us recklessly devalue their reserves by the day! Now you see why the Octopus is reaching out its tentacles to Ukraine: it is not merely to add that great agricultural prize to its many dependencies. What a nice distraction from its own domestic woes! Besides, after West Asia, the other great treasure trove of oil and natural gas is Russia—and its neighbors (Europe has always viewed Eurasia, slaveringly, as its own colonial semi-periphery).

It remains to be seen whether even a giant octopus can swallow a whale. And so it goes. One minor point: it is often claimed that the US 'won' the Cold War. I would have to demur. I have already presented summary data on the US economy. *It is, in stark terms, close to being a failed economy and a faltering society—governed by a predatory state.*

Russia is a growing, increasingly stable, quasi-democracy—with a clearly competent government: it fares better, today, compared *both* to the insolvent G-7 and the US. Compared to the latter's shrill clamor, and chest-thumping histrionics, Russia (and China) appears sobrietous, calm, and measured. They are not there yet, but Russia, India and China may well be the *future leaders of the 'free' world* (though a truly free world, unlike a pack of hounds, would not require any such tribal chieftains). Looks to me, therefore, like *they* won.

And the future? Belongs, for now, to the BRICS: they will bring order and stability, and revive the prospect of a *polycentric* world all over again—if they can avert World War III. There will be no need for empire, nor a 'reserve currency'— which is, mainly, a tool of empire. Deploying serious checks to rampant capitalist predations—*i.e., greed*—is all that is needed to make this a reasonably hospitable planet, subject to the many weaknesses of *men* (gender intended).

If markets are to exist, then the marketeers had better be resolutely, nay warily, regulated. As Smith warned us: '*People of the same trade seldom meet together, even for merriment and diversion, but the conversation ends in a conspiracy against the public, or in some contrivance to raise prices.*' And, after 2008, we should all know about 'conspiracies against the public.'

Bounded greed is a whole lot better than unbounded greed. Corporates can be downsized, held to social account, and compelled to behave. Banks could be trimmed of their 'credit creation' functions: and currency could be issued by the Central authority (Treasury) directly—free of their current 'debt loading.' The Fed would have no special *raison d'être* after that, as an entity. Initially, as the dollar is revalued, perhaps after a bank holiday, at the local level, we may all have to learn the provident economies of *barter. And such an economy, howsoever temporary, might help kindle (or is it rekindle?) an entire panoply of mutually sustaining hospitalities that most ordinary people carry, under their skin, away from sight: people, everywhere, are a mite better than they appear to be (or are permitted to be by their overseers), once freed of the duress of Big Brother.*

Once again, antic tribal wisdom may come in handy, when modernist sophistication not merely fails, but quite undermines us. The 'Indians' of the time are routinely derided for having 'sold' Manhattan to the Dutch for but 60 Guilders worth of trade goods (the celebrated 'beads' may, or may not, have been in that mix). If they had known what it would be turned into, centuries later, by the inheritors of that estate, perhaps they might not have gifted it away! *What is to be Undone*, on this scale of things, could be a really long list. So, a bit of good housekeeping is due. But all that is for tomorrow, the *Day After.*

You see, Europe, and its New World Offshoots, gave us WW1 and WW2: now they are screeching for a Grand Sequel. It is that fatal *Temptation of Empire— to get something for nothing—*that they have battened on since the 1600's. It is sort of 'second nature' with them. *But this time they will not prevail.* For they are not merely financially, but morally, bankrupt as well.

NATO, under tutelage of its Master of Revels, has blithely violated international covenants, *willy-nilly*, preying upon the weak and the helpless like a heedless carnivore—reminding us all of *their* (*i.e.,* its constituent nations) not-so-old-style history of double-standards and imperial drives. Africa, Asia and South America know them, and their designs, by now, all too well—indeed, are all fairly up on their learning curves. And Auden's ringing lines apply to them all:

> *In the nightmare of this dark. All the dogs of Europe bark*
> *And the living nations, wait Each sequestered in its hate;*
> *Intellectual disgrace Strares from every human face,*
> *And the seas of pity lie Locked and frozen in each eye.*

The world's longest lived *rentiers* will now have to, finally, manage their households, trim their sails, and cut their coats according to such cloth as is available (without embezzling the resources of the *Other*). Prudence, discipline, and parsimony sounds like the good old Protestant Ethic to me. Time *they* embraced it, centuries after preaching it to other. After all, *any 'ethic'* is, perhaps, better than no *ethics*.

Part VII

Eurocentrism

40

Eurocentrism 101

A Primer

History is first made/unmade by Conquerors: and then, regrettably, written by them—or their hacks. Which leaves historical truth a hapless, pathetic hostage of the ruling ploys of the hegemonic *demiurge* at issue. *So it is that Eurocentrism—in the sciences, arts, politics, governance, medicine, et al.—dominates the planet today, having intruded into its farthest recesses.* So deep, wide, and encompassing is this ideology that its premises and prognoses have been largely internalized by governing elites the world over, all but unconsciously.

Culture is difference: and until the onset of this monotonic contagion, the world was blessed, for millennia, by a refreshing *plurality* of outlooks, practices, and beliefs. *Then came the European.* And *his* (gender intended) relentless expansion into every corner of the globe, for some 400 years, turned most of the world's cultures inside out. First, they were warped materially: looted, plundered, as the European saw fit. Next, they were, in that state of despoliation, *morally* (or shall I say mortally?) distorted, with their intellectual elites systematically cleansed of their own native philosophies, material and moral, and schooled instead in the extant modes of European ideas and practices.

Even 'dissent,' originating amongst the Colonized, had to be of a brand duly licensed, so that the 'dissenters' remained no more than His European Majesty's Loyal Opposition. Any other *indigenous* opposition would be branded as *'nativist'* (not least by the created brand of such 'loyal dissenters'), and crushed *tout a fait*. Recall the fate of the 2000 plus Native American Nations who 'dissented' from the invading European Colonists' plans for them—and you get the point. European 'international' institutions rule the entire world today, as intended. The UN, the World Bank, the WTO, the GATT: or the various 'Conventions,' from Geneva, Berne, and Basel—governing this, or ordaining that.

The *Non-European* world had little to do with the manufacture of such *fora*, but participate nonetheless—as second, third, or fourth class, members (decades ago, I knew an Indian economist who was seconded to the World Bank as a Director: he spent most of his time away from his 'job.' Why? It was ceremonial only. He was filling, back then, an unimportant 'India slot,' since the nation, being 'non-aligned' in the Cold War, was given short shrift. He was expected only to draw his paycheck—and take in the sights of D.C.).

An ex-Colony could be wholly redesigned, pole-to-pole, on the basis of a *Mother Country Template*. In India, some years ago, I met a senior Education Minister and said to him: What is Indian about India today? The Educational system was planted by Lord Macaulay, the Indian Penal Code is British, oddly enough, also masterminded by Macaulay; the Parliamentary system is British, as is the organization of the Indian army, judiciary, *etc.* Did India lack the basic organs of (self) government prior to the arrival of the Brits? *Did an India that scribed the world's first written grammar, its earliest classics of poetry and literature, its earliest algebra and calculus; that founded its earliest cities, its earliest science-cum-metaphysics, its earliest metallurgy, its earliest universities—really have to shamefacedly 'borrow' 'nineteenth century,' British Colonial, administrative, leftovers of faltering empire, after 'independence,' simply to plod on?*

He had nothing to say: the matter had never occurred to him. One can multiply such examples. To state it simply, European Hegemony is, was, *total*. And we all know what happens, even now in the twenty-first century, if any culture, nation, or people chooses to go its own way. Which makes the European (policy maker) the greatest, most inveterate, Hegemon in history. Genghis Khan may have conquered much of the world, but left its cultures intact. It is this wholesale *totalitarianism* that gets very little vent in the discourse of our times.

Small wonder: since the world's major media are also, not accidentally, European. A while ago a daring Senegalese educator, Amadou-Mahtar M'Bow, upon becoming the first African to head the Agency (UNESCO) commissioned the 'MacBride Report' that asked for a 'New Information Order' (to break the Western monopoly on information), in 1980. Of course, the West found a swift way to depose him: and the monopoly continues on, undisturbed.

True, Russia and China, the 'natural' *Other* retain a certain qualified 'autonomy': but, for how long? And to what effect? Recall China gave up its 'Maoism,' under European pressure: and the Soviets, their 'Communism.' And now they are, inevitably, yet being pressured, to yield even more than they likely ever realized. Suffice it to say—and this is not, as yet, widely understood—*that these good North Atlantic folk will not rest until they have girdled the globe twice over with their vanities*: and then once more—just for surety. Where does that leave the non-European Periphery today? Living precariously, and not at all by their *own* norms and institutions.

I fear there can be no greater anthropic tragedy than cultures forced to abide by the norms of others. 'Culture-death' may be the ultimate catastrophe in the process of societal extinction: one has only to witness the plight of the Aboriginals down-under, or Native Americans closer home to understand this. *Euromodernism now, like a great pall, Envelopes All.* Africa, South America and much of Asia, were *en route* to their own divergent paths to 'modernizing'—when their societies were overrun by the 'westernizing' impulses of Europeans. Indeed, Japan, in the twentieth century was farthest along that road (so would India have been, save for being 'arrested' by the British blight).

And then we know what happened. Today, Japan is yet another 'puppet' state of the West, despite its viable economy and competent technologies. Anglo-Amstyle Capitalism is/was thrust upon *all* by dint of force: legal, economic, diplomatic, political, and military—as needed. The UN requires adoption of Keynesian accounting, the WTO requires 'open economies,' and so forth: their set of 'pre-requisites' proliferate. And whatever the West wishes, becomes, effectively, Global Policy (and good for humanity).

Remember 'birth-control,' and the Malthusian bogey of the Post-WWII period? It is all a bit *passé* now. It was the Cold War yesteryear, then the War against Terror, next the Financialization of the world economy, and so on: doubtless, with even more such overarching universal mobilizations yet to come.

North America blinks: and even the mighty EU is ready to jump. How, indeed, can weaker societies hope to fare any better? European *productivism* plus North American *consumerism* are now the *sine qua non* of all nations, regardless of suitability, preference, or need. The mushrooming '*Global University*' delivers both, *universally*: the natural sciences turn out commercial and military technologies, the social sciences the requisite norms of social submission and consumer acquiescence. *Theirs to Produce, as they choose fit, at any cost, societal or natural: Yours but to work, consume, obey—and be silent.*

Every error of Euromodernism, in economics, in politics, in ecology is now, perforce, repeated worldwide. Having fortified themselves with enough explosives to detonate the earth, several times over, they now stimulate similar build-ups, complete with pretextual 'crises,' everywhere, defense Corps being amongst the largest of the Transnationals.

The issue is *not* simply that their economic model spells rank serfdom for toilers, today—and their political model a democracy where quiescent masses vote for representatives who are then bought out by Corporate lobbies, giving us, everywhere, '*the best government money can buy*' (without even the older eyewash as to guaranteed liberties). The issue is that *Alternatives* to the Great European Way are not allowed to even be seriously conceptualized, let alone implemented. A Buddhist economy, or any such with a semblance of economic *autarky*, cannot be tolerated. Similarly, a Tribalist, Communal, Polity is not permissible (save on 'reservations,' and in 'Bantustans').

A non-European, non-Consumerist, Culture cannot exist—if it is at odds with the 'culture' of Coco-Cola and McDonald's. And so a flat, monotonic, uniform, homogeneous, atomized, fragmented, alienated Amero-European denizen, living in privatized, individualized, isolate, tenements, with a gamut of ever multiplying gadgets as companions: *that* becomes the export template for all societies. *You know what I mean: it is that quintessentially European, gluttonous, paradise where 'hell is other people.'*

Angola to Australia, the same lush adverts ply the luxury, leisure, tropes of resort hotels, beach paradises, fast cars, private airplanes, fine wines and fashion shows—as though humanity was collectively, and merrily, *en vacance*—in these times of mass austerity and privation. *Civilizations take millennia to evolve: yet they can, sadly, succumb to vulgar materialist philistinism in but two generations.* It is not an edifying sight to witness: India, *e.g.,* stands poised on the brink of being stripped of its own motley 'Indianness' by this engulfing tide of globalized forces. Of course, the process of disintegration began over two centuries ago, with steadily encroaching British occupation: but has rapidly accelerated under the hothouse globalization of the past decades, spreading from urban enclaves to rural hinterlands. It is in some danger, if trends continue, of being, duly '*Singaporeanized*': *i.e.,* all GDP and no native, living, *culture* to speak of.

And all GDP, and no culture, makes Jack (or Janaka), to say the least, a very dull kid.

The European tried to convince his Colonies that double-entry bookkeeping and compound interest are the very *alpha* and *omega* of *civilization* (the latter being understood as 'Modernization,' Euro style). Where such ephemera govern all things, they are but signs of the real atrophy of affective, co-respective, societal relations (*giving us, as an end product, the American reality of a casino economy, a video culture, and an acquiescent polity*).

Europe itself, prior to its own Modernist *Devolution*, understood as much: as evidenced in the many medieval prohibitions/strictures of so-called 'Canon Law,' that were duly subverted by the Reformation, and cheered on by emergent commercial interests. Similarly, one might also recall that so-called 'economics'— *the hegemonic crown jewel of Euromodernism*—was once part of *Moral Philosophy*. Yes, *Moral* Philosophy. Adam Smith, whom average economists ignorantly, if not disingenuously, revere as a sort of a 'First Economist,' held the Chair of *Moral Philosophy* at Glasgow. Yet, the Chronicle of Higher(!) Education, thoughtfully, lists Economics under the rubric of *'Business,'* within its Job Listings. Perhaps, it knows better than to think the latter-day economist incorporates any 'moral philosophy' in his/her nostrums.

So much for the *Devolution of Values*.

At any rate, civilization is, amongst other *non-things*, the *pacification of anthropic existence*. And that is achieved in our species by the domestication, amidst affective ties of emotive reciprocity, of predatory masculinist drives by the *moral* modalities and metaphors of kinship. So civilization subsists, *prima facie*, on a shared *morality. It was the fate of Europe, in mistaken genius, to deconstruct that antic paradigm in favor of a 'contractual society' built, instead, on material 'interests.'*

In short, the moral basis of society was discarded in favor of a material base (oddly enough, even the putatively 'Christian' maxim—though the idea actually predates Christianity—of 'Do unto others as you would have others do unto you' is not a *moral* rule, in the first instance, much as it is *a reciprocating principle of contractual, mutually beneficial exchanges*. A mother's concern for a child is *not* conducted on the basis of a *'mutuality of benefit'*—but of a *'unilateral'* caring).

In effect, Europe embraced *Amorality* as a dominant societal norm (whence 'Economics' divested itself swiftly of the encumbrance of 'moral philosophy'), thereby leaving the lineage of anthropic, human society behind. *In sum, 'civilization' is a willful 'choice' made to avoid the low road to a materialist El Dorado (which is, sadly, also the road to Tartarus). Tribal societies, not yet devolved to the masculinist temptation of Empire, exemplify such a choice. In that sense, the European is not yet ascended to civilization (vide* Gandhi's celebrated quip): and, as past and present events confirm, *ad nauseam*, the pacification of existence is not even remotely a policy interest in their global Agenda—*au contraire*, arguably, *they are, quite enduringly, still the most warlike of tribes in history.*

Selecting but one fact, at random, *e.g.*, *there is not one major world crisis in the past 100 years that is not European in origin.* They remain implacably the world's premier destabilisers, regime-changers, interventionists, and warmongers. And they account, directly or indirectly, for virtually *All* of global economic, financial, ecological, and societal instability (though China, India, and Russia are playing 'catch-up' at least in the area of ecological destruction).

That is why 'Eurocentrism'—*a grand synthesis of a philosophy of Materialism, a self-serving notion of Progress measured in material indices, a near blind 'faith' in the protocols of Science, and a readiness to use force to achieve any/all of its 'modernist' Policy ends*—is the real, encompassing, scourge of our times, a fact that needs be understood in all its baleful entirety. This is not merely to help resist that advancing avalanche of distorted priorities that threaten all, including the planet: though that is, surely, vital enough as a task for our times. I suggest, also, that *Non-Europeans*, in a very profound sense, effectively *'do not know who they are'* (this is not dissimilar, epistemically, to women not knowing who they really are, when reared within the ideology of Patriarchy) for having been reared, for generations, in the *unnaturally assumed pseudo-identities of Euro-Modernist discourse*—at grievous, irretrievable cost of the virtual annihilation of their own received culture, tradition, and heritage.

Transcendence may only be contingent, therefore, upon such a deep, revelatory, comprehension of what I see as modern history's *Greatest Transgression.*

41

Toward Dissolution

In this short piece, I clarify the standpoint of my *Critique* of EuroModernism (in the second section of this Note). I have tried to argue, in various previous papers, that EuroModernism is the demoralizing, totalizing, specter that haunts the globe today—albeit now in its very last tremors (though its ghoulish tail lasheth at us all, willy-nilly). Its expungement will be, I have written, a great boon to humanity, globally, not least to European societies themselves that were its very first victims.

I have not claimed this as a *moral* imperative, though it certainly is so. Nor have I forwarded it as an *a priori* political judgment, though the Argument might not be diminished by such a stance. Instead, I have merely posited the requisites of *real,* anthropic societies: and suggested that all of Modernist presumptions run plainly contrary to their basic presumptions. In effect, Modernist ontology and epistemology are inherently *anti-anthropic* in their thrust: and will, if allowed full rein, destroy our anthropic existence entirely—thereby fully arresting human evolution. The prospect of a *Transhuman* future, which is not far off—if unchecked— is quite ineradicably written into Modernist dogmas.

To the 'progressivist' Modernist such a critique will appear *un'dialectical,'* equivalent to 'throwing the baby out, alongside the bathwater.' Stated differently, the *Loyal Critics of His Modernist Majesty* have it that it is kosher to criticize

Modernist *realities,* but not Modernist *ideals* (that they, apparently, share)—omitting to remember the critical, umbilical, cord connecting the one to the other.

Indeed, Modernism 'creates' a wholly *mutant* social form, alien to the anthropic essence, and antithetical to its hospitable survival, in a relatively equable natural world. It replaces the vital nexus of *kinship* with *contractual* relations, to the point of viewing society itself as a 'contract' rather than an *affective* compact. It postulates, and idealizes, an *asocial* 'individual' who is prompted with *self-seeking* conduct as the ontological 'building block' of this 'civil' society. It also vests this luckless creature—doomed henceforth to live out the dual, if still monotonic, destinies of a producer/consumer—with illimitable material drives, that keep it at the wheel, like caged hamsters, for the duration of its days.

After performing this radical *caesarean*, it compensates this disabled, rootless, entity with the promise of a slew of meretricious *'rights'*: equality, liberty, *et al.* Where/when these dubious benefices are found insufficient in themselves (as ever!), there is that standby, gaudy, glut of commodities that might help while away the idle, empty hour, where such time is available at all; away, that is, from the daily, lifelong, grind of *laboring*—usually for the profit of *others,* which is the abject lot of the vast majority.

Even were these 'rights' to be 'real' (*i.e.,* realizable) they would only help solidify the *alienated* individual, forlornly within his/her personalized domain of cold, 'rational' *anomie,* floundering without the crucial rudders of care and consideration, manifestly essential to anthropic well-being. But they are *tendentious* promises only, run through, and razed, by the designs of the rich and the powerful—who manage the 'system,' one way or other, for their own ends.

To live and die within the solitary confinement of such a lightless, privatized, existence, formally 'equal' to others suffering similarly under the same common fate, does not, somehow, appear to represent a cornucopia of psychic riches to be envied, or marveled at: let alone being the apex of human attainment, as Euro-Modernism views itself. Indeed, it is a condition that, perhaps somewhat more obviously, moves sentient, feeling, creatures to the very margins of debauchery and destruction (of the Self, or Others)—as befitting a state of rudderless *anomie.*

Paradoxically, the more normless, and *amoral,* the real societal state of being, on average, the more glaring the Modernist flaunt of Constitutions, Codes, and Rulebooks (yes, it is an *Empire,* any time of day, blest with a commanding largesse of Laws). In fact, even a casual glance at the civil/social statistics of EuroModernist societies would help confirm the very palpable *psychic* suffering, *alienation,* if you will, that accompanies a life *spent*—not lived!—in such an arid terrain of perpetual, pitiless competition, one-upmanship, and despoiling, extirpative, conflict.

It becomes, inescapably, a nasty, boorish, Hobbesian world where, as has justly been remarked and iterated often in this work, 'hell is other people.' The urban jungles of the lead Modernist entity, the US, illustrate this ineffable quality of hellishness, almost in caricature. Small wonder that desperation, existential *angst*, and coruscating, irrequitable *loneliness* is the lot of so many of the true believers who still worship at the Modernist altar (even whilst being sacrificed on it). Indeed, the frantically utopian yearnings of the sensitized, within them, are a reflex only of the unbearable, destituting, burdens of that prostrating *geist*.

The conclusion may well be indefeasible: *that EuroModernism is little other than sheer fraud, a scurrilous Libel upon the—admittedly slender reeds of beneficence of—the Human Race. For desocialization is, for us humans, dehumanization.*

Stated differently, the eclipse of *gemeinschaft* communities by the hypertrophic *gesellschaft* formations so favored by Modernist Corporatism—for it is their choice creation!—presages only the slow, suffocating, extinction of the civilities, nay decencies, of anthropic life. With the latter, dies *morality*—a societal norm deriving from the domestic sphere of *child rearing* (the domain, *in extremis*, of societal care and consideration). Whence arises the *amoral* 'human' (a real oxymoron), now rendered fair game for manipulation, robotization, and exploitation—by the powers that be.

I have tried to point out that deep underneath the unprecedentedly egregious Crises of our times is a real, titanic struggle between the 'mammals' (warm blooded/heat-seeking) and the 'reptiles' (cold blooded/calculating). I have no doubt that given *time*, our *species-being* will, eventually, assert itself: but it could be this very vital resource that may be insufficient to ensure such an outcome—given the overflowing Tribe of Dr. Strangeloves (and worse) that today populates, in increasing overswell, the extant halls of Power and Governance.

EuroModernism is, in short, misanthropy, writ large.

❊

Standpoints, in such analyses of the here, and the hereafter, are clearly important. Any philosophy or 'social science' that elides a sound knowledge of a realist anthropology of the species is, thereby, simply gratuitous. Regrettably, almost all of European speculative *philosophy*, since the so-called 'enlightenment'—including its 'social sciences'—has had nothing but thin air as its presumptive, ontic foundation (whether pronounced piously or pompously).

Marx's Tenth Thesis on Feuerbach says: *The standpoint of the old materialism is civil society; the standpoint of the new is human society, or social humanity.* It can now be seen that both the 'standpoints' referred to, above, are flawed. 'Civil

Society' is the quintessential artifact of EuroModernism, that negates every axiom of anthropic society, in its constitution, being the playground (or is it the battle-ground?) of 'universal egoism'—where each sees the other, and society itself, as a means to his/her personal ends. But the novel 'standpoint' he proffers, in its stead, is also pure fiction: indeed, what *realist* basis exists for such a fantasy?

Now, to the extent that his 'human society' is none other than *tribal* forma-tions—first overrun by European conquistadores and then eulogized as '*primitive communism*'—there would be, thence, a solid base for a very real, *already achieved,* 'Utopia.' But it is not at all clear that that is what is being referred to: 'primi-tive communism' was, undeniably, an original point of departure for Marx, and others—but his later ideas left that inspiration behind, as he went on to embrace a radical, 'left-wing' version of Liberal EuroModernist ideas (I am aware that, in his very last years, Marx changed his mind about many such issues, in his jottings on the so-called 'Russian Road,' but his legacy and legators did not scale that into their plans).

As I have written elsewhere, the underlying vision of Marx, like so many of his 'progressive' contemporaries, is not too far apart—with some hyperbole—from a secular version of the Judeo-Christian 'kingdom of heaven.' The irony of other-wise materialist philosophers, plim with fanciful ideals is far from a trifling one. Most European 'enlightenment' philosophers, in this *genre,* theorized even more 'speculatively,' much like the US 'declaration of independence' positing boldly, one presumes with a divinely granted perspicacity, various human attributes given us by an invisible 'Creator.' I do not, given such discouraging precedents, advo-cate, in turn, yet another 'pie-in-the-sky' Program leading to a Promised Land: instead, I point to 'actually achieved utopia,' *i.e.,* the innocuous, self-sustaining, anthropic communities that lived contentedly (if within unbreachable anthropic limits), on the basis of *affective, kindred based, convivial relations*—almost 'dialec-tically' antipodal to any and all versions of EuroModernist societies.

As I have written, we can't simply 'imagine' ourselves into a 'new world,' on the basis of a grand, even noble, '*camaraderie of ideals*': which is largely the way EuroModernists went about their plans to unscalable human misery, such as has characterized social engineering, Capitalist and Socialist, in the twentieth cen-tury. Anthropic society is real: it is not difficult to fathom—if studied seriously, without the aids of colored or discolored lenses. *It is neither good nor bad: it is what it is.*

I argue that the essence of our *species-being* lies in *kinship*: and, accordingly, I suggest that societies that are based on that live *possibly* more satisfying lives, in consequence. I point to the universality of the *family* as the ultimate warren of nurturance, care, and warmth for the human animal as providing powerful testimony in support of that supposition.

This is not utopian 'banner-waving,' nor does it constitute unduly wishful thinking: *au contraire*, it is a serious argument that is as yet, providentially?, verifiable empirically: given that a few such societies still exist where, by sheer inadvertence, the Modernists, be they European or *Other*wise, have not annihilated them completely. As such, the *Argument* is in point of fact, for better or for worse, *realist* in the extreme.

One Final matter: Modernism is the motherlode from which both Capitalism and Socialism derive. Putting aside Socialism, that derived from an appreciation of the more egregious defaults of EuroCapitalism (obvious to both Dickens and Engels, for example, in England), the issue might be posed: *which came first, Modernism or Capitalism?* Unlike the chicken-or-the-egg conundrum ('solved,' apparently, leastways to their own satisfaction by Brit researchers, recently), this one is rather easy.

It is Modernism that first validates individualized, unilateral (*i.e.*, *un*-social, and *anti*-social) *self-interest*, unmindful of the community interest, as socially appropriate: it is this glaring watershed that separates not only Europe from its own history, but also from the history of All existing societies, globally. That idea found its resonance in the subsequent approval of the ill-fated *Profit-motive* (that so disfigures all scapes of Europe, forever after) which is the mantra, and mainstay, of Modernist capitalism.

So, yes, EuroModernism was the foster-nurse, and midwife, of EuroCapitalism.

42

Eurocentrism and EuroModernism

I have defined *Euro-Modernism*, in another Work (Kanth, 2005), as consisting of some *Four* signal attributes: a less than critical *'faith'* in Science, a self-congratulatory notion of *'Progress'* (measured, for the most part, in *material* terms), an over-riding philosophy of *Materialism*, and a willingness to deploy *force* to 'modernize' (or, as even the Liberal saint, J.S. Mill averred, to *'force people to be free':* the vaunted 'freedom' understood in terms of the perspective of the 'liberator' rather than the 'to-be-liberated'—on the broad lines of Robespierre's 'Virtue without Terror is ineffective' idea) peoples.

In my reckoning *Euro-Modernism* is virtually identical to *Eurocentrism,* and subsumes both 'Capitalism' and 'Socialism' within it. So, whilst any society can 'modernize' (*i.e., evolve in its own terms*), *Euro-Modernism* is driven by a very schematic, rigid, and monovalent agenda that has, *by force,* cloned itself globally—to the everlasting destruction of *Non-European and/or Pre-Modern* cultures and civilizations. As such, it is wholly and ruthlessly *'totalitarian,'* in scope, and represents the most inexorable force for wholesale vandalism that history has ever witnessed.

I view the ensuing *struggle—of Other Cultures (and Contra currents within the European world)* trying to survive its onslaughts—as a struggle between the *'Mammals'* and the *'Reptiles' (i.e.,* between the 'warm-blooded' and the 'cold-blooded'), or between *Civilization* and *Barbarism.*

Implicit in the notions, above, is the idea that materialism (scientific and philo-sophical) which undergirds the Great European Way is false—both as metaphysics and science. Advances in *Physics* (*via Quantum* discoveries) are steadily confirming the *scientific inadequacy* of materialism; and one has only to glance at the state of the world today *vis-à-vis* economy, society, culture, environment, and morality, to fathom the consequences of the materialist *Weltanschauung* on the mundane and extra-mundane world.

Finally, it is European *'social science' (which is no more than Protestantism, in secular form)* that 'delivers' the *mantras* of *Eurocentrism* to all and sundry today.

43

Racism

A Personal Discursus

I present, here, my personal reflections on this scourge of humankind. Why personal? Because I am 'privileged' to have experienced it directly (satisfying, one might say, the 'participant observation' requirement of Anthropology), in the very specific sense in which I will be defining the term, at the hands, not of the Aryan Nation, but very cultivated and urbane people: colleagues, friends, et al., who champion, in public, quite contrary ideals.

It is, of course, no 'privilege' at all that European society compels Non-Europeans (who choose to live within it) to be daily reminded of it, endlessly: and in all interactions. The sheer ennui of that defies description, and far outweighs the ensuing outrage and indignation.

In that sense the European who makes this topic an object of scholarly interest is exercising no more than a 'choice,' out of a large palette of options: au contraire, the Non-European can scarcely fail to be engaged with it, even against his/her will. I know I resent this enforced 'waste' and 'misdirection' of my time and interests even more than the more mundane stigmata one accepts as a recipient of racialist policy and practice. The racially targeted minority lives, permanently in a psychological gulag that stunts and crimps the normal fluencies of a human life irreparably.

*One necessary caveat. My obiter dicta may/may not endorse any received opin-
ion on the matter: indeed, I have always called it as I have viewed it, than with a
mind to staying on the right side of any norm of 'political correctness' (the latter is yet
another well consecrated myth outfitted to imply that despite the fact that we live in
a vividly abhorrent world of iniquity and oppression, it is still the 'best of all possible
worlds'—since we at least pay lip service to high ideals in our gracious parlor room
conversations).*

✻

President Mugabe, strongman of Zimbabwe, and no favorite of the West, at a
recent Summit in India, as Chairperson of the African Union, thanked India
for supporting African causes w/out 'dehumanizing' Africans. He hit it (as far as
defining the essence of racism).

There are many forms of racism, many definitions, and many theories of it.
Perhaps it is most potent in the form it has taken, in the European world, whose
basic configuration Mr. Mugabe summarized in just one word.

It were well if Racism were thought of, at its apex, as exactly that: the *dehumanization* of a fellow species—quite apart from its baggage of economic, political, legal, and other cultural deprivations, that, more generally, occupy public
policy attention.

I have said 'European,' in a generic sense, because one or other form of racism
has been a European penchant for centuries: and shows little, serious, sign of abating. And, within that praxis and ideology, Anglo-Norman stances have been the
most pronounced (why this may be so is a subject worthy of speculation, and this
short piece may offer a clue, by allusion). This would be true even if white police
officers didn't routinely murder unarmed Afro-Americans, as a near-monthly
staple in the land of the free—with virtual impunity.

The hypocrisy of the Media, the Authorities, *et al.,* in this area is quite striking,
even exemplary. Not to omit the Universities, and their well-provisioned intelligentsia, who, if in expectedly effete fashion, do little more than, ritually—when
at all—affirm minority rights, *en générale*, and leave it at that. The hegemony of
empire conceivably needs such a tonic, now and then.

Afro-Americans may well head the list of victims, but the stance is/was also
operative with various other non-Europeans as well, if history—past and present—is to be recalled. Native peoples, Chinese, or 'Orientals' more generally,
Hispanics, *et al.* Of course, the Game is stacked against *all* Non-Europeans: in
particular, when so many amongst the latter fall easily prey to divide and rule

strategies, where blind individualism, as a prior default, has not had them fail to affiliate with their own reference groups/strata.

Regardless of whether the vast majority of people of European origin share this ideology of dehumanization, they are, nonetheless, inevitably (if unequally) 'beneficiaries' of it. Not dissimilarly, males 'benefit,' as a class, from systematic misogyny.

Now, to need to clear the ground for some other, related issues. There is a Caste-system within European tribes that has engendered victimization of entire peoples (as with Irish, Italians, *etc.,* in the early history of the US, *e.g.*), historically. Similarly, the endemic anti-Semitism of Christian Europe has oppressed Jewish people, for millennia—and is even today very far from extinct (this remained true even in the 'socialist' Europe of yesteryear: my late friend, Wlodzimierz Brus, a noted Polish economist and partisan, left his native land for the sanctuary of Oxford owing to, he told me, the sharpness of Polish prejudice at the highest levels of state. That may not have been the whole story, but it was real all the same). Yet, I believe, outright genocide has not been their lot as recurrently as the unbroken, wanton slaughter of Non-Europeans by Europeans, for at least four centuries.

This last statement is quite critical. Non-Europeans are anything but incapable of intolerance. Indeed, cultural chauvinism, to some degree or other, is a near universal, usually, once we step outside the matrix of simpler, tribal social formations (such as, *e.g.,* the Australian Aboriginals). Religious bigotry is another, similar, prejudice that offers a parallel: the Abrahamic faiths are emblematic in this area, accounting for the vast majority of instances of religiously based violence and oppression in the world, and being at least a party to most such conflicts. Oft, even within a religion, internal schisms lead to horrors: *e.g.,* Shia vs Sunni in Islam, caste conflicts in India, and Protestant *vs* Catholic in Christianity.

So, yes, human society, *en générale*, is run through with all manner of prejudice, intolerance, and violent hatred. But, I will maintain the Argument that overriding all these malevolent forms of social rejection, in terms of scale, continuity, and depth, European racism has no parallel in human history, especially in the Era of European Modernism—dating broadly from the fifteenth century.

Today, racism is the silent, unwritten code of European governors (it by no means remains insulated at that level, but percolates down to all segments of society). What makes Euro-racism particularly repugnant is its stark, even stunning, contrast with the never-ending declaration of high societal morality, rights, and freedoms that also, monotonically, emanate from the same provenance.

This is an important point. If one believes in inequality, special innate superiority, and 'might is right' ideas, then oppression follows logically—and not at all inconsistently. But this is not the case with Modern Europe.

They, in other words, followed justly infamous double standards to a nicety: boldly preaching one philosophy, and brazenly practicing another. I will not stoop to provide examples (to the educated, they are common knowledge: others may need to do some homework). Most of the non-European world made no such strident declarations of universal piety and benevolence as Europe did in the ascendant phase of its Modernist Revolutions.

In other words, they were ingenuous enough to match their iniquitous ideas with suitably invidious actions. The Taleban stone women to death for adultery: but, in their eyes, *they are adhering to norms, not breaking them.*

No, I do not mean that consistency is a virtue: rather, that hypocrisy is not.

❄

How are we to explain this European uniqueness? One strong explanation is that conquest of the world, and domination over the world's peoples, as accomplished by Europeans, gave them a 'charged' confidence in this area that they may have lacked otherwise.

However, I will add a dimension to this discussion that is, possibly, novel. And it pertains to the 'dehumanization' idea, previously mentioned. It could be that my observations may apply only, or with unusual force, to Anglo-Norman formations since they are the dominant force in the world today—on most scales. I don't know. Other analysts may have to follow through this notion to test the range of its applicability.

My understanding—if it is that—comes from British India (and the US), if only because I know that segment better than the colonial exploits of other colonizing nations. I have ever been struck with the oft-noticed, yet practically ignored, fact that, in their multi-generational sojourn in India, there is one abiding feature: that, in all that time, the Brits maintained virtually no relationship with the natives, rarely troubling even to learn the language, let alone customs, or traditions—relying, instead, for the most part, on paid native informers (much like early colonial anthropologists), or native hostages.

Why? It makes little practical sense because hegemony may have been easier, more economically, and more swiftly, achieved—had they 'fraternized' more. Why didn't they? Now let's bring in the 'dehumanization' idea. At essence, the term implies that the subject, at issue, is not a 'valid' human entity (in all malignant irony, Hollywood made a film titled 'a man named horse,' where this accusation is turned against Native Americans by a White Settler). Where does this denial of 'humanness' stem from?

Why did the Brits so thoroughly shun the peoples they ruled in India to the point of complete occlusion? I now bring in my speculation. There is a self-absorption to Europeans that is, in my perception, a cultural *singularity.* One might call it, for want of a better word, an advanced form of *autism.* To state the matter: it is almost as if, in a manner of speaking, the '*Other*' simply did not exist, so that their wholesale exclusion was less an act of will, or policy, but rather 'intrinsic'— in the sense of not being 'thought out.'

If this idea can be sustained, it will become apparent that, at issue, was not virulent antipathy, or violent revulsion, but a simple, anthropological act, or non-act: of 'non-perception.' In other words, the ruled—in India, in this instance—did not appear, to the Brits, as human 'wholes,' but as temporal-functional entities only: *i.e.,* as native workers, soldiers, mutineers, *etc.* It is this cloak of 'invisibility' thrust upon them that perspicuous Non-Europeans have found incomprehensible, applying normal human criteria.

I will not cite examples, but just one instance may provide a clue. At the infamous Jallianwala Bagh (British India, *circa* 1919), General Dyer ordered steady and continuous machine-gun firing into a crowd of peacefully gathered men, women, and children, coolly, calmly and, quite unemotionally (examples of such actions are legion: from the hunting of Aboriginals in Australia to the outrages in the Belgian Congo). It was not an act of unbridled passion, such as (presumably) moved the Turkish massacre of Armenians, Upper caste Hindu atrocities against Dalits, or Sunni murders of Sh'ites (or *vice versa*) in West Asia. It was not even 'rational' in the sense of being anything even remotely close to being 'required' to achieve the intended effect—of pacification.

Nor was it sheer wild, cruelty-driven, bestial, male savagery, on display during wars, for example, amongst all peoples. Nor was it located in some presumed period of a Lapsarian pre-history, but in the twentieth century, and by a culture that saw itself as refinement itself (though I do refer to them—leastways their ruling elites—as the '*Brutish Isles*').

Au contraire, it was done mechanically, and unreflectively, in the same way people snuff out vermin in their households: by not viewing them at all as forms of life. No doubt General Dyer went on to sip his port, and peruse his copy of *The Times* that evening, routinely—for it was, after all, just another working day. I suggest that even the dropping of nuclear devices on Japan (rather than fellow-European Germany) was carried out in that remarkably 'non-sentient' way.

Now, normally, in 'social science,' one seeks—and finds—'material' explanations, so racism is often thought of as a tool of political economy. I think it certainly bears that function, but I am arguing that, prior to any such utilitarian calculus, Non-Europeans were, just possibly, already 'damned' to non-recognition—simply for being just that.

An example: one might argue that Afro-Ams are looked down upon today because of their history of slavery: but *vice versa* might also be true—that they were enslaved because they were looked down upon (so, it also may not be an Either/Or issue). *Remarkably, it's almost as if the 'Other' was not even that, and bore no anthropic existence whatsoever.*

I recommend catching Hollywood at it—faithful mirror as it has ever been of racism, sexism, and xenophobia—like a powerful and glamorous Fifth Estate, propping up empire in its own unique way. The old movie *Hatari* comes to mind: where a stellar white cast is adventuring, on safari, in Africa. It may not be too much of an exaggeration to say that *African animals have more speaking parts in it than the African Coolies:* who are featured endlessly bearing trays, fetching things, and generally being obedient Sambos. Now, this is a Post-WW II American film, and not set in the nineteenth century in some antic, historical tale. Educated folk wrote the script, produced it, directed it, and acted in it: but it didn't occur to them that there was anything out of the ordinary.

Or, I can refer to the even more self-absorbed Brits: a major mystery series, on television (produced for ITV), Inspector Lewis, leastways in its early phase, ran multiple episodes with no significant non-white roles in it: set in Oxford, an international university town no less, an otherwise savvy camera somehow also failed to 'spot' minorities anywhere, even as background noise. Even worse, if this were to be pointed out to the producers, I doubt they would have blanched.

You see such things happen not by fault, but by default. So, rather than prejudice, I am suggesting something more immanent, and ineffable, for which I find the 'autism' idea serviceable. The non-European appeared a jot more than just 'dehumanized'—which yet suggests some volition: rather, as simply non-Human in the eyes of the European. This is—if very roughly—ideationally equivalent to a dog, presumed color blind, being unable, as such, to see green or red (*btw,* recently, this has been discovered to be untrue). One can't blame the dog for a disability.

The continuing atrocities against non-Europeans by Europeans (in particular the indiscriminate drone-killings with a 90% collateral casualty rate, is significantly reminiscent of General Dyer's insouciant murders), in the current era, may well lend some credence to this notion: though today, admittedly, the crass political economy of an Age of Imperium overrides any need for subtler, more intrinsic, explanations.

I do not mean to suggest that this idea replaces more conventional explanations of racism: but that it may well be a useful, and novel, supplement to them.

❈

My own personal experience in the US/UK—not to be trivialized after Michael Polanyi's pathbreaking *Personal Knowledge* work, all but ignored by ruling opinion in academe—also confirms that strong impression. I need hardly say more.

If true, then this points to the importance of the notion of latent 'propensities' that Euro-Modernism denies strenuously (I have argued elsewhere, *e.g.,* that men and women are instinctually different—whether 'culture' accentuates that difference, or attempts to blot it out).

But, as a more general argument—though a certain cadre of the anthropocentred is uncomfortable with the notion—it is quite demonstrably true. Instincts, for example, undeniably, guide animal conduct. The Bonobos (pacific), *e.g.,* are quite different from Chimps (aggressive). And we are, *contra* many genres of religious ideology (inclusive of Judeo-Christian ideas), for all our anthropic conceit, little more than animals.

In humans, culture is the agency of *difference,* so the 'propensities' I alluded to would be vested in specific cultures: and so, unsurprisingly, Danish capitalism is a thing apart from American capitalism—and a shared 'economic system' does not obliterate that difference.

Modernism cleverly elides culture (whence difference)—so as to posit a homogeneous, standardized 'society' globally—the better to manage and manipulate it as needed. Yet, today, a continued future for humankind may well rest upon such minutiae of difference as actually exist (despite efforts to stamp them out). At any rate, we should now know why materialist 'political economy' perspectives dominate analyses of racism. It is because, in so dissolving it within a bland, universal soup, the unique peculiarities of Europeans in this matter are quite veiled over.

This is akin to blaming a generic 'capitalism' for all the ills of the modern world, whereas it is unmistakably Anglo-Norman extremist drives within it that have precipitated its ruinously calamitous nature: Icelandic capitalism, *e.g.,* is not, and will never be, a threat to human survival. Put another way, there are unique *cultural* endowments that lead to the very same 'structure' producing different outcomes.

More bluntly, one important effect of the Anglo-Norman domination of the world has been the virtual excision of any critical studies of *their* own specific social anthropology. It is that *genre* of historical inquiry, that I sometimes term *'reverse anthropology,'* that still awaits its Copernicus.

At any rate, as may be apparent, I do not deny the pellucid economics and politics of racism, but I do stress the fact that Euro-racism is a unique breed apart; so, the notion that 'we are all racists' that is the implied residual of such approaches palters, I believe, very seriously, with the truth.

On the other hand, I am open enough to offer this hunch/hypothesis to the acid test of facts: submitting it to their verdict IF they do, clearly and convincingly, militate against it.

The dehumanization idea, it needs be pointed out, cuts both ways, defining both victim and persecutor: since the presumed autism of the oppressor may be a sign of their being, say, *quasi*-human?

It might also allow for a somewhat unexpected 'out' to our worthy, Hesperian cousins: we may have to echo Biblical sentiment in that, just possibly: *they know not what they do.*

44

Explaining a Critique

(Euro)Modernism: Delusions, Debacles, and Defaults

It is time to explain, for these are things that have never been said before. I have suggested that *all* of (Euro)Modernist ideology (or, EM)—Philosophy, 'Social Science,' what have you—is essentially misconceived: *since it is not based on a sound knowledge of our real Anthropic State of Being.* EuroModernist (many different modernisms were afoot, when Europe, by dint of conquest, imposed its own brand as the *only* approved brand on the world) thinking often simply carried over, in its general *weltanschauung*, various arcana of Christian theology—flights of fancy so to speak—onto a secular plane, with its parallel view of a 'pilgrim's progress,' onto salvation (if, only, *via* purgatory, be it of the Left or the Right), in so many 'stages.'

Marx's 'communism,' *e.g.,* is little more than a secular heaven—indeed, his Early Works reek gaily of a warm, Christian romanticism—much like the other 'utopias' that preceded his work (as with Thomas More). To be sure, until Darwin's publication, an *adequate* biology—*i.e.,* that we are *animals,* likely not made in the 'image of god,' unless, perchance, god was an ape—was not available to the many canonical figures in that tradition: though, on the *autre* hand, anthropology was not at all so hindered.

Now, to come to the crux, *it is impossible to set up—meaningful—societal 'ideals,' let alone comment on Wo(Man's) 'eternal state,' without real knowledge of the latter.* Yet, that is exactly how it got done. As such, it was *all*, only *speculative*—and not in the best sense of that word, either. One has only to read Freud's facile fabrications—his entire slew of this or that 'complexes'—to understand the inaneness of it all. Perhaps, had he lived amongst the Masai, or the Aboriginals, he might have reconsidered his 'Oedipal Complex' flaunt, amongst other such solecisms. But his was only arrant armchair anthropology—*study a few Viennese, so to speak, and you have the world in your palms!*—of a markedly three-legged nature (a rebuke that Levi-Strauss once directed against Sartre, under similar circs).

Philosophy fared no better, for the same reasons. Schopenhauer's rabid travesties, as but one example, about the 'nature of women,' are shot through with rank misogyny, posing as serious commentary: again, based on little other than personal whimsy. Hegel's notions of the 'Orient' were also but late repeats of Aristotle's stellar ignorance in such matters. It was all rather shabby ethnocentrism—*i.e.*, *Eurocentrism*—minus even a modicum of self-awareness.

Politically, this took to rather wild sloganeering: just glance at the—self-eulogizing—French and American Revolutionary Declarations, for instance. Did they seriously imagine that yodelling from pulpits, or barricades, could radically alter our real anthropic state? *But they did*: owing, partly, again, to the legacy of Christian notions of 'perfectibility' (which gets transmuted into secular ideas of 'progress' that dominate Modernist ideology).

In another vein, take Rousseau's specious 'man is born free, but everywhere is in chains,' declaration, that so stirred the imaginations of the (feckless) intelligentsia. Did they stop to think, for an instant, that not all 'chains' are morbid: had they never experienced the 'chains' of caring, of love, or compassion? Apparently not—and in consequence they easily smote all chains, including the vital (societal) ties that heal, and succor: and, to make it worse, helped forge new chains that tied the mass of the populace to the wheel of capital accumulation—for others to leech on.

In their (apparent) revolutionary zeal for 'freedom,' they 'freed' most of us from the very social compact that gave us that sense of identity without which we are rootless, lost, and forlorn, individuals. In another sense, the *'moral'* economy, resting on affective ties, was expunged in favor of the *'material'* economy, based on acquisitive motivations (though this remains an invidious process, still far from completed). To an extent, also, speaking in large scapes, the ancient subsistence-based *social economy of women* (a vital base of the moral economy) was undermined by the emergent, expansionary, *political economy of men*. Indeed, what dire catastrophes were not unleashed amongst our species in the name of 'progress'!

In effect, they 'forgot' (again owing to a theology that held humans in the image of the Supra-Human) that we are *animals,* close kin, no more, of Chimps, and Bonobos—and, perhaps, only slightly more elevated (in fact, both fatefully and sadly, we took after Chimps, and not Bonobos, though nearly equi-distant from both). So, a real, tragic history saw to it that such manner of vacuous ideals got duly shattered, and the ill-fated cannon fodder who fought for such day-dreams perished in large numbers at the hands of their new 'leaders'—in both capitalist and socialist revolutions.

❅

But, the obvious lessons from such debacles have, sadly, not yet been learnt: at least, not fully. For such 'movements' yet surge on, in our times: to certain, and predictable, disaster. The anthropic male is, instinctually, both aggressive and turf-conscious—and the urge to dominate boils over, wherever power is to be availed of: in particular, when/where there is no weighted countervailing anthropic norm (such as colligating kinship rules) to obstruct it. In other words, male power-struggles, outside of a social-moral vacuum, subvert any/all 'utopian' urges, regularly.

This is our history: it has been our history—and it will be our history (His story, to be accurate). Modernism is 'open-season' for such struggles, because it enters the world *via* the prior, and on-going, destruction of kinship-communal ties that could, albeit limitedly, restrain and contain such ruinous drives.

Now, it is easy to understand why the 'utopian' impulse takes hold in Europe when it does—*circa* More's work in the sixteenth century: just when kin-based *gemeinschaft* communities were eroding in North-Western Europe, under pressure of the force and fraud of the commercializing ruling classes (enclosures, monetization, *et al.).* It was, thereby, no more than a *cri de cœur.* In effect, the votaries of EM were seeking, blindly as it were, and oft in metaphor, what they themselves had first eviscerated on the mundane plane. In pitiable irony, having first forsaken the felicities of 'home,' they went about seeking sanctuary everywhere else—to no success.

There you have, in summary form, the contours of late European angst, and anomie, writ large. Neither a consumer cornucopia, nor an idealized 'communism,' can ever still that pain, though it was obviously hoped it would.

❅

Now I am not suggesting that anthropology is destiny. It is possible to overcome, albeit with nothing short of eternal vigilance!, male aggression: in fact that is what makes (mainly, not exclusively, matrilineal) tribal societies of antiquity so very interesting and instructive. They worked out familial /emotive/kinship restraints, such that murderous male violence was at least out of bounds *within* intra-tribal boundaries (which is a huge accomplishment, given the record in Modernist societies where 'incestuous' killing sprees, and mini 'civil wars,' of one kind or other, are ever rampant, specially within the lead EM formation: the US).

Au contraire, EM eliminates such natural-social restraints by disabling community, and devalorizing kinship ties: thereby leaving the field wide open for *amoral* depredations. The real, ontic basis of anthropic morality is the *kin-based societal entity—indeed its provenance lies in the evolutionary need to sustain the vulnerable human infant safely within the insecure minefields of male aggression*—when that is uprooted, only a formal, vacuous 'legality' steps in, *viz.,* the beginning of the end of social-moral standards. *Stated differently, desiccated legalisms begin, where (communal) morality ends.*

All EM societies exist in this unnatural state of legal fictions and, thereby—very tenuously. At any rate, knowledge of our anthropic state imposes caution as regards the hype—or is it cant?—about equality and freedom. Where indeed has Modernism achieved this vaunted 'equality'? If anything, it has only reproduced pre-Modernist levels of inequality, in these latter days of Late Modernism. Though, I will grant that we are certainly gifted a very definite 'equality': of misery, alienation, and loneliness, sequestered, as we are, in our little, isolating, individual, cells.

And freedom? Yes, the tramp is yet 'free' to walk into the Plaza, order *haute cuisine,* and to sleep under a bridge right after (unless security, or the police, block both options—as is likely, in these times). Perhaps Janis Joplin (why not?: insight is far from being an academic monopoly) said it best, in a justly famous One-Liner: (EuroModernist) *freedom's just another word for nothing left to lose.*

We are first 'freed' of our means of moral sustenance, even before the Modernist Game begins: freed of our human entitlement, given of a timeless Antiquity, to survive and thrive within our communal spaces, without required recourse to forced labor, and/or commercial exchange—*outside of traditionally accepted emotive-societal bonds.*

I can take care of my pet dog as my obligation and charge: or set it 'free' to roam its way, on the streets, to an early demise. It is this latter 'freedom' that EM guarantees us all, within limits: and has done so for four centuries, with much trumpery—and tragic effect.

❋

It is this mind-set that has produced, first within the ruling Anglo-Norman *demiurge,* the scourge of the *Amoral Society* (the subject of my *The Post-Human Society,*

Kanth, 2015) where any general concept of a societal morality itself is expunged—for lacking any utilitarian value. That kind of 'structural' morality in our era is radically reduced to the confines of the nuclear family, in such mode of societies, if not even less—since that familial unit is itself under threat of decay/debasement.

Now it were not vastly important to the human condition if such epistemes were to be restricted to Anglo-Norman formations. However, there is a *Gresham's Law of Cultures*, which I will state thus: *bad culture, i.e., Barbarism, drives good culture, i.e., Civilization, out of circulation.* I am not really being capricious in this regard: only direct. *Civilization is little other than the pacification of our conditions of existence, societal and natural.* And, Anglo-Norman societies have defied all civil bounds in flouting this precept: one shouldn't need to guess at the most militarized society in the world, in every sense of that term, and—until recently—the nation most responsible for the degradation of the environment, *via* its reckless consumer and producer mores. Ask yourself, additionally: who both invented, and deployed, the Ultimate Weapon(s) of *species-suicide*, in all reckless lunacy? Truly, what other definition of barbarism is needed?

If one adds to these delinquencies, the rampant ills of *racism* as *social policy* (not to mention the far more universal bane of *sexism*) rather than as merely an internalized *animus*, it would appear that our vaunted 'western civ' is not even skin-deep. At any rate, this death of morality is no less than the demise of anthropic society itself, leading to what I have called the *Post Human Society* (Kanth, 2015). The next step can only be the *Trans-Human* one, now busily being constructed, with suicidal fervor, and the help of robotics and biotech: in effect, creating a radical *caesura* in Evolution—from which we may, as a species, never return. At any rate, when rulers are faced with crises (be it of their own creation), even such skimpy and/or specious 'freedoms' as exist are quickly revoked—in favor of conscription, and/or other forms of mandatory service. Recently, *e.g.,* *habeas corpus,* the crown jewel of EM legalisms, was, casually, and to no great public stir, 'revoked' in a nation I do not need to name.

And, where has any EM society 'guaranteed' us the freedoms that really matter: *freedom from want, from insecurity, from indignity?* Never mind the 'huddled masses': *I don't have them myself in the wretched 'land of the free,' for lacking proper ethnic credentials* (let my more fortunate friends of European ethnicity take due note). Yet, even the Bushmen possessed that set of vital survival rights (thankfully, without the fanfare and prattle). But we deem their kind as 'savages': whereas our EM folks pose as the very acme of anthropic civilization. Or so the—self-congratulatory—EM books have it. And you know how it goes: *if it is in writing (perfect-bound, and priced high), it must be true.*

At any rate, the philosophy and social theory emanating from the European 'Enlightenment,' as much as the practices they sanctioned, have led us all now, howsoever unexpectedly, to the very brink of annihilation (World War I, World War II, and still counting…). Its egregious faults—errors, omissions, and elisions—are little short of legion.

Partly, was it a set of canny dissemblings: to convince the lower orders into supporting a new cadre of rulers, with sweat and blood (take the case, *e.g.*, of the Chartists in England who labored, and struggled on the streets—only to help invest the bourgeois with suffrage, in 1832: the so-called Reform Act cannily left its erstwhile allies, *i.e.*, workers, out of it). Partly, it was pure fantasy, such as inspired by free flowing claret, that social relations embracing human warmth could still be retained within a so-called 'civil society' of 'universal egoism' (Hegel's delectable phrase), where each sees the other as a means to a personal, private end: ending up, predictably, in a misanthropic, Hobbesian state of being, where, as per Sartre, 'hell is Other people.'

The vulgar, 'materialist' cast of EM was yet another default: that a growing mess of GDP pottage was worth the rending of communal, kinship-based, affective ties upon which anthropic society had rested for millennia. Thus did the sordid norm of 'pushpin is as good as poetry' (Bentham) become enshrined as the singularly Anglo-Norman 'gift' to civilization.

The generalization of an individualized self-interest *motif*, overriding our natural, and hence societal, motivations of communal co-operation was another nail in the coffin of the 'Convivial Society' (understood, with some obvious hyperbole, as represented by the tribal formations of Antiquity). *Yes, I do exaggerate, simply to make the important point—as a species, our fondest urge is simply to huddle, not to draft manifestos, proclaim utopias, or seek salvation: unless provoked by a radical excision of the affective norms that bind.*

The near-eternal, werewolf, 'wanderlust' of EM—restless, wanting ever more, aiming for the improbable—is a mark of rank alienation only: alienation from the mainsprings of our *species-being*. Divested of primal contentments, as only available in the ancient felicities of hearth and home, it is little wonder that our EM folk pursued—and still pursue—the will-o'-the-wisp, the chimera, of an ever elusive 'happiness': to the point where the pursuit is itself become the only misguided 'salve' they derive from living (so we should now know why the *Stones* never got, nor could ever hope to derive, any real 'satisfaction,' *a la* the lyrics of their famous song, regardless of effort(s) invested).

Despite EM pretensions, we are, for the most part, rather humble heat-seeking, not light-seeking animals: like most other animals. Regrettably, such misguided EM notions have helped transmute us warm-blooded mammals into cold-blooded reptiles, speaking in tropes. As the Beatles sang it, in yesteryear: *it's (only) a fool (or a knave) that 'plays it cool.'*

❄

The sop offered us all to accept such obvious pathologies was pathetic: a purely formal 'equality,' and a specious 'liberty'—that meant, effectively, little more than a ruthless abnegation of responsibility towards fellow-beings, with the principle of 'devil-take-the-hindmost' as the ruling motto. Another ideological fraud was to insist that men and women were, more or less, the same, thereby saddling women, gratuitously, with the received sins of men, aside from significantly misreading our species-traits. In point of fact, men and women are distinctly different, at the instinctual level (a level not recognized by EM ideology for being viewed as 'natural,' since it claims that 'we' are, unlike animals, 'nature-free,' so to speak—another Judeo-Christian trope that situates the 'human' on an undeserved pedestal): *in fact, it is arguably the most significant 'difference' that exists in the anthropic world, vested with momentous consequence(s) for human history* (I have, elsewhere—in my *Against Eurocentrism* work—spoken of the 'paradigm of masculinity' and the 'paradigm of femininity,' to distinguish between the two as 'clusters of traits').

Thus would a Levi-Strauss, in a flush of rationalist excess, proudly declaim that instincts explain nothing; rather that it is they that need to be explained. EM hates *difference:* since it prefers a uniform, homogeneous world, so very economical for a smooth run of exploitations.

I could go on: but the points are (mostly) made.

EM ideologues declaimed like commissioned prophets (and some were indeed so contracted), to rationalize the emergent needs of the stewards of commercial society: and now, having sown wildly in the wind, we, their unwitting heirs, are all set to reap the whirlwind—of global disaster, perhaps even the extinction of our species. So, in sum: a truant philosophy concocted of 'thin air,' innocent of any insights into human anthropology, has enveloped this world, for some four centuries now, as an asphyxiating miasma—racing from error to error, debacle to debacle.

And yet, even now, is there no learning curve: for all their astonishing achievements in science and technology (one very important *caveat*: what the Euro Enlightenment owes to the *Other*, is a field of research that awaits its Copernicus. I have, in other papers, noted the colossal debt that Northern Europe owes to *Southern* Europe, or what I term *Mediterranean Civ*: *i.e.,* Italy, Greece, Egypt, *et al.,* themselves seeded by India and China; and, of course, Asia for much of its inspirations. The colonial pirating, in effect, was *not* merely of *material* resources), and great credit is truly, and totally, due their ilk, Anglo-Norman cultures fail abysmally in *One* significant Area—*of connecting the dots.*

I would hazard the (educated) guess that their thinking trajectory is radically *micro*-oriented, and reductionist, *in extremis.* They can break things down, *ad infinitum,* and with great, even consummate, ingenuity, into their constituent elements: but are at something of a loss, at putting the pieces back together. Now that might well serve as a metaphor for what they have done to this Planet, and why.

The Dystopia of today is, unmistakably, their, loving creation (I stress *Anglo-Normans* in this Note: since others in the EM bandwagon, today—be they European or non-European—are all, or mostly, little more than Vassal States. Russia, China, and parts of West Asia, are in, various ways, of course, yet resistive of their hegemony).

Eastern traditions, and tribal ideologies, *en générale,* remain their permanent, polar opposite: for being always, perhaps ineluctably, holistic in their visions. And, as the noble Siddhartha said it, eons ago, in his very first utterances: 'as you think, you are.'

❆

Can IT all be rolled back? Can we, so to speak, rediscover our real, anthropic humanity (outside of the claptrap of EM discourse), before the eleventh hour? It is an important question: just have a glance at the current setting of the Doomsday Clock, if you think otherwise. As I have argued, a profound lack of self-knowledge, *i.e., ignorance,* lies at the root of the Great Crisis of EuroModernism, emanating inexorably from the original epistemic base of all its facile fabrications.

One way to really understand the (negative) potency of EM is to view it as a powerful, secular *theology*: with the stress on the noun. Empires may, perhaps, not be rationalized by anything less. Misanthropy and misogyny are a part of it, but only as secondary traits. *And, Error flows inevitably from Ignorance, as a rivulet from a spring.* This is interesting also because the ancient Indian epics, the *Vedas,* speak similarly of the real provenance of the ills of the world. But they attributed 'error' to *Maya,* or the delusive nature of reality; perhaps we may see EM, also, as such a species of 'false consciousness'?

At any rate, the rulers of the universe today, doubtless, will ride even a sinking iceberg into a polar sea, so long as short-term gains are in tow. But it is not impossible, I think, for a radical, epistemic break to still occur: though not without some prior, and serious, 'setback,' that helps stir mass imagination out of its stupor. Here, some, non-exhaustive, possibilities (if we are spared a fiery extinction to begin with), noted only abstractly, though with an important caveat: *we do not really know the inherent properties of our own anthropic species-being, for simply viewing it, for long, via fatally flawed EM lenses.*

Nature may, unexpectedly, provide such a warning—that may not be ignored (the query needs be posed: *are we the only 'self-conscious' part of the universe, or is it all, in some as yet unfathomed way, 'self-aware'* (to use a phrase of Quantum Physicist Amit Goswami)? Or, perhaps, a partial (even accidental?) nuclear conflict that may strike (!) just the right note of terror, to provoke serious rethinking. Or, a unique personage, vested with *charisma,* that ineffable quality (as remarked, there is much about us as hominids that we still do not fully know) that raises some to 'abnormal'—yet entirely social—influence over others, arisen to point the Way.

Or, perhaps, women, after millennia of pacific forbearance, may, *qua* women, finally, step up to stop the rot wrought by 'Patriarchy Unbound'—and deliver us all from bondage: if, in unprecedented, and unforeseeable, ways.

Or, *all* of the above?

❄

To conclude: EM is a misguided mélange of diverse elements involving: a specious, quantitative, view of 'progress,' a related materialist calculus of happiness, a misplaced, suicidal stress on asocial individuation as a societal ideal, a stark reduction of human roles solely to their part in the accumulation process (producer, consumer, *etc.*), a reductionist *scientism* that is also privileged as a theology which must be obeyed, a philosophical flaunt of elevating the human as 'above' nature, with the latter seen as no more than a manipulable, disposable tool, and a ruthless proclivity to use force, ironically, to 'free' us all of any vestiges of any 'culture' that disdains its vulgar visions.

In sum, we have (all) read ourselves wrongly, owing to EM persuasions. *And, as we read, we write*—scripts that have had us construct, and look to, Doomsday Clocks, no less. It were time, I think, to *Rethink* it all, before it is too late. And late is the operative word. For since *they* discovered atomic fission, let no one be mistaken, our species has existed on a very narrow, slender, plane of borrowed time.

45

Ancient Vedic Wisdom

Key Concepts

Atman (the inner Self, part of *Purusa,* the Unchanging Spirit) and *Brahman* (the Final Cause, the Ultimate Reality) are One only in the universe of pure consciousness, outside of space-time. In the mundane world (or *Prakrti,* the changeable material world, itself governed by *Maya,* or illusion), *Ahamkara* (the Ego-Self, the I-Self) is rendered separate from *Vijnana* (wisdom) by base matter: and sentience.

Like a mug inside a jug: the wall of the mug interrupts the flow of the common air (consciousness) of the jug. That wall is matter, and that matter is the non-local wave function 'disguised' as a macro particle, owing to the operation of Maya.

So, we are apart from one another owing to the barrier of the body-shell, and the perception/memory of the mental Ego 'Self'—that give the latter a distinct ID. Of course, we can, given enough *Jnana* (knowledge) 'look beyond,' and recognize the delusion of separateness. But, 'down to earth', the delusion is a *lived* process: we are born, love, suffer, and die—in that domain of material separateness.

Now that 'materiality' is a delusion born of our senses: for the mug, 'really,' has no wall separating it from the jug. But, such delusions, though false conceptualisations, are also material facts: the delusion of a sinkhole can still drown us. So to say *Atman* and *Brahman* are One, is to be both right and wrong. For *Purusa* and *Prakrti* are not one in the space-time world.

The Mug exists within the Jug, but yet, in its own self-perception, appears distinct from it. Neither does the jug, 'really' exist.

We may come from a Non-local universe, and return to it: but we 'live' and struggle, in a mundane world, perhaps only a hologram, itself part of a space-time universe.

In the One, *Atman* and *Brahman* are One: in the Other, *Atman,* devolved to *Ahamkara,* becomes 'alienated' from its host. The very fact that there is a definable Local and a non-Local domain defies any simple notion of One-ness. Not to mention the entity (?) doing the 'defining'.

So: how many delusions does it take to constitute it All? Well, we are about 7.3 billion on this planet. Plus the mundane universe. Of course, the space-time universe (being co-dependent) may disappear if we were to cease to exist, given the 'observer' effect. And that may make the entire mundane universe a grand delusion.

But, paradoxically, this delusional universe of appearances is also 'real' for us 'participant-observers' (!): since it limits the observers themselves, *via* its laws that are effective, in an evolving frame no less, leastways in time and space: *e.g.,* we 'observers' are not all born, nor die, at once.

But are we, 'really,' the 'observers' or, are we also, perhaps, the observed?

So it is not just that we are delusional, or/and that the (material) universe is itself a delusion. It is that we, conjointly, the observed and the observed, are the delusion. Neither exists, except within a larger, mutual delusion.

The accounting, perhaps, would run thus: we observers devolve from a non-Local Universe of pure consciousness, and our sense-perceptions then 'create,' and mirror, the space-time universe (which derives from *paticcasamuppda,* or dependent origination).

In that sense we create our own universe(s). No wonder the universe is Self-aware (as Amit Goswami argues): for it reflects our own self-awareness. And I argue it is also Self-fulfilling: for all our *Mahabarathas* (an epic, Vedic, morality battle), dubious or not, are played out within *consciousness.* We exist, and the Universe exists, entirely within it.

Indeed, the magniloquently opulent Buddhist tradition, slightly different from its Vedic roots, identifies no less than 89 different kinds of consciousness, across the scale: from mundane to the supramundane.

So, in this universe, both the observer and the observed may be no more than fleeting creations of *Leela,* the Cosmic Game of (playful) Creativity. All this, whilst the vast universe of pure consciousness, in the non-terrestrial domain, from which all universes descend, and toward which all universes tend, slumbers on.

And when we pass, if at all successful in ridding ourselves of *Avidya* (the ignorance that veils our truth), we re-enter that exalted exit of *Nirvana* (release) that cometh after *Moksha* (emancipation) where we transcend the ignorance, error, and delusions of *Samsara* (the material world) resting shakily on the protean face of *Prakrti* (ever changing cause and effect).

Whence we 'return,' to merge with *Brahman*: the ultimate, and sole, reality.

Postface

Beyond Eurocentrism: The Next Frontier

Breaking with the Enlightenment, and its delusional Modes of Discourse, involves necessarily returning to our Organic Roots in Anthropic Society, radically rent for centuries by Modernist Revolutions. We need therefore to reconfigure our placement in the Universe, both Social and Natural, and Reclaim our Natural State of *Autonomy* and Self-Regulation. I offer here, in pithy '*Thesis*' format, an unravelment of Modernism, in favor of the real *Organa of Anthropic Existence.*

1. In its most basic sense, *Politics, en générale,* is simply the Relations between *Competing Orders of Men.* More specifically, it refers to the *Modalities of Masculinity* as expressed in the '*Public*' Domain whose very illimitable extension is an index of the Atrophy of the '*Domestic Economy of Affections,*' *i.e., Convivial Relations.*

2. *Economics,* on the other hand, refers to the *Momenta of the Material Life,* and takes Two general forms: (a) *One,* the efforts invested in garnering a conventional subsistence which is originally a '*Feminine,*' *Non-Modernist* activity, involving various Reciprocities with/within both Natural and Communitarian resources; and the Other (b), the uniquely Male-driven

search for *'Command over Resources,'* i.e., a *'Surplus,'* potential or actual, involving Asymmetrical and Adversarial relations between *Disparate Cadres of Men*, in overlordship over 'Other' Men and Women, Other Species, and Nature. It is this *latter* thrust [peaking under Modernism, but far from unique to it] that merges concordantly with the Masculinist *Politics* described above.

3. The *'Social'* is simply the *Matrix of Familial Relations* centered on the Modalities of Child Rearing, and Child-Care, and is therefore, again, a uniquely Feminine site of *Praxis*.

   Theorem# A: *Women and Children form the irreducible Familial Units of Anthropic Society, upon which Men impinge and intrude as Itinerants only.*

   a) The ordinary Anthropic State is one of *Tribalism*—the Anthropic version of Mammalian Herds—which is an extension of the Familial/Kin Principle.

   b) In essence, Humans exist as both Pack and Herd animals. *Modernism breaks the Tribal Tie*, by invention of the Novel Domain of *'Civil Society'*—not an Anthropic Society at all—which is the ultimate home of the arid, *Masculinist*, Paradigm shorn of all *Affective Affinities*.

4. *Culture is a Hierarchical ordering of Values, Tastes, and Preferences*, whose tone, form, and content, are set by the historically specific *Gender Balance of Ideologies and Practices* extant in a given eco-society, at a given Moment of Evolution. The wide divergence in the *Cultures of Patriarchy* is accounted for by this, amongst other factors.

5. And *Civilization*, i.e., the *Pacification of Anthropic Existence*, is the extent to [and intensity with] which essentially *Feminine Hospitalities*, as conceived within the Familial Moment, are extended in evolution—with, by, and through the consent of the Ruling Patriarchs, who are ever the *Final Arbiters of Power*—in a given culture, to the full range of Anthropic activities and possibilities.

   a) Stated differently, Theorem# B: *'Civilization' is simply the extent to which the 'Feminine Principle' trumps inherent Masculinist proclivities;*

   b) As such, Theorem# C: *Gender struggles, not Class struggles, are the true determinant of this 'Civilizing' process.*

6. Women are, perennially, not merely the prime *Bearers of Conviviality*, but through their affective activities essentially found (and are the progenitors of) the *Affective Society*, and become the *Guarantors*, even in Patriarchal Empires, of what we might understand as the *Prerequisites of Civilization*.

7. Religion is not necessarily, 'false consciousness,' despite infiltration into its discourse by ruling orders that seek to manipulate it, but is our *Original Paradigm of Anthropic Awareness* of the Universe. It needs only the on-going enrichment of *Non-Modernist* Science and Philosophy, as available in all Pre-Modernist frames, to arrive at profundity. It can serve as Opiate, but is more often, an Amphetamine.

   Theorem# D: *Religion is uniquely Pre-Modernist [the bulk of it is NonEuropean as well; the only heartfelt religion Modernist Europe has bequeathed us is the Worship of Mammon] in provenance; its late surrogates within later-day Modernism are but desperate, reactive efforts to counter/resist burgeoning Modernist Inhospitalities.*

8. In European history, Church and State fought it out because Catholic Ideology was resistant to the needs of Capital Accumulation.

   Theorem# E: *There is no need for us all to universalize, permanently, a passing footnote in European History.*

   Theorem# F: *The Protestant Revolution 'modernized,' i.e., subverted, the Anti-Materialist import of Classical Christianity.*

   In Eastern/Traditional Formations, Religion provided, as in Medieval Europe, both a *Code of Propriety* and Conduct and a *Repository* of Anthropic Knowledge. In ancient *Vedic Civilization*, for example, Science, Religion, and Philosophy, are virtually indistinguishable.

   Theorem# G: *This integration of Religion and Science is equally true* of all Tribal and Traditional Formations. Modernism virtually invents/concocts the *Self-Divisive Society*, par excellence, permanently at War with Itself. Besides, to ask why we are here in the first place is the very *First* Anthropic Query, and is the *locus classicus* of the Religious Impulse: Modernist Science has little to offer here, and can claim no monopoly on Answers to such queries.

   Theorem# H: *We must not impose Modernist Divisive Grids on such organically integrated systems. Modernist Knowledge, where it is not blatantly counterfactual, is purchased at the dear, and dire, cost of Traditional Wisdoms.*

9. Formal '*Equality*,' the dissembling slogan of Modernism, is far from being an Anthropic virtue, and is absent as a serious demand, in all Non-Modernist Formations. As an ideology, *Modernist Equality* is arguably the *Alien, Individualist, Antidote* to *Caring, Civility, and Corespective* behaviors.

Theorem# I: *Anthropic Hierarchies, based on Trusteeship, are Anthropic Universals, and are not inferior to abstract, barren, and, more to the point, fictitious Modernist Equalities which leave us cold, separate, isolate, and uncared for.*

10. 'Liberty,' in its Modernist usage, is, similarly, a *Negative, Anti-social Ideology* born again of a Reactionary Corporatism. *Substantively* understood, it is emphatically not a Modernist invention, nor even a *Modernist Condition*, except in its characteristically Anti-social, Corporatist, and Alien(at-ing) form. Under European conditions, *Libertarian sloganeering* devolved from the need of emergent industrial oligarchies to be free of customary, traditional restraints that curbed their *Manifests of Expropriation*. And, in its *Individualist Variant*, as pervades the *Subject Orders within Modernism*, it privileges only a *Hobbesian Estrangement* from others, which is no great boon. Indeed, such *Asocial Liberties* would spell, and have so spelt, the moral failure [collapse] of society at the very moment of their success.
    Theorem# J: *Modernism has invented neither Individuals nor Individualism, except in their Asocial, Misanthropic, and perverse forms.*

11. Putative *Democracy*, reducing only to a *formal voting rule*, is not a virtue, either, and is again a tendentious *Tool of Modernism*, an artifice originally to resolve differences peaceably *within* the Ruling Strata. *Majority Rule*, its concomitant, is both divisive and corrosive, and breeds only anger and discontent. Traditional formations pursue a far more effective and satis-factory Mode of Participation: *Consensus-building*—which takes eons to achieve, but which leaves none behind.
    Theorem# K: *Hominids seek Autonomy, which is Communitarian, and Cultural, in the extreme, not abstract freedoms.*
    Theorem# L: *Modernism destroys all Autonomies, in favor of mechanical Dependencies, created by either Market or State.*

12. The *Anthropic Family* is an exemplary, pedagogical model of a natural and traditional institution; it is not based on Equality, Freedom, or Democ-racy—and yet offers the human animal *all the nurturance vitally necessary for survival*. Now imagine, in context, the madness of the High Modern-ist Marx and Engels who hoped, astonishingly, in some of their wilder fantasies, to 'abolish the family.'
    Theorem# M: *In much the same way that Economics has no understanding of Anthropic Needs, Modernism has no understanding of our Species-Being, or our real, flesh and blood, State of Being.*

Whilst knowing better, despite its long-standing *Physics-Envy,* Modernism tendentiously likens us *to free-fending Atoms, i.e.,* standard, homogeneous and, above all, *Manipulable* Entities.

13. *The Escape from Alienation* is given by *Delinking*—be it Individually, in Groups, and/or as Communities—Epistemically and Ontically, from the variegated *Logics of Modernism,* so we can reconstruct our lives free from Modernist Delusions/Practices. This does not involve, at least directly, any need to '*seize the Winter Palace,*' or confront power violently, which is the Eternal *Masculinist Temptation.* In effect, Modernism is *Self-Subverting; minus our willful consent to its Epistemes, its Hegemony simply ceases to be.*

14. More explicitly, to be *Whole,* we need to bring our Lives and Labors under *Self-Direction,* and infuse all our inherited, arid, and barren, Modernist roles, which confer no benediction, with *real meaning.* So, the next time you say '*have a nice day*' in that routine, disembodied all-American way: *mean it,* and you might even surprise yourself,

    Theorem# N: *Modernism fails to survive scrutiny when confronted seriously with its own Myths.*

    To challenge Modernism we need to Quiz/Query the *Formal* Rationality of the System with *Substantive* Rationality, Formal Justice with *Substantive* Justice, Formal Education with *Real* Education, and so on, in our daily lives.

    Theorem# O: *By Demanding the Impossible, as above, albeit in a routine way, we expose convincingly the hollow Charades of Modernism.*

15. *Life, just possibly, is meant to be lived, not theorized.*

    Theorem# P: *There is no need for a Social Science, only Social Empathy.*

    In effect, the most pervasive Transcendent *Anthropic Need* is to huddle. Even within Masculinist Patriarchy, we are *Heat seeking,* not *Light seeking* Animals.

16. Theorem# Q: *To tame/contain the Murderous Predations of Masculinity is the Permanent Challenge for Anthropic Civilization: It can only be so calmed within the Matrix of Kinship, or the Social Economy of Affections.*

    This is what *Tribal, i.e., Familial,* society achieves super abundantly. It is the real Anthropic Paradise we Modernist subjects have lost.

17. The current, *Epochal Struggle* between the *Mammals and the Reptiles* will not be won by Modernism, since Nature may not be supplanted for long by the *Artifice of Culture.*

18. The world over, Religion, which stands today for an *Anti-Modernist, Transcendent Ethics*, is in revolt against Modernist tyranny. Its Power to Mobilize is simply inexhaustible.

19. In the end, and we are fairly close to that Climacteric, the Spontaneous *Moral Economy* constituted by Women, Toilers still close to their Peasant Roots, and Traditional Cultures, will both survive and triumph.

20. We *Custodians of Abstract Words* can assist their struggles, but only if we so choose.

    Theorem# R: We are the Planet—and do not dwell apart from it—and the Planet, through us, is/will be fighting back.

    Theorem# S: *Planets likely survive, but Recalcitrant Species don't: Therein lies our Warning. Nature, eventually, Repairs all Trespasses against her Weal.*

21. The Challenge for Sentient/Thinking beings is to intrude the *Sympathy of Life* into all our nostrums, and engage Modernism critically in all domains, in particular Science, Politics, and Everyday Living. Indeed, a simple slogan suffices to define this posture, as from the NonEurocentered to the Eurocentric: '*You are not the Standard; We are not on Trial.*'

22. But the *real* Challenge of Eurocentrism is to *Reclaim our Anthropic Natures* once more: and strip the imposed, delusory, material veils within which we sadly, but daily, hide our true *Anthropic Affinities,* from both ourselves, and each other.

Note

1. This Paper was presented in a Special Event at the American Economic Association Meetings, Chicago, January 4, 2007: '*The Challenge of Eurocentrism: A Global Review of Parameters: Festschrift Celebration of the Life and Work of Rajani Kannepalli Kanth.*'

Bibliography

Arya, Ravi Prakash, and Joshi, K.L. (eds). *The Four Vedas: Rgveda, Samaveda, Yajurveda, Atharvaveda* (9 Vols.: Translators: H.H. Wilson and Bhasya of Sayanacarya). Varanasi: Indica Books, 2002.

Bernal, Martin. *Black Athena: The Afroasiatic Roots of Classical Civilization*, 3 Vols. NJ: Rutgers University Press, 1987.

Bohm, David. *Wholeness and the Implicate Order*. London: Routledge, 2002.

Buddha, Gautama. *The Dhammapada* [Trans. Ananda Maitreya, Foreword.Thich Nhat Hanh]. Reprint edition. Berkeley: Parallax Press, 2001.

Capra, Fritjof. 'The Dance of Shiva: The Hindu View of Matter in the Light of Modern Physics,' *Main Currents in Modern Thought. Minnesota: Centre for Integrated Education*, 1972.

Chomsky, Noam. *Year 501: The Conquest Continues*. Cambridge: South End Press, 1993.

Feyerabend, P. *Farewell to Reason*. London: Verso, 1987.

Goswami, Amit. *The Self-Aware Universe*. New York, NY: Tarcher Perigee, 1995.

Illich, Ivan. *Tools for Conviviality,* London: Marion Boyars, 2001.

Kanth, Rajani. *The Post-Human Society: Elemental Contours of the Aesthetic Economy of the United States*. Munich: De Gruyter, 2015.

———, (ed.). *The Challenge of Eurocentrism: Global Perspectives, Policy and Prospects*. New York, NY: Macmillan, 2009.

———. *Against Eurocentrism: A Transcendent Critique of Modernist Science, Society, and Morals*. New York, NY: Palgrave Macmillan, 2005.

———. *Against Economics: Rethinking Political Economy.* London, UK: Avebury, 1997a.

———. *Breaking with the Enlightenment: The Twilight of History and the Rediscovery of Utopia.* Atlantic Highlands, NJ: Humanity Books, 1997b.

———, (ed.). *Paradigms in Economic Development: Classic Perspectives, Critiques and Reflections.* Armonk: M.E. Sharpe, 1994.

———. *Capitalism and Social Theory.* Armonk, NY: M.E. Sharpe, 1992.

———. *Political Economy and Laissez-Faire: Economics and Ideology in the Ricardian Era.* Totowa, NJ: Rowman & Littlefield Publishers, 1986.

———. 'Two Lectures on Eurocentrism.' Chicago, IL, 2007. https://www.youtube.com/watch?v=ZDwQrpfom9M

Kohl, Christian Thomas. 'Pratityasamutpada in Eastern and Western Modes of Thought.' *International Association of Buddhist Universities* 4 (2012):68–80.

Nagarjuna. *The Fundamental Wisdom of the Middle Way: Nagarjuna's Mulamadhyamakakarika,* (J. L. Garfield, Translator). Oxford: Oxford University Press, 1995.

Petersen, Aage. 'The Philosophy of Niels Bohr', *Bulletin of the Atomic Scientists*, Vol. 19, No. 7 September, 1963.

Planck, Max. 'Das Wesen der Materie' (The Nature of Matter), a 1944 speech in Florence, Italy. Source: Archiv zur Geschichte der Max—Planck—Gesellschaft, Abt. Va, Rep. 11 Planck, Nr. 1797.

Polanyi, Michael, *Personal Knowledge: Towards a Post-Critical Philosophy.* Chicago: University of Chicago Press, 1958.

Shiva, Vandana. *Staying Alive: Women, Ecology and Survival in India.* New Delhi: Kali for Women, 1988.

Thich Nhat Hahn. *The Heart of the Buddha's Teaching.* New York, NY: Three Rivers Press, 1999.

Wallerstein, Immanuel. *European Universalism: The Rhetoric of Power.* 1st edition. New York: The New Press, 2006.

Young, Robert, J.C. *White Mythologies: Writing History and the West.* London: Routledge, 1991.

Index

A

Aboriginals. *see* Australian Aboriginals

accounting
fabrications of economists, 25
GAAP-based vs. cash-based, 2
UN requiring Keynesian, 30–31, 44–45, 241

Adversarial Society
masculinist politics and, 274
Modernists leaving behind divided, 115
from unbridled Greed, 163

Affective Society
Anthropic Society as enduring balance of, 138
destroyed by Modernism, 201
how to return to Eden, 123–124
human animal ruled by, 147
social economy of, 87–88
Women as bearers of, 274

Africa
conquering of, 168–169
en route to modernizing before overrun, 241
European Barbarism in South, 222
Europeans creating wretchedness in, 172–173
Northern Europeans ransacking, 49, 167
on western aid to, 224

Afro-Americans
gaining right to vote, 160
leading list of racial victims, 253–254
reason they are looked down upon, 257
white police routinely murdering unarmed, 117, 253

Against Eurocentrism (Kanth, 2005), 44, 64, 70, 164, 266

Age of Discontent, 142, 212

Age of Quantity, xii, 151–152

Ahamkara (Ego-Self), Vedic wisdom, 77, 269

Alienation
meaning of/antidote for, xxix
moving beyond Eurocentrism and, 277
wanderlust of EM as mark of, 265

"All Men are created Equal," 81, 114

E

Modernism's false promise of, 212, 246
negative vs. positive, 115
unabashed rollback of, 11
limited democracy, 160
linguistics, 154

M

M2 (cash + checking deposits + time deposits)
velocity, erosion of, 4
macroeconomics. *see* Keynesian (macroeco-
nomic) ideas
Madoff, Bernie, 34, 38
males. *see* Masculine Principle
Malthus, Robert, 99
Mammals
in arrested anthropic evolution, 144
countries set apart from reptiles, 174
Heat-seeking essence of, 138
Modernist Europe giving up heritage of,
171
morphing into reptiles, 59, 115, 151, 266
Struggle between Reptiles and, 192–193
Manu Smriti document, 183
Manufacturing, redefinitions of, 25
Maoism, 241
Marx, Karl
on capitalism deriding all values, 6
on civil vs. human society, 59, 247–248
on economics, 43
on emerging alienation, 17–18
Judeo-Christian ideology of, xxvi, 140, 153
on Primitive Communism, 89
secular heaven of communism, 260
Masculine Principle. *see also* Paradigm of
Masculinity (POM)
beyond Eurocentrism, 273–274
exploiting power, 49
instinct to kill, xxiii–xxiv, xxviii, 67–68
Instincts as real anthropology, 156
kinship tempering aggression of, 211, 263
leading to universal egoism, 193
male/female dyad, 66–67

material economy driven by, 211–212
no special tilt toward equity/justice, xxiv
Oppression of Women, 68
political economy of, 261
universal archetype of, xxiv–xxv
women as solution to societal ills of,
63–64, 72
Material Economy, Moral Economy vs., 261
Material Economy of Interests, 147
Materialism
abandoning discredited, 148
all required to subscribe to, 44–45
building via extraction of resources, 136
Chinese vs. European, 200
Civilization as moral choice to avoid, 57,
243
crisis of Anglo-Am capitalism, 15
driven by masculine principle, 212–213
effects of globalization on culture, 53–56
Euro-philosophy of, 73
governing classes using crass form of,
73–74
human/non-human costs of, 127–128
injurious to our anthropic values, 200–201,
220–221
Material vs. Moral Economy, 88
need to jettison world world-view of, 147
of non-European formations, 121
provoking European expansion globally,
188
Quantum Physics and, 115
rampant in Modernism, xix, xxiv, 121
Rationality and, 65–66
scientific and philosophical, 73, 144, 229
staggering Anglo-Saxon achievement of,
190–192
why EuroModernism succeeded, 215–217
world upside-down today due to, 199–200
as wrong in EuroModernism, 173, 251,
265
matter-energy dyad, 74–75
Maya (delusion), Vedic wisdom, 76–77, 227,
229–230, 269
McDonaldization of food, 192